Granger In

AMERICAN PROSE

AMERICAN PROSE

HAWTHORNE: IRVING: LONGFELLOW:
WHITTIER: HOLMES: LOWELL:
THOREAU: EMERSON.

WITH INTRODUCTIONS AND NOTES

BY HORACE E. SCUDDER

Granger Index Reprint Series

 BOOKS FOR LIBRARIES PRESS
FREEPORT, NEW YORK

First Published 1880
Reprinted 1971

INTERNATIONAL STANDARD BOOK NUMBER:
0-8369-6242-7

LIBRARY OF CONGRESS CATALOG CARD NUMBER:
70-149117

PRINTED IN THE UNITED STATES OF AMERICA

PREFACE.

IN making a selection of *American Prose* the
principle which controlled in *American Poems*
has been followed. The book does not profess to
be representative of the authors included, but complete papers or stories have been taken of a length
permitting a fair display of some of the author's
characteristics. The object has been to set before
the reader some of the higher forms of prose art
as interpreted by American writers, and to cultivate a taste for the enduring elements of literature.
As before, an attempt has been made to lead the
student from the simpler to the more involved and
subtle forms, and throughout the book the literature of knowledge has been less regarded than the
literature of power. The best result will be reached
if those who use this volume are impelled to ask
for the fuller works of the authors whose acquaintance as writers of prose they may here make.

In *American Poems* a brief biographical sketch
of each writer was given, and since a similar plan
in this volume would have required some repetition, the editor has preferred to make the introductions more general in character, with a view to suggesting points of critical inquiry in literature, for
such a volume as this offers a good opportunity for
directing young students toward a more thoughtful
attention in reading. Prose, with its familiar forms
and its more intimate relations to other studies, is
often a better field for practice in criticism than
poetry, especially as the student has the advantage of using it himself. The writing of poetry
frequently helps in a critical interpretation of
poetical forms, but to most such exercises have an
element of unreality, while prose, as the mother
tongue of all, affords a material which is never
strange. It is worth while, therefore, to show the
young what fine qualities exist in that which all
men are using.

The more expanded character of prose makes
annotation less necessary than in poetry. Besides,
the interruption of an obscure reference is less
fatal to enjoyment than in poetry. The editor,
therefore, has given fewer notes than in *American*

Poems, and has purposely left work to be done by the reader, the doing of which will add a zest to his reading. This is most noticeable in the case of Emerson's essay on *Books.* It would be an admirable exercise for any young student to edit this paper by making full references to the array of points presented in it. A similar exercise in local historical study could be found in commenting upon Hawthorne's sketch of *Howe's Masquerade.*

CONTENTS.

viii CONTENTS.

NATHANIEL HAWTHORNE.

INTRODUCTION.

IT was Hawthorne's wont to keep note-books, in which he recorded his observations and reflections; sometimes he spoke in them of himself, his plans, and his prospects. He began the practice early, and continued it through life, and after his death selections from these note-books were published in six volumes, under the titles: *Passages from the American Note-Books of Nathaniel Hawthorne, Passages from the English Note-Books of Nathaniel Hawthorne*, and *Passages from the French and Italian Note-Books of Nathaniel Hawthorne*. In these books, and in prefaces which appear in the front of the volumes containing his collected stories, one finds many frank expressions of the interest which Hawthorne took in his work, and the author appeals very ingenuously to the reader, speaking with an almost confidential closeness of his stories and sketches. Then the *Note-Books* contain the unwrought material of the books which the writer put out in his lifetime. One finds there the suggestions of stories, and frequently pages of

1

observation and reflection, which were afterward
transferred, almost as they stood, into the author's
works.   It is a very interesting labor to trace Hawthorne's stories and sketches back to these records
in his note-books, and to compare the finished work
with the rough material.   It seems, also, as if each
reader was admitted into the privacy of the author's
mind.   That is the first impression, but a closer
study reveals two facts very clearly.   One is stated
by Hawthorne himself in his preface to *The Snow-
Image and other Twice-Told Tales :* " I have been
especially careful [in my Introductions] to make
no disclosures respecting myself which the most
·indifferent observer might not have been acquainted
with, and which I was not perfectly willing that
my worst enemy should know. . . . . I have taken
facts which relate to myself [when telling stories]
because they chance .to be nearest at hand, and
likewise are my own property.   And, as for ego-
tism, a person who has been burrowing, to his
utmost ability, into the depths of our common nature for the purposes of psychological romance —
and who pursues his researches in that dusky region,
as he needs must, as well by the tact of sympathy
as by the light of observation — will˙smile at in-
curring such an imputation in virtue of a little
preliminary talk about his external habits, his abode,
his casual associates, and other matters entirely
upon the surface.   These things hide the man
instead of displaying him.   You must make quite
another kind of inquest, and look through the

whole range of his fictitious characters, good and evil, in order to detect any of his essential traits."

There has rarely been a writer of fiction, then, whose personality has been so absolutely separate from that of each character created by him, and at the same time has so intimately penetrated the whole body of his writing. Of no one of his characters, male or female, is one ever tempted to say, This is Hawthorne, except in the case of Miles Coverdale in *The Blithedale Romance*, where the circumstances of the story tempt one into an identification; yet all of Hawthorne's work is stamped emphatically with his mark. Hawthorne wrote it, is very simple and easy to say of all but the merest trifle in his collected works; but the world has yet to learn who Hawthorne was, and even if he had not forbidden a biography of himself, it is scarcely likely that any life could have disclosed more than he has chosen himself to reveal.

The advantage of this is that it leaves the student free to concentrate his attention upon the writings rather than on the man. Hawthorne, in the passage quoted above, speaks of himself as one " who has been burrowing, to his utmost ability, into the depths of our common nature for the purposes of psychological romance," and this states, as closely as so short a sentence can, the controlling purpose and end of the author. The vitality of Hawthorne's characters is derived but little from any external description; it resides in the truthfulness with which they respond to some permanent and controlling operation of the human soul. Looking into his own heart, and always, when studying others, in search of fundamental rather than occasional motives, he proceeded to develop these motives in conduct and life.   Hence he had a leaning toward the allegory, where human figures are merely masks for spiritual activities, and sometimes he employed the simple allegory, as in *The Celestial Railroad.*   More often in his short stories he has a spiritual truth to illustrate, and uses the simplest, most direct means, taking no pains to conceal his purpose, yet touching his characters quietly or playfully with human sensibilities, and investing them with just so much real life as answers the purpose of the story.   This is exquisitely done in *The Snow-Image.*   The consequence of this " burrowing into the depths of our common nature " has been to bring much of the darker and concealed life into the movement of his stories.   The fact of evil is the terrible fact of life, and its workings in the human soul had more interest for Hawthorne than the obvious physical manifestations.   Since his observations are less of the men and women whom everybody sees and recognizes than of the souls which are hidden from most eyes, it is not strange that his stories should often lay bare secrets of sin, and that a somewhat dusky light should seem to be the atmosphere of much of his work. Now and then, especially when dealing with childhood, a warm, sunny glow spreads over the pages of his books ; but the reader must be prepared for the most part to read stories which lie in the shadow of life.

There was one class of subjects which had a peculiar interest for Hawthorne, and in a measure affected his work. He had a strong taste for New England history, and he found in the scenes and characters of that history favorable material for the representation of spiritual conflict. He was himself the most New English of New Englanders, and held an extraordinary sympathy with the very soil of his section of the country. By this sympathy, rather than by any painful research, he was singularly acquainted with the historic life of New England. His stories, based directly on historic facts, are true to the spirit of the times in something more than an archæological way. One is astonished at the ease with which he seized upon characteristic features, and reproduced them in a word or phrase. Merely careful and diligent research would never be adequate to give the life-likeness of the images in *Howe's Masquerade.*

There is, then, a second fact discovered by a study of Hawthorne, that while one finds in the *Note-Books*, for example, the material out of which stories and sketches seem to have been constructed, and while the facts of New England history have been used without exaggeration or distortion, the result in stories and romances is something far beyond a mere report of what has been seen and read. The charm of a vivifying imagination is the crowning charm of Hawthorne's stories, and its medium is a graceful and often exquisitely apt diction. Hawthorne's sense of touch as a writer is very fine. He knows when to be light, and when to press heavily; a very conspicuous quality is what one is likely to term quaintness, — a gentle pleasantry which seems to spring from the author's attitude toward his own work, as if he looked upon that, too, as a part of the spiritual universe which he was surveying.

Hawthorne spent much of his life silently, and there are touching passages in his note-books regarding his sense of loneliness and his wish for recognition from the world. His early writings were short stories, sketches, and biographies, scattered in magazines and brought together into *Twice-Told Tales*, in two volumes, published, the first in 1837, the second in 1842 ; *Mosses from an Old Manse*, in 1846 ; *The Snow-Image and other Twice-Told Tales*, in 1851. They had a limited circle of readers. Some recognized his genius, but it was not until the publication of *The Scarlet Letter*, in 1850, that Hawthorne's name was fairly before the world as a great and original writer of romance. *The House of the Seven Gables* followed in 1851. *The Blithedale Romance* in 1852. He spent the years 1853–1860 in Europe, and the immediate result of his life there is in *Our Old Home: A Series of English Sketches*, published in 1863, and *The Marble Faun, or the Romance of Monte Beni*, in 1864. For young people he wrote *Grandfather's Chair*, a collection of stories from New England history, *The Won-*

der-Book and *Tanglewood Tales*, containing stories out of classic mythology. There are a few other scattered writings which have been collected into volumes and published in the complete series of his works.

Hawthorne was born July 4, 1804, and died May 19, 1864.

The student of Hawthorne will find in G. P. Lathrop's *A Study of Hawthorne*, and Henry James Jr.'s *Hawthorne*, in the series *English Men of Letters*, material which will assist him. Dr. Holmes published, shortly after Hawthorne's death, a paper of reminiscences which is included in *Soundings from the Atlantic;* and Longfellow welcomed *Twice-Told Tales* with a glowing article in the *North American Review*, xlviii. 59, which is reproduced in his prose works. The reader will find it an agreeable task to discover what the poets, Longfellow, Lowell, Stedman, and others have said of this man of genius.

THE SNOW–IMAGE:

A CHILDISH MIRACLE.

ONE afternoon of a cold winter's day, when the sun shone forth with chilly brightness, after a long storm, two children asked leave of their mother to run out and play in the new-fallen snow. The elder child was a little girl, whom, because she was of a tender and modest disposition, and was thought to be very beautiful, her parents, and other people who were familiar with her, used to call Violet. But her brother was known by the style and title of Peony, on account of the ruddiness of his broad and round little phiz, which made everybody think of sunshine and great scarlet flowers. The father of these two children, a certain Mr. Lindsey, it is important to say, was an excellent but exceedingly matter-of-fact sort of man, a dealer in hardware, and was sturdily accustomed to take what is called the common-sense view of all matters that came under his consideration. With a heart about as tender as other people's, he had a head as hard and impenetrable, and therefore, perhaps, as empty, as one of the iron pots which it was a part of his busi-

ness to sell. The mother's character, on the other
hand, had a strain of poetry in it, a trait of unworldly beauty, — a delicate and dewy flower, as
it were, that had survived out of her imaginative
youth, and still kept itself alive amid the dusty realities of matrimony and motherhood.

So Violet and Peony, as I began with saying,
besought their mother to let them run and play in
the new snow; for, though it had looked so dreary
and dismal, drifting downward out of the gray sky,
it had a very cheerful aspect now that the sun was
shining on it. The children dwelt in a city, and
had no wider play-place than a little garden before
the house, divided by a white fence from the street,
and with a pear-tree and two or three plum-trees
overshadowing it, and some rose-bushes just in front
of the parlor windows. The trees and shrubs, however, were now leafless, and their twigs were envel-
oped in the light snow, which thus made a kind of
wintry foliage, with here and there a pendent icicle
for the fruit.

" Yes, Violet, — yes, my little Peony," said their
kind mother; " you may go out and play in the
new snow."

Accordingly, the good lady bundled up her darlings in woollen jackets and wadded sacks, and put
comforters round their necks, and a pair of striped
gaiters on each little pair of legs, and worsted mit-
tens on their hands, and gave them a kiss apiece,
by way of a spell to keep away Jack Frost. Forth
sallied the two children, with a hop-skip-and-jump

that carried them at once into the very heart of a
huge snow-drift, whence Violet emerged like a snow-
bunting, while little Peony floundered out with his
round face in full bloom.   Then what a merry time
had they !   To look at them, frolicking in the wintry garden, you would have thought that the dark
and pitiless storm had been sent for no other purpose but to provide a new plaything for Violet and
Peony ; and that they themselves had been created,
as the snow-birds were, to take delight only in the
tempest, and in the white mantle which it spread
over the earth.

At last, when they had frosted one another all
over with handfuls of snow, Violet, after laughing
heartily at little Peony's figure, was struck with a
new idea.

"You look exactly like a snow-image, Peony,"
said she, " if your cheeks were not so red.   And
that puts me in mind !   Let us make an image out
of snow, — an image of a little girl, — and it shall
be our sister, and shall run about and play with us
all winter long.   Won't it be nice ? "

"Oh, yes ! " cried Peony, as plainly as he could
speak, for he was but a little boy.   " That will be
nice !   And mamma shall see it ! "

" Yes," answered Violet ; " mamma shall see the
new little girl.   But she must not make her come
into the warm parlor ; for, you know, our little
snow-sister will not love the warmth."

And forthwith the children began this great business of making a snow-image that should run about ;

while their mother, who was sitting at the window and overheard some of their talk, could not help smiling at the gravity with which they set about it. They really seemed to imagine that there would be no difficulty whatever in creating a live little girl out of the snow. And to say the truth, if miracles are ever to be wrought, it will be by putting our hands to the work in precisely such a simple and undoubting frame of mind as that in which Violet and Peony now undertook to perform one, without so much as knowing that it was a miracle. So thought the mother; and thought, likewise, that the new snow, just fallen from heaven, would be excellent material to make new beings of, if it were not so very cold. She gazed at the children a moment longer, delighting to watch their little figures, — the girl, tall for her age, graceful and agile, and so delicately colored that she looked like a cheerful thought, more than a physical reality; while Peony expanded in breadth rather than height, and rolled along on his short and sturdy legs as substantial as an elephant, though not quite so big. Then the mother resumed her work; what it was I forget, but she was either trimming a silken bonnet for Violet, or darning a pair of stockings for little Peony's short legs. Again, however, and again, and yet other agains, she could not help turning her head to the window to see how the children got on with their snow-image.

Indeed, it was an exceedingly pleasant sight, those bright little souls at their tasks! Moreover,

it was really wonderful to observe how knowingly
and skilfully they managed the matter.   Violet assumed the chief direction, and told Peony what to
do, while, with her own delicate fingers, she shaped
out all the nicer parts of the snow-figure.   It
seemed, in fact, not so much to be made by the
children, as to grow up under their hands, while
they were playing and prattling about it.   Their
mother was quite surprised at this ; and the longer
she looked the more and more surprised she grew.

"What remarkable children mine are ! " thought
she, smiling with a mother's pride ; and, smiling at
herself, too, for being so proud of them.   "What
other children could have made anything so like a
little girl's figure out of snow at the first trial ?
Well ; — but now I must finish Peony's new frock,
for his grandfather is coming to-morrow, and I want
the little fellow to look handsome."

So she took up the frock, and was soon as busily
at work again with her needle as the two children
with their snow-image.   But still, as the needle
travelled hither and thither through the seams of
the dress, the mother made her toil light and happy
by listening to the airy voices of Violet and Peony.
They kept talking to one another all the time, their
tongues being quite as active as their feet and hands.
Except at intervals, she could not distinctly hear
what was said, but had merely a sweet impression
that they were in a most loving mood, and were
enjoying themselves highly, and that the business
of making the snow-image went prosperously on.

Now and then, however, when Violet and Peony
happened to raise their voices, the words were as
audible as if they had been spoken in the very parlor where the mother sat. Oh, how delightfully
those words echoed in her heart, even though they
meant nothing so very wise or wonderful, after
all !

But you must know a mother listens with her
heart much more than with her ears ; and thus she
is often delighted with the trills of celestial music,
when other people can hear nothing of the kind.

" Peony, Peony ! " cried Violet to her brother,
who had gone to another part of the garden, " bring
me some of that fresh snow, Peony, from the very
farthest corner, where we have not been trampling.
I want it to shape our little snow-sister's bosom
with. You know that part must be quite pure,
just as it came out of the sky ! "

" Here it is, Violet ! " answered Peony, in his
bluff tone, — but a very sweet tone, too, — as he
came floundering through the half-trodden drifts.
" Here is the snow for her little bosom. O Violet,
how beau-ti-ful she begins to look ! "

" Yes," said Violet, thoughtfully and quietly ;
" our snow-sister does look very lovely. I did not
quite know, Peony, that we could make such a
sweet little girl as this."

The mother, as she listened, thought how fit and
delightful an incident it would be, if fairies, or,
still better, if angel-children were to come from
paradise and play invisibly with her own darlings,

and help them to make their snow-image, giving it the features of celestial babyhood! Violet and Peony would not be aware of their immortal playmates, — only they would see that the image grew very beautiful while they worked at it, and would think that they themselves had done it all.

"My little girl and boy deserve such playmates, if mortal children ever did!" said the mother to herself; and then she smiled again at her own motherly pride.

Nevertheless, the idea seized upon her imagination; and, ever and anon, she took a glimpse out of the window, half dreaming that she might see the golden-haired children of paradise sporting with her own golden-haired Violet and bright-cheeked Peony.

Now, for a few moments, there was a busy and earnest, but indistinct, hum of the two children's voices, as Violet and Peony wrought together with one happy consent. Violet still seemed to be the guiding spirit, while Peony acted rather as a laborer, and brought her the snow from far and near. And yet the little urchin evidently had a proper understanding of the matter, too!

"Peony, Peony!" cried Violet; for her brother was again at the other side of the garden. "Bring me those light wreaths of snow that have rested on the lower branches of the pear-tree. You can clamber on the snow-drift, Peony, and reach them easily. I must have them to make some ringlets for our snow-sister's head!"

" Here they are, Violet!" answered the little boy. "Take care you do not break them. Well done! Well done! How pretty!"

" Does she not look sweetly?" said Violet, with a very satisfied tone; "and now we must have some little shining bits of ice, to make the brightness of her eyes. She is not finished yet. Mamma will see how very beautiful she is; but papa will say, ' Tush! nonsense! — come in out of the cold!'"

" Let us call mamma to look out," said Peony; and then he shouted lustily, "Mamma! mamma!! mamma!!! Look out, and see what a nice little girl we are making!"

The mother put down her work, for an instant, and looked out of the window. But it so happened that the sun — for this was one of the shortest days of the whole year — had sunken so nearly to the edge of the world that his setting shine came obliquely into the lady's eyes. So she was dazzled, you must understand, and could not very distinctly observe what was in the garden. Still, however, through all that bright, blinding dazzle of the sun and the new snow she beheld a small white figure in the garden that seemed to have a wonderful deal of human likeness about it. And she saw Violet and Peony, — indeed, she looked more at them than at the image, — she saw the two children still at work; Peony bringing fresh snow, and Violet applying it to the figure as scientifically as a sculptor adds clay to his model. Indistinctly as she discerned the snow-child, the mother thought to herself that never before was there a snow-figure so cunningly made, nor ever such a dear little girl and boy to make it.

" They do everything better than other children," said she, very complacently. " No wonder they make better snow-images ! "

She sat down again to the work, and made as much haste with it as possible; because twilight would soon come, and Peony's frock was not yet finished, and grandfather was expected, by railroad, pretty early in the morning. Faster and faster, therefore, went her flying fingers. The children, likewise, kept busily at work in the garden, and still the mother listened, whenever she could catch a word. She was amused to observe how their little imaginations had got mixed up with what they were doing, and were carried away by it. They seemed positively to think that the snow-child would run about and play with them.

" What a nice playmate she will be for us, all winter long ! " said Violet. " I hope papa will not be afraid of her giving us a cold ! Shan't you love her dearly, Peony ? "

" Oh, yes ! " cried Peony. " And I will hug her, and she shall sit down close by me, and drink some of my warm milk ! "

" Oh, no, Peony ! " answered Violet, with grave wisdom. " That will not do at all. Warm milk will not be wholesome for our little snow-sister. Little snow-people, like her, eat nothing but icicles. No, no, Peony; we must not give her anything warm to drink ! "

There was a minute or two of silence; for Peony, whose short legs were never weary, had gone on a pilgrimage again to the other side of the garden. All of a sudden Violet cried out, loudly and joyfully, —

" Look here, Peony ! Come quickly ! A light has been shining on her cheek out of that rose-colored cloud ! and the color does not go away ! Is not that beautiful ! "

" Yes ; it is beau-ti-ful," answered Peony, pronouncing the three syllables with deliberate accuracy. " O Violet, only look at her hair ! It is all like gold ! "

" Oh, certainly," said Violet, with tranquillity, as if it were very much a matter of course. " That color, you know, comes from the golden clouds that we see up there in the sky. She is almost finished now. But her lips must be made very red, — redder than her cheeks. Perhaps, Peony, it will make them red if we both kiss them ! "

Accordingly, the mother heard two smart little smacks, as if both her children were kissing the snow-image on its frozen mouth. But, as this did not seem to make the lips quite red enough, Violet next proposed that the snow-child should be invited to kiss Peony's scarlet cheek.

" Come, 'ittle snow-sister, kiss me ! " cried Peony.

" There ! she has kissed you," added Violet, " and now her lips are very red. And she blushed a little, too ! "

" Oh, what a cold kiss ! " cried Peony.

2

Just then came a breeze of the pure west-wind, sweeping through the garden and rattling the parlor windows. It sounded so wintry cold that the mother was about to tap on the window-pane with her thimbled finger, to summon the two children in, when they both cried out to her with one voice. The tone was not a tone of surprise, although they were evidently a good deal excited ; it appeared rather as if they were very much rejoiced at some event that had now happened, but which they had been looking for, and had reckoned upon all along.

" Mamma! mamma! We have finished our little snow-sister, and she is running about the garden with us ! "

" What imaginative little beings my children are ! " thought the mother, putting the last few stitches into Peony's frock. " And it is strange, too, that they make me almost as much a child as they themselves are ! I can hardly help believing, now, that the snow-image has really come to life ! "

" Dear mamma ! " cried Violet, " pray look out and see what a sweet playmate we have ! "

The mother, being thus entreated, could no longer delay to look forth from the window. The sun was now gone out of the sky, leaving, however, a rich inheritance of his brightness among those purple and golden clouds which make the sunsets of winter so magnificent. But there was not the slightest gleam or dazzle, either on the window or on the snow ; so that the good lady could look all over the garden, and see everything and everybody in

it. And what do you think she saw there? Violet and Peony, of course, her own two darling children. Ah, but whom or what did she see besides?
Why, if you will believe me, there was a small figure of a girl, dressed all in white, with rose-tinged
cheeks and ringlets of golden hue, playing about the
garden with the two children ! A stranger though
she was, the child seemed to be on as familiar terms
with Violet and Peony, and they with her, as if all
the three had been playmates during the whole of
their little lives. The mother thought to herself
that it must certainly be the daughter of one of the
neighbors, and that, seeing Violet and Peony in the
garden, the child had run across the street to play
with them. So this kind lady went to the door,
intending to invite the little runaway into her comfortable parlor; for, now that the sunshine was
withdrawn, the atmosphere out of doors was already growing very cold.

But, after opening the house-door, she stood an
instant on the threshold, hesitating whether she
ought to ask the child to come in, or whether she
should even speak to her. Indeed, she almost
doubted whether it were a real child, after all, or
only a light wreath of the new-fallen snow, blown
hither and thither about the garden by the intensely
cold west-wind. There was certainly something
very singular in the aspect of the little stranger.
Among all the children of the neighborhood, the
lady could remember no such face, with its pure
white, and delicate rose-color, and the golden ring-

lets tossing about the forehead and cheeks. And as for her dress, which was entirely of white, and fluttering in the breeze, it was such as no reasonable woman would put upon a little girl, when sending her out to play, in the depth of winter. It made this kind and careful mother shiver only to look at those small feet, with nothing in the world on them except a very thin pair of white slippers. Nevertheless, airily as she was clad, the child seemed to feel not the slightest inconvenience from the cold, but danced so lightly over the snow that the tips of her toes left hardly a print in its surface; while Violet could but just keep pace with her, and Peony's short legs compelled him to lag behind.

Once, in the course of their play, the strange child placed herself between Violet and Peony, and taking a hand of each, skipped merrily forward, and they along with her. Almost immediately, however, Peony pulled away his little fist, and began to rub it as if the fingers were tingling with cold; while Violet also released herself, though with less abruptness, gravely remarking that it was better not to take hold of hands. The white-robed damsel said not a word, but danced about, just as merrily as before. If Violet and Peony did not choose to play with her she could make just as good a playmate of the brisk and cold west-wind, which kept blowing her all about the garden, and took such liberties with her that they seemed to have been friends for a long time. All this while the mother stood on the threshold, wondering how a little girl could look so much like a flying snow-drift, or how a snow-drift could look so very like a little girl.

She called Violet, and whispered to her.

"Violet, my darling, what is this child's name?" asked she. "Does she live near us?"

"Why, dearest mamma," answered Violet, laughing to think that her mother did not comprehend so very plain an affair, "this is our little snow-sister, whom we have just been making!"

"Yes, dear mamma," cried Peony, running to his mother, and looking up simply into her face. "This is our snow-image! Is it not a nice 'ittle child?"

At this instant a flock of snow-birds came flitting through the air. As was very natural, they avoided Violet and Peony. But — and this looked strange — they flew at once to the white-robed child, fluttered eagerly about her head, alighted on her shoulders, and seemed to claim her as an old acquaintance. She, on her part, was evidently as glad to see these little birds, old Winter's grand-children, as they were to see her, and welcomed them by holding out both her hands. Hereupon, they each and all tried to alight on her two palms and ten small fingers and thumbs, crowding one another off, with an immense fluttering of their tiny wings. One dear little bird nestled tenderly in her bosom; another put its bill to her lips. They were as joyous, all the while, and seemed as much in their element as you may have seen them when sporting with a snow-storm.

Violet and Peony stood laughing at this pretty sight; for they enjoyed the merry time which their new playmate was having with these small-winged visitants almost as much as if they themselves took part in it.

"Violet," said her mother, greatly perplexed, "tell me the truth, without any jest. Who is this little girl?"

"My darling mamma," answered Violet, looking seriously into her mother's face, and apparently surprised that she should need any further explanation, "I have told you truly who she is. It is our little snow-image, which Peony and I have been making. Peony will tell you so, as well as I."

"Yes, mamma," asseverated Peony, with much gravity in his crimson little phiz; "this is 'ittle snow-child. Is not she a nice one? But, mamma, her hand, is oh, so very cold!"

While mamma still hesitated what to think and what to do, the street-gate was thrown open, and the father of Violet and Peony appeared, wrapped in a pilot-cloth sack, with a fur cap drawn down over his ears, and the thickest of gloves upon his hands. Mr. Lindsey was a middle-aged man, with a weary and yet a happy look in his wind-flushed and frost-pinched face, as if he had been busy all the day long, and was glad to get back to his quiet home. His eyes brightened at the sight of his wife and children, although he could not help uttering a word or two of surprise at finding the whole

family in the open air, on so bleak a day, and after
sunset too. He soon perceived the little white
stranger, sporting to and fro in the garden, like a
dancing snow-wreath, and the flock of snow-birds
fluttering about her head.

"Pray, what little girl may that be?" inquired
this very sensible man. "Surely her mother must
be crazy, to let her go out in such bitter weather
as it has been to-day, with only that flimsy white
gown and those thin slippers!"

"My dear husband," said his wife, "I know no
more about the little thing than you do. Some
neighbor's child, I suppose. Our Violet and Peony,"
she added, laughing at herself for repeating so ab-
surd a story, "insist that she is nothing but a snow-
image, which they have been busy about in the
garden almost all the afternoon."

As she said this, the mother glanced her eyes
toward the spot where the children's snow-image
had been made. What was her surprise, on per-
ceiving that there was not the slightest trace of so
much labor! — no image at all! — no piled-up heap
of snow! — nothing whatever save the prints of
little footsteps around a vacant space!

"This is very strange!" said she.

"What is strange, dear mother?" asked Violet.
"Dear father, do not you see how it is? This is
our snow-image, which Peony and I have made,
because we wanted another playmate. Did not
we, Peony?"

"Yes, papa," said crimson Peony. "This be our

'ittle snow-sister. Is she not beau-ti-ful? But she gave me such a cold kiss!"

"Poh, nonsense, children!" cried their good, honest father, who, as we have already intimated, had an exceedingly common-sensible way of looking at matters. "Do not tell me of making live figures out of snow. Come, wife; this little stranger must not stay out in the bleak air a moment longer. We will bring her into the parlor; and you shall give her a supper of warm bread and milk, and make her as comfortable as you can. Meanwhile, I will inquire among the neighbors; or, if necessary, send the city crier about the streets, to give notice of a lost child."

So saying, this honest and very kind-hearted man was going toward the little white damsel, with the best intentions in the world. But Violet and Peony, each seizing their father by the hand, earnestly besought him not to make her come in.

"Dear father," cried Violet, putting herself before him, "it is true what I have been telling you! This is our little snow-girl, and she cannot live any longer than while she breathes the cold west-wind. Do not make her come into the hot room!"

"Yes, father," shouted Peony, stamping his little foot, so mightily was he in earnest, "this be nothing but our 'ittle snow-child! She will not love the hot fire!"

"Nonsense, children, nonsense, nonsense!" cried the father, half vexed, half laughing at what he considered their foolish obstinacy. "Run into the house, this moment! It is too late to play any longer now. I must take care of this little girl immediately, or she will catch her death-a-cold!"

"Husband! dear husband!" said his wife, in a low voice, — for she had been looking narrowly at the snow-child, and was more perplexed than ever, — "there is something very singular in all this. You will think me foolish, — but — but — may it not be that some invisible angel has been attracted by the simplicity and good-faith with which our children set about their undertaking? May he not have spent an hour of his immortality in playing with those dear little souls? and so the result is what we call a miracle. No, no! Do not laugh at me; I see what a foolish thought it is!"

"My dear wife," replied the husband, laughing heartily, "you are as much a child as Violet and Peony."

And in one sense so she was; for all through life she had kept her heart full of childlike simplicity and faith, which was as pure and clear as crystal; and, looking at all matters through this transparent medium, she sometimes saw truths so profound that other people laughed at them as nonsense and ab surdity.

But now kind Mr. Lindsey had entered the garden, breaking away from his two children, who still sent their shrill voices after him, beseeching him to let the snow-child stay and enjoy herself in the cold west-wind. As he approached the snow-birds took to flight. The little white damsel, also, fled backward, shaking her head, as if to say, " Pray do not touch me!'' and roguishly, as it appeared, leading him through the deepest of the snow.   Once, the good man stumbled, and floundered down upon his face, so that, gathering himself up again, with the snow sticking to his rough pilot-cloth sack, he looked as white and wintry as a snow-image of the largest size.   Some of the neighbors, meanwhile, seeing him from their windows, wondered what could possess poor Mr. Lindsey to be running about his garden in pursuit of a snow-drift, which the west-wind was driving hither and thither!   At length, after a vast deal of trouble, he chased the little stranger into a corner, where she could not possibly escape him.   His wife had been looking on, and, it being nearly twilight, was wonder-struck to observe how the snow-child gleamed and sparkled, and how she seemed to shed a glow all round about her ; and when driven into the corner, she positively glistened like a star!   It was a frosty kind of brightness, too, like that of an icicle in the moon-light.   The wife thought it strange that good Mr. Lindsey should see nothing remarkable in the snow-child's appearance.

" Come, you odd little thing!" cried the honest man, seizing her by the hand, " I have caught you at last, and will make you comfortable in spite of yourself.   We will put a nice, warm pair of worsted stockings on your frozen little feet, and you shall have a good thick shawl to wrap yourself in.   Your poor white nose, I am afraid, is actually frost-bitten. But we will make it all right.   Come along in."

And so, with a most benevolent smile on his sagacious visage, all purple as it was with the cold, this very well-meaning gentleman took the snow-child by the hand and led her towards the house. She followed him, droopingly and reluctant; for all the glow and sparkle was gone out of her figure; and whereas just before she had resembled a bright, frosty, star-gemmed evening, with a crimson gleam on the cold horizon, she now looked as dull and languid as a thaw. As kind Mr. Lindsey led her up the steps of the door, Violet and Peony looked into his face, — their eyes full of tears, which froze before they could run down their cheeks, — and again entreated him not to bring their snow-image into the house.

" Not bring her in ! " exclaimed the kind-hearted man. " Why, you are crazy, my little Violet ! — quite crazy, my small Peony ! She is so cold, already, that her hand has almost frozen mine, in spite of my thick gloves. Would you have her freeze to death ? "

His wife, as he came up the steps, had been taking another long, earnest, almost awe-stricken gaze at the little white stranger. She hardly knew whether it was a dream or no ; but she could not help fancying that she saw the delicate print of Violet's fingers on the child's neck. It looked as if, while Violet was shaping out the image, she had given it a gentle pat with her hand, and had neglected to smooth the impression quite away.

" After all, husband," said the mother, recurring

to her idea that the angels would be as much delighted to play with Violet and Peony as she herself was, — " after all, she does look strangely like a snow-image! I do believe she is made out of snow!"

A puff of the west-wind blew against the snow-child, and again she sparkled like a star.

" Snow!" repeated good Mr. Lindsey, drawing the reluctant guest over his hospitable threshold. " No wonder she looks like snow. She is half frozen, poor little thing! But a good fire will put everything to rights."

Without further talk, and always with the same best intentions, this highly benevolent and common-sensible individual led the little white damsel — drooping, drooping, drooping, more and more — out of the frosty air, and into his comfortable parlor. A Heidenberg stove, filled to the brim with intensely burning anthracite, was sending a bright gleam through the isinglass of its iron door, and causing the vase of water on its top to fume and bubble with excitement. A warm, sultry smell was diffused throughout the room. A thermometer on the wall farthest from the stove stood at eighty degrees. The parlor was hung with red curtains, and covered with a red carpet, and looked just as warm as it felt. The difference betwixt the atmosphere here and the cold, wintry twilight out of doors, was like stepping at once from Nova Zembla to the hottest part of India, or from the North Pole into an oven. Oh, this was a fine place for the little white stranger!

The common-sensible man placed the snow-child on the hearth-rug, right in front of the hissing and fuming stove.

" Now she will be comfortable ! " cried Mr. Lindsey, rubbing his hands and looking about him with the pleasantest smile you ever saw. " Make yourself at home, my child."

Sad, sad and drooping, looked the little white maiden, as she stood on the hearth-rug, with the hot blast of the stove striking through her like a pestilence. Once, she threw a glance wistfully toward the windows, and caught a glimpse, through its red curtains, of the snow-covered roofs, and the stars glimmering frostily, and all the delicious intensity of the cold night. The bleak wind rattled the window-panes, as if it were summoning her to come forth. But there stood the snow-child, drooping, before the hot stove !

But the common-sensible man saw nothing amiss.

" Come, wife," said he, " let her have a pair of thick stockings and a woollen shawl or blanket directly ; and tell Dora to give her some warm supper as soon as the milk boils. You, Violet and Peony, amuse your little friend. She is out of spirits, you see, at finding herself in a strange place. For my part, I will go around among the neighbors, and find out where she belongs."

The mother, meanwhile, had gone in search of the shawl and stockings ; for her own view of the matter, however subtle and delicate, had given way, as it always did, to the stubborn materialism of her husband. Without heeding the remonstrances of his two children, who still kept murmuring that their little snow-sister did not love the warmth, good Mr. Lindsey took his departure, shutting the parlor-door carefully behind him. Turning up the collar of his sack over his ears, he emerged from the house, and had barely reached the street-gate, when he was recalled by the screams of Violet and Peony, and the rapping of a thimbled finger against the parlor window.

" Husband ! husband ! " cried his wife, showing her horror-stricken face through the window-panes. " There is no need of going for the child's parents ! "

" We told you so, father ! " screamed Violet and Peony, as he reëntered the parlor. " You would bring her in ; and now our poor — dear — beau-ti-ful little snow-sister is thawed ! "

And their own sweet little faces were already dissolved in tears ; so that their father, seeing what strange things occasionally happen in this every-day world, felt not a little anxious lest his children might be going to thaw too ! In the utmost perplexity, he demanded an explanation of his wife. She could only reply, that, being summoned to the parlor by the cries of Violet and and Peony, she found no trace of the little white maiden, unless it were the remains of a heap of snow, which, while she was gazing at it, melted quite away upon the hearth-rug.

" And there you see all that is left of it ! " added she, pointing to a pool of water in front of the stove.

" Yes, father," said Violet, looking reproachfully at him, through her tears, " there is all that is left of our dear little snow-sister ! "

" Naughty father ! " cried Peony, stamping his foot, and — I shudder to say — shaking his little fist at the common-sensible man. " We told you how it would be ! What for did you bring her in ? "

And the Heidenberg stove, through the isinglass of its door, seemed to glare at good Mr. Lindsey, like a red-eyed demon, triumphing in the mischief which it had done !

This, you will observe, was one of those rare cases, which yet will occasionally happen, where common-sense finds itself at fault. The remarkable story of the snow-image, though to that sagacious class of people to whom good Mr. Lindsey belongs it may seem but a childish affair, is, nevertheless, capable of being moralized in various methods, greatly for their edification. /One of its lessons, for instance, might be, that it behooves men, and especially men of benevolence, to consider well what they are about, and, before acting on their philanthropic purposes, to be quite sure that they comprehend the nature and all the relations of the business in hand. What has been established as an element of good to one being may prove absolute mischief to another ; even as the warmth of the parlor was proper enough for children of flesh and blood, like Violet and Peony, — though by no means very wholesome, even for them, — but involved nothing short of annihilation to the unfortunate snow-image.

But, after all, there is no teaching anything to wise men of good Mr. Lindsey's stamp. They know everything, — oh, to be sure ! — everything that has been, and everything that is, and everything that, by any future possibility, can be. And, should some phenomenon of nature or providence transcend their system, they will not recognize it, even if it come to pass under their very noses.

" Wife," said Mr. Lindsey, after a fit of silence, " see what a quantity of snow the children have brought in on their feet ! It has made quite a puddle here before the stove. Pray tell Dora to bring some towels and sop it up ! "

II.

THE GREAT STONE FACE.

One afternoon, when the sun was going down, a mother and her little boy sat at the door of their cottage, talking about the Great Stone Face. They had but to lift their eyes, and there it was plainly to be seen, though miles away, with the sunshine brightening all its features.

And what was the Great Stone Face?

Embosomed amongst a family of lofty mountains there was a valley so spacious that it contained many thousand inhabitants. Some of these good people dwelt in log huts, with the black forest all around them, on the steep and difficult hillsides. Others had their homes in comfortable farm-houses, and cultivated the rich soil on the gentle slopes or level surfaces of the valley. Others, again, were congregated into populous villages, where some wild, highland rivulet, tumbling down from its birthplace in the upper mountain region, had been caught and tamed by human cunning, and compelled to turn the machinery of cotton-factories. The inhabitants of this valley, in short, were numerous, and of many modes of life. But all of them, grown people and children, had a kind of familiarity with the Great Stone Face, although some possessed the gift of distinguishing this grand natural phenomenon more perfectly than many of their neighbors.

The Great Stone Face, then, was a work of Nature in her mood of majestic playfulness, formed on the perpendicular side of a mountain by some immense rocks, which had been thrown together in such a position as, when viewed at a proper distance, precisely to resemble the features of the human countenance. It seemed as if an enormous giant, or a Titan, had sculptured his own likeness on the precipice. There was the broad arch of the forehead, a hundred feet in height; the nose, with its long bridge; and the vast lips, which, if they could have spoken, would have rolled their thunder accents from one end of the valley to the other. True it is, that if the spectator approached too near he lost the outline of the gigantic visage, and could discern only a heap of ponderous and gigantic rocks, piled in chaotic ruin one upon another. Retracing his steps, however, the wondrous features would again be seen ; and the farther he withdrew from them, the more like a human face, with all its original divinity intact, did they appear ; until, as it grew dim in the distance, with the clouds and glorified vapor of the mountains clustering about it, the Great Stone Face seemed positively to be alive.

It was a happy lot for children to grow up to manhood or womanhood with the Great Stone Face before their eyes, for all the features were noble, and the expression was at once grand and sweet, as if it were the glow of a vast, warm heart, that embraced all mankind in its affections, and had room for more. It was an education only to look at it. According to the belief of many people, the valley owed much of its fertility to this benign aspect that was continually beaming over it, illuminating the clouds, and infusing its tenderness into the sunshine.

As we began with saying, a mother and her little boy sat at their cottage-door, gazing at the Great Stone Face, and talking about it. The child's name was Ernest.

"Mother," said he, while the Titanic visage smiled on him, " I wish that it could speak, for it looks so very kindly that its voice must needs be pleasant. If I were to see a man with such a face, I should love him dearly."

" If an old prophecy should come to pass," an-

swered his mother, " we may see a man, some time
or other, with exactly such a face as that."

" What prophecy do you mean, dear mother? "
eagerly inquired Ernest. " Pray tell me all about
it ! "

So his mother told him a story that her own
mother had told to her, when she herself was
younger than little Ernest; a story, not of things
that were past, but of what was yet to come; a
story, nevertheless, so very old, that even the Indians, who formerly inhabited this valley, had heard
it from their forefathers, to whom, as they affirmed,
it had been murmured by the mountain streams,
and whispered by the wind among the tree-tops.
The purport was, that, at some future day, a child
should be born hereabouts, who was destined to
become the greatest and noblest personage of his
time, and whose countenance, in manhood, should
bear an exact resemblance to the Great Stone Face.
Not a few old-fashioned people, and young ones
likewise, in the ardor of their hopes, still cherished
an enduring faith in this old prophecy. But others,
who had seen more of the world, had watched and
waited till they were weary, and had beheld no
man with such a face, nor any man that proved to
be much greater or nobler than his neighbors, concluded it to be nothing but an idle tale. At all
events, the great man of the prophecy had not yet
appeared.

" O mother, dear mother ! " cried Ernest, clap-
ping his hands above his head, " I do hope that I
shall live to see him ! "

His mother was an affectionate and thoughtful woman, and felt that it was wisest not to discourage the generous hopes of her little boy. So she only said to him, " Perhaps you may."

And Ernest never forgot the story that his mother told him. It was always in his mind, whenever he looked upon the Great Stone Face. He spent his childhood in the log cottage where he was born, and was dutiful to his mother, and helpful to her in many things, assisting her much with his little hands, and more with his loving heart. In this manner, from a happy yet often pensive child, he grew up to be a mild, quiet, unobtrusive boy, and sun-browned with labor in the fields, but with more intelligence brightening his aspect than is seen in many lads who have been taught at famous schools. Yet Ernest had had no teacher, save only that the Great Stone Face became one to him. When the toil of the day was over, he would gaze at it for hours, until he began to imagine that those vast features recognized him, and gave him a smile of kindness and encouragement, responsive to his own look of veneration. We must not take upon us to affirm that this was a mistake, although the Face may have looked no more kindly at Ernest than at all the world besides. But the secret was, that the boy's tender and confiding simplicity discerned what other people could not see ; and thus the love, which was meant for all, became his peculiar portion.

About this time, there went a rumor throughout

the valley, that the great man, foretold from ages long ago, who was to bear a resemblance to the Great Stone Face, had appeared at last. It seems that, many years before, a young man had migrated from the valley and settled at a distant seaport, where, after getting together a little money, he had set up as a shopkeeper. His name — but I could never learn whether it was his real one, or a nickname that had grown out of his habits and success in life — was Gathergold. Being shrewd and active, and endowed by Providence with that inscrutable faculty which develops itself in what the world calls luck, he became an exceedingly rich merchant, and owner of a whole fleet of bulky-bottomed ships. All the countries of the globe appeared to join hands for the mere purpose of adding heap after heap to the mountainous accumulation of this one man's wealth. The cold regions of the north, almost within the gloom and shadow of the Arctic Circle, sent him their tribute in the shape of furs ; hot Africa sifted for him the golden sands of her rivers, and gathered up the ivory tusks of her great elephants out of the forests ; the East came bringing him the rich shawls, and spices, and teas, and the effulgence of diamonds, and the gleaming purity of large pearls. The ocean, not to be behindhand with the earth, yielded up her mighty whales, that Mr. Gathergold might sell their oil, and make a profit on it. Be the original commodity what it might, it was gold within his grasp. It might be said of him, as of Midas in the fable, that whatever he touched with his finger immediately glistened, and grew yellow, and was changed at once into sterling metal, or, which suited him still better, into piles of coin. And, when Mr. Gathergold had become so very rich that it would have taken him a hundred years only to count his wealth, he bethought himself of his native valley, and resolved to go back thither, and end his days where he was born. With this purpose in view, he sent a skilful architect to build him such a palace as should be fit for a man of his vast wealth to live in.

As I have said above, it had already been rumored in the valley that Mr. Gathergold had turned out to be the prophetic personage so long and vainly looked for, and that his visage was the perfect and undeniable similitude of the Great Stone Face. People were the more ready to believe that this must needs be the fact, when they beheld the splendid edifice that rose, as if by enchantment, on the site of his father's old weather-beaten farm-house. The exterior was of marble, so dazzlingly white that it seemed as though the whole structure might melt away in the sunshine, like those humbler ones which Mr. Gathergold, in his young play-days, before his fingers were gifted with the touch of transmutation, had been accustomed to build of snow. It had a richly ornamented portico, supported by tall pillars, beneath which was a lofty door, studded with silver knobs, and made of a kind of variegated wood that had been brought from beyond the sea. The windows, from the floor

to the ceiling of each stately apartment, were composed, respectively, of but one enormous pane of
glass, so transparently pure that it was said to be
a finer medium than even the vacant atmosphere.
Hardly anybody had been permitted to see the interior of this palace; but it was reported, and with
good semblance of truth, to be far more gorgeous
than the outside, insomuch that whatever was iron
or brass in other houses was silver or gold in this;
and Mr. Gathergold's bedchamber, especially, made
such a glittering appearance that no ordinary man
would have been able to close his eyes there. But,
on the other hand, Mr. Gathergold was now so in-
ured to wealth, that perhaps he could not have
closed his eyes unless where the gleam of it was
certain to find its way beneath his eyelids.

In due time, the mansion was finished; next came
the upholsterers, with magnificent furniture; then
a whole troop of black and white servants, the har-
bingers of Mr. Gathergold, who, in his own majestic person, was expected to arrive at sunset. Our
friend Ernest, meanwhile, had been deeply stirred
by the idea that the great man, the noble man, the
man of prophecy, after so many ages of delay, was
at length to be made manifest to his native valley.
He knew, boy as he was, that there were a thousand ways in which Mr. Gathergold, with his vast
wealth, might transform himself into an angel of
beneficence, and assume a control over human affairs as wide and benignant as the smile of the
Great Stone Face. Full of faith and hope, Ernest

doubted not that what the people said was true, and that now he was to behold the living likeness of those wondrous features on the mountain-side. While the boy was still gazing up the valley, and fancying, as he always did, that the Great Stone Face returned his gaze and looked kindly at him, the rumbling of wheels was heard, approaching swiftly along the winding road.

" Here he comes ! " cried a group of people who were assembled to witness the arrival. " Here comes the great Mr. Gathergold ! "

A carriage drawn by four horses dashed round the turn of the road. Within it, thrust partly out of the window, appeared the physiognomy of a little old man, with a skin as yellow as if his own Midas-hand had transmuted it. He had a low forehead, small, sharp eyes, puckered about with innumerable wrinkles, and very thin lips, which he made still thinner by pressing them forcibly together.

" The very image of the Great Stone Face ! " shouted the people. " Sure enough, the old prophecy is true ; and here we have the great man come, at last ! "

And, what greatly perplexed Ernest, they seemed actually to believe that here was the likeness which they spoke of. By the roadside there chanced to be an old beggar-woman and two little beggar-children, stragglers from some far-off region, who, as the carriage rolled onward, held out their hands and lifted up their doleful voices, most piteously beseeching charity. A yellow claw — the very same that had clawed together so much wealth — poked itself out of the coach-window, and dropped some copper coins upon the ground; so that, though the great man's name seems to have been Gathergold, he might just as suitably have been nicknamed Scattercopper. Still, nevertheless, with an earnest shout, and evidently with as much good faith as ever, the people bellowed, —

"He is the very image of the Great Stone Face!"

But Ernest turned sadly from the wrinkled shrewdness of that sordid visage, and gazed up the valley, where, amid a gathering mist, gilded by the last sunbeams, he could still distinguish those glorious features which had impressed themselves into his soul. Their aspect cheered him. What did the benign lips seem to say?

"He will come! Fear not, Ernest; the man will come!"

The years went on, and Ernest ceased to be a boy. He had grown to be a young man now. He attracted little notice from the other inhabitants of the valley; for they saw nothing remarkable in his way of life, save that, when the labor of the day was over, he still loved to go apart and gaze and meditate upon the Great Stone Face. According to their idea of the matter, it was a folly, indeed, but pardonable, inasmuch as Ernest was industrious, kind, and neighborly, and neglected no duty for the sake of indulging this idle habit. They knew

not that the Great Stone Face had become a teacher
to him, and that the sentiment which was expressed
in it would enlarge the young man's heart, and fill
it with wider and deeper sympathies than other
hearts.   They knew not that thence would come a
better wisdom than could be learned from books,
and a better life than could be moulded on the defaced example of other human lives.   Neither did
Ernest know that the thoughts and affections which
came to him so naturally, in the fields and at the
fireside, and wherever he communed with himself,
were of a higher tone than those which all men
shared with him.   A simple soul, — simple as when
his mother first taught him the old prophecy, — he
beheld the marvellous features beaming adown the
valley, and still wondered that their human counterpart was so long in making his appearance.

By this time poor Mr. Gathergold was dead and
buried; and the oddest part of the matter was, that
his wealth, which was the body and spirit of his
existence, had disappeared before his death, leaving
nothing of him but a living skeleton, covered over
with a wrinkled, yellow skin.   Since the melting
away of his gold, it had been very generally conceded
that there was no such striking resemblance, after
all, betwixt the ignoble features of the ruined merchant and that majestic face upon the mountain-
side.   So the people ceased to honor him during
his lifetime, and quietly consigned him to forgetful-
ness after his decease.   Once in a while, it is true,
his memory was brought up in connection with the

magnificent palace which he had built, and which
had long ago been turned into a hotel for the ac-
commodation of strangers, multitudes of whom came
every summer to visit that famous natural curiosity,
the Great Stone Face. Thus, Mr. Gathergold, being discredited and thrown into the shade, the man
of prophecy was yet to come.

It so happened that a native-born son of the valley, many years before, had enlisted as a soldier,
and, after a great deal of hard fighting, had now become an illustrious commander. Whatever he may
be called in history, he was known in camps and
on the battle-field under the nickname of Old Blood-
and-Thunder. This war-worn veteran, being now
infirm with age and wounds, and weary of the tur-
moil of a military life, and of the roll of the drum
and the clangor of the trumpet, that had so long
been ringing in his ears, had lately signified a purpose of returning to his native valley, hoping to
find repose where he remembered to have left it.
The inhabitants, his old neighbors and their grown-
up children, were resolved to welcome the re-
nowned warrior with a salute of cannon and a public
dinner; and all the more enthusiastically, it
being affirmed that now, at last, the likeness of
the Great Stone Face had actually appeared. An
aide-de-camp of Old Blood-and-Thunder, travelling
through the valley, was said to have been struck
with the resemblance. Moreover the schoolmates
and early acquaintances of the general were ready
to testify, on oath, that, to the best of their recol-

lection, the aforesaid general had been exceedingly like the majestic image, even when a boy, only that the idea had never occurred to them at that period. Great, therefore, was the excitement throughout the valley ; and many people, who had never once thought of glancing at the Great Stone Face for years before, now spent their time in gazing at it, for the sake of knowing exactly how General Blood-and-Thunder looked.

On the day of the great festival, Ernest, with all the other people of the valley, left their work, and proceeded to the spot where the sylvan banquet was prepared. As he approached, the loud voice of the Rev. Dr. Battleblast was heard, beseeching a blessing on the good things set before them, and on the distinguished friend of peace in whose honor they were assembled. The tables were arranged in a cleared space of the woods, shut in by the surrounding trees, except where a vista opened eastward, and afforded a distant view of the Great Stone Face. Over the general's chair, which was a relic from the home of Washington, there was an arch of verdant boughs, with the laurel profusely intermixed, and surmounted by his country's banner, beneath which he had won his victories. Our friend Ernest raised himself on his tip-toes, in hopes to get a glimpse of the celebrated guest ; but there was a mighty crowd about the tables anxious to hear the toasts and speeches, and to catch any word that might fall from the general in reply ; and a volunteer company, doing duty as a guard, pricked ruthlessly with their bayonets at any particularly quiet person among the throng. So Ernest, being of an unobtrusive character, was thrust quite into the background, where he could see no more of Old Blood-and-Thunder's physiognomy than if it had been still blazing on the battle-field. To console himself, he turned towards the Great Stone Face, which, like a faithful and long-remembered friend, looked back and smiled upon him through the vista of the forest. Meantime, however, he could over- hear the remarks of various individuals, who were comparing the features of the hero with the face on the distant mountain-side.

" 'T is the same face, to a hair ! " cried one man, cutting a caper for joy.

" Wonderfully like, that 's a fact ! " responded another.

" Like ! why, I call it Old Blood-and-Thunder ..imself, in a monstrous looking-glass ! " cried a third. " And why not ? He 's the greatest man of this or any other age, beyond a doubt."

And then all three of the speakers gave a great shout, which communicated electricity to the crowd, and called forth a roar from a thousand voices, that went reverberating for miles among the mountains, until you might have supposed that the Great Stone Face had poured its thunder-breath into the cry. All these comments, and this vast enthusiasm, served the more to interest our friend ; nor did he think of questioning that now, at length, the moun- tain-visage had found its human counterpart. It is true, Ernest had imagined that this long-looked-for personage would appear in the character of a man of peace, uttering wisdom, and doing good, and making people happy. But, taking an habitual breadth of view, with all his simplicity, he contended that Providence should choose its own method of blessing mankind, and could conceive that this great end might be effected even by a warrior and a bloody sword, should inscrutable wisdom see fit to order matters so.

"The general! the general!" was now the cry. "Hush! silence! Old Blood-and-Thunder's going to make a speech."

Even so; for, the cloth being removed, the general's health had been drunk amid shouts of applause, and he now stood upon his feet to thank the company. Ernest saw him. There he was, over the shoulders of the crowd, from the two glittering epaulets and embroidered collar upward, beneath the arch of green boughs with intertwined laurel, and the banner drooping as if to shade his brow! And there, too, visible in the same glance, through the vista of the forest, appeared the Great Stone Face! And was there, indeed, such a resemblance as the crowd had testified? Alas, Ernest could not recognize it. He beheld a war-worn and weather-beaten countenance, full of energy, and expressive of an iron will; but the gentle wisdom, the deep, broad, tender sympathies, were altogether wanting in Old Blood-and-Thunder's visage; and even if the Great Stone Face had assumed his look

ɔf stern command, the milder traits would still have
tempered it.

"This is not the man of prophecy," sighed Ernest
to himself, as he made his way out of the throng.
"And must the world wait longer yet?"

The mists had congregated about the distant
mountain-side, and there were seen the grand and
awful features of the Great Stone Face, awful but
benignant, as if a mighty angel were sitting among
the hills and enrobing himself in a cloud-vesture of
gold and purple. As he looked, Ernest could hardly
believe but that a smile beamed over the whole
visage, with a radiance still brightening, although
without motion of the lips. It was probably the
effect of the western sunshine, melting through the
thinly diffused vapors that had swept between him
and the object that he gazed at. But — as it always did — the aspect of his marvellous friend
made Ernest as hopeful as if he had never hoped in
vain.

"Fear not, Ernest," said his heart, even as if the
Great Face were whispering him, — "fear not,
Ernest; he will come."

More years sped swiftly and tranquilly away.
Ernest still dwelt in his native valley, and was now
u man of middle age. By imperceptible degrees,
he had become known among the people. Now,
as heretofore, he labored for his bread, and was the
same simple-hearted man that he had always been.
But he had thought and felt so much, he had given
ꬱo many of the best hours of his life to unworldly

hopes for some great good to mankind, that it seemed as though he had been talking with the angels, and had imbibed a portion of their wisdom unawares. It was visible in the calm and well-considered beneficence of his daily life, the quiet stream of which had made a wide green margin all along its course. Not a day passed by that the world was not the better because this man, humble as he was, had lived. He never stepped aside from his own path, yet would always reach a blessing to his neighbor. Almost involuntarily, too, he had become a preacher. The pure and high simplicity of his thought, which, as one of its manifestations, took shape in the good deeds that dropped silently from his hand, flowed also forth in speech. He uttered truths that wrought upon and moulded the lives of those who heard him. His auditors, it may be, never suspected that Ernest, their own neighbor and familiar friend, was more than an ordinary man; least of all did Ernest himself suspect it; but, inevitably as the murmur of a rivulet, came thoughts out of his mouth that no other human lips had spoken.

When the people's minds had had a little time to cool, they were ready enough to acknowledge their mistake in imagining a similarity between General Blood-and-Thunder's truculent physiognomy and the benign visage on the mountain-side. But now, again, there were reports and many paragraphs in the newspapers, affirming that the likeness of the Great Stone Face had appeared upon the broad

shoulders of a certain eminent statesman. He, like
Mr. Gathergold and Old Blood-and-Thunder, was a
native of the valley, but had left it in his early days,
and taken up the trades of law and politics. Instead
of the rich man's wealth and the warrior's sword,
he had but a tongue, and it was mightier than both
together. So wonderfully eloquent was he, that
whatever he might choose to say, his auditors had
no choice but to believe him; wrong looked like
right, and right like wrong; for when it pleased
him he could make a kind of illuminated fog with
his mere breath, and obscure the natural daylight
with it. His tongue, indeed, was a magic instrument; sometimes it rumbled like the thunder;
sometimes it warbled like the sweetest music. It
was the blast of war, — the song of peace; and it
seemed to have a heart in it, when there was no
such matter. In good truth, he was a wondrous
man; and when his tongue had acquired him all
other imaginable success, — when it had been heard
in halls of state, and in the courts of princes and
potentates, — after it had made him known all over
the world, even as a voice crying from shore to
shore, — it finally persuaded his countrymen to
select him for the Presidency. Before this time,
— indeed, as soon as he began to grow celebrated,
.— his admirers had found out the resemblance between him and the Great Stone Face; and so much
were they struck by it that throughout the country
this distinguished gentleman was known by the
name of Old Stony Phiz. The phrase was cou-

4

sidered as giving a highly favorable aspect to his political prospects; for, as is likewise the case with the Popedom, nobody ever becomes President without taking a name other than his own.

While his friends were doing their best to make him President, Old Stony Phiz, as he was called, set out on a visit to the valley where he was born. Of course, he had no other object than to shake hands with his fellow-citizens, and neither thought nor cared about any effect which his progress through the country might have upon the election. Magnificent preparations were made to receive the illustrious statesman; a cavalcade of horsemen set forth to meet him at the boundary line of the State, and all the people left their business and gathered along the wayside to see him pass. Among these was Ernest. Though more than once disappointed, as we have seen, he had such a hopeful and confiding nature, that he was always ready to believe in whatever seemed beautiful and good. He kept his heart continually open, and thus was sure to catch the blessing from on high, when it should come. So now again, as buoyantly as ever, he went forth to behold the likeness of the Great Stone Face.

The cavalcade came prancing along the road, with a great clattering of hoofs and a mighty cloud of dust, which rose up so dense and high that the visage of the mountain-side was completely hidden from Ernest's eyes. All the great men of the neighborhood were there on horseback; militia officers, in uniform; the member of Congress; the

sheriff of the county ; the editors of newspapers ;
and many a farmer, too, had mounted his patient
steed, with his Sunday coat upon his back. It
really was a very brilliant spectacle, especially as
there were numerous banners flaunting over the
cavalcade, on some of which were gorgeous portraits
of the illustrious statesman and the Great Stone
Face, smiling familiarly at one another, like two
brothers. If the pictures were to be trusted, the
mutual resemblance, it must be confessed, was marvellous. We must not forget to mention that there
was a band of music, which made the echoes of the
mountains ring and reverberate with the loud triumph of its strains ; so that airy and soul-thrilling
melodies broke out among all the heights and hollows, as if every nook of his native valley had
found a voice to welcome the distinguished guest.
But the grandest effect was when the far-off mountain precipice flung back the music ; for then the
Great Stone Face itself seemed to be swelling the
triumphant chorus, in acknowledgment that, at
length, the man of prophecy was come.

All this while the people were throwing up their
hats and shouting, with enthusiasm so contagious
that the heart of Ernest kindled up, and he likewise
threw up his hat, and shouted, as loudly as the
loudest, " Huzza for the great man ! Huzza for
Old Stony Phiz ! " But as yet he had not seen
him.

" Here he is, now ! " cried those who stood near
Ernest. " There ! There ! Look at Old Stony

Phiz and then at the Old Man of the Mountain, and see if they are not as like as two twin-brothers ! "

In the midst of all this gallant array, came an open barouche, drawn by four white horses ; and in the barouche, with his massive head uncovered, sat the illustrious statesman, Old Stony Phiz himself.

" Confess it," said one of Ernest's neighbors to him, " the Great Stone Face has met its match at last ! "

Now, it must be owned that, at his first glimpse of the countenance which was bowing and smiling from the barouche, Ernest did fancy that there was a resemblance between it and the old familiar face upon the mountain-side. The brow, with its massive depth and loftiness, and all the other features, indeed, were boldly and strongly hewn, as if in emulation of a more than heroic, of a Titanic model. But the sublimity and stateliness, the grand expression of a divine sympathy, that illuminated the mountain visage, and etherealized its ponderous granite substance into spirit, might here be sought in vain. Something had been originally left out, or had departed. And therefore the marvellously gifted statesman had always a weary gloom in the deep caverns of his eyes, as of a child that has outgrown its playthings, or a man of mighty faculties and little aims, whose life, with all its high performances, was vague and empty, because no high purpose had endowed it with reality.

Still Ernest's neighbor was thrusting his elbow into his side, and pressing him for an answer.

"Confess! confess! Is not he the very picture of your Old Man of the Mountain?"

"No!" said Ernest, bluntly, "I see little or no likeness."

"Then so much the worse for the Great Stone Face!" answered his neighbor; and again he set up a shout for Old Stony Phiz.

But Ernest turned away, melancholy, and almost despondent; for this was the saddest of his disappointments, to behold a man who might have fulfilled the prophecy, and had not willed to do so. Meantime, the cavalcade, the banners, the music, and the barouches swept past him, with the vociferous crowd in the rear, leaving the dust to settle down, and the Great Stone Face to be revealed again, with the grandeur that it had worn for untold centuries.

"Lo, here I am, Ernest!" the benign lips seemed to say. "I have waited longer than thou, and am not yet weary. Fear not; the man will come."

The years hurried onward, treading in their haste on one another's heels. And now they began to bring white hairs, and scatter them over the head of Ernest; they made reverend wrinkles across his forehead, and furrows in his cheeks. He was an aged man. But not in vain had he grown old: more than the white hairs on his head were the sage thoughts in his mind; his wrinkles and furrows were inscriptions that Time had graved, and in which he had written legends of wisdom that had been tested by the tenor of a life. And Ernest had ceased to be obscure. Unsought for, undesired, had come the fame which so many seek, and made him known in the great world, beyond the limits of the valley in which he had dwelt so quietly. College professors, and even the active men of cities, came from far to see and converse with Ernest; for the report had gone abroad that this simple husbandman had ideas unlike those of other men, not gained from books, but of a higher tone, — a tranquil and familiar majesty, as if he had been talking with the angels as his daily friends. Whether it were sage, statesman, or philanthropist, Ernest received these visitors with the gentle sincerity that had characterized him from boyhood, and spoke freely with them of whatever came uppermost, or lay deepest in his heart or their own. While they talked together his face would kindle, unawares, and shine upon them, as with a mild evening light. Pensive with the fulness of such discourse, his guests took leave and went their way ; and passing up the valley, paused to look at the Great Stone Face, imagining that they had seen its likeness in a human countenance, but could not remember where.

While Ernest had been growing up and growing old, a bountiful Providence had granted a new poet to this earth. He, likewise, was a native of the valley, but had spent the greater part of his life at a distance from that romantic region, pouring out his sweet music amid the bustle and din of cities. Often, however, did the mountains which had been familiar to him in his childhood lift their snowy peaks into the clear atmosphere of his poetry. Neither was the Great Stone Face forgotten, for the poet had celebrated it in an ode which was grand enough to have been uttered by its own majestic lips. This man of genius, we may say, had come down from heaven with wonderful endowments. If he sang of a mountain, the eyes of all mankind beheld a mightier grandeur reposing on its breast, or soaring to its summit, than had before been seen there. If his theme were a lovely lake, a celestial smile had now been thrown over it, to gleam forever on its surface. If it were the vast old sea, even the deep immensity of its dread bosom seemed to swell the higher, as if moved by the emotions of the song. Thus the world assumed another and a better aspect from the hour that the poet blessed it with his happy eyes. The Creator had bestowed him, as the last best touch to his own handiwork. Creation was not finished till the poet came to interpret, and so complete it.

The effect was no less high and beautiful when his human brethren were the subject of his verse. The man or woman, sordid with the common dust of life, who crossed his daily path, and the little child who played in it, were glorified if he beheld them in his mood of poetic faith. He showed the golden links of the great chain that intertwined them with an angelic kindred; he brought out the hidden traits of a celestial birth that made them worthy of such kin. Some, indeed, there were, who thought to show the soundness of their judgment by affirming that all the beauty and dignity of the natural world existed only in the poet's fancy. Let such men speak for themselves, who undoubtedly appear to have been spawned forth by Nature with a contemptuous bitterness; she having plastered them up out of her refuse stuff, after all the swine were made. As respects all things else, the poet's ideal was the truest truth.

The songs of this poet found their way to Ernest. He read them after his customary toil, seated on the bench before his cottage door, where for such a length of time he had filled his repose with thought, by gazing at the Great Stone Face. And now as he read stanzas that caused the soul to thrill within him, he lifted his eyes to the vast countenance beaming on him so benignantly.

" O majestic friend," he murmured, addressing the Great Stone Face, " is not this man worthy to resemble thee ? "

The Face seemed to smile, but answered not a word.

Now it happened that the poet, though he dwelt so far away, had not only heard of Ernest, but had meditated much upon his character, until he deemed nothing so desirable as to meet this man, whose untaught wisdom walked hand in hand with the noble simplicity of his life. One summer morning, therefore, he took passage by the railroad, and, in the decline of the afternoon, alighted from the cars at no great distance from Ernest's cottage. The great hotel, which had formerly been the palace of Mr. Gathergold, was close at hand, but the poet, with his carpet-bag on his arm, inquired at once where Ernest dwelt, and was resolved to be accepted as his guest.

Approaching the door, he there found the good old man, holding a volume in his hand, which alternately he read, and then, with a finger between the leaves, looked lovingly at the Great Stone Face.

"Good evening," said the poet. "Can you give a traveller a night's lodging?"

"Willingly," answered Ernest; and then he added, smiling, "Methinks I never saw the Great Stone Face look so hospitably at a stranger."

The poet sat down on the bench beside him, and he and Ernest talked together. Often had the poet held intercourse with the wittiest and the wisest, but never before with a man like Ernest, whose thoughts and feelings gushed up with such a natural freedom, and who made great truths so familiar by his simple utterance of them. Angels, as had been so often said, seemed to have wrought with him at his labor in the fields; angels seemed to have sat with him by the fireside; and, dwelling with angels as friend with friends, he had imbibed the sublimity of their ideas, and imbued it with the sweet and lowly charm of household words. So thought the poet. And Ernest, on the other hand, was moved and agitated by the living images which the poet flung out of his mind, and which peopled all the air about the cottage door with shapes of beauty, both gay and pensive. The sympathies of these two men instructed them with a profounder sense than either could have attained alone. Their minds accorded into one strain, and made delightful music which neither of them could have claimed as all his own, nor distinguished his own share from the other's. They led one another, as it were, into a high pavilion of their thoughts, so remote, and hitherto so dim, that they had never entered it before, and so beautiful that they desired to be there always.

As Ernest listened to the poet, he imagined that the Great Stone Face was bending forward to listen too. He gazed earnestly into the poet's glowing eyes.

" Who are you, my strangely gifted guest ? " he said.

The poet laid his finger on the volume that Ernest had been reading.

" You have read these poems," said he. " You know me, then, — for I wrote them."

Again, and still more earnestly than before, Ernest examined the poet's features ; then turned towards the Great Stone Face ; then back, with an uncertain aspect, to his guest. But his countenance fell ; he shook his head, and sighed.

" Wherefore are you sad ? " inquired the poet

" Because," replied Ernest, " all through life I have awaited the fulfilment of a prophecy ; and, when I read these poems, I hoped that it might be fulfilled in you."

"You hoped," answered the poet, faintly smiling, "to find in me the likeness of the Great Stone Face. And you are disappointed, as formerly with Mr. Gathergold, and Old Blood-and-Thunder, and Old Stony Phiz. Yes, Ernest, it is my doom. You must add my name to the illustrious three, and record another failure of your hopes. For — in shame and sadness do I speak it, Ernest — I am not worthy to be typified by yonder benign and majestic image."

"And why?" asked Ernest. He pointed to the volume. "Are not those thoughts divine?"

"They have a strain of the Divinity," replied the poet. "You can hear in them the far-off echo of a heavenly song. But my life, dear Ernest, has not corresponded with my thought. I have had grand dreams, but they have been only dreams, because I have lived — and that, too, by my own choice — among poor and mean realities. Sometimes even — shall I dare to say it? — I lack faith in the grandeur, the beauty, and the goodness, which my own works are said to have made more evident in nature and in human life. Why, then, pure seeker of the good and true, shouldst thou hope to find me in yonder image of the divine?"

The poet spoke sadly, and his eyes were dim with tears. So, likewise, were those of Ernest.

At the hour of sunset, as had long been his frequent custom, Ernest was to discourse to an assemblage of the neighboring inhabitants in the open air. He and the poet, arm in arm, still talk-

ing together as they went along, proceeded to the
spot. It was a small nook among the hills, with
a gray precipice behind, the stern front of which
was relieved by the pleasant foliage of many creeping plants, that made a tapestry for the naked
rock, by hanging their festoons from all its rugged
angles. At a small elevation above the ground,
set in a rich framework of verdure, there appeared
a niche, spacious enough to admit a human figure,
with freedom for such gestures as spontaneously
accompany earnest thought and genuine emotion.
Into this natural pulpit Ernest ascended, and
threw a look of familiar kindness around upon his
audience. They stood, or sat, or reclined upon the
grass, as seemed good to each, with the departing
sunshine falling obliquely over them, and mingling
its subdued cheerfulness with the solemnity of a
grove of ancient trees, beneath and amid the boughs
of which the golden rays were constrained to pass.
In another direction was seen the Great Stone
Face, with the same cheer, combined with the
same solemnity, in its benignant aspect.

Ernest began to speak, giving to the people of
what was in his heart and mind. His words had
power, because they accorded with his thoughts;
and his thoughts had reality and depth, because
they harmonized with the life which he had always
lived. It was not mere breath that this preacher
uttered; they were the words of life, because a life
of good deeds and holy love was melted into them.
Pearls, pure and rich, had been dissolved into this

precious draught. The poet, as he listened, felt that the being and character of Ernest were a nobler strain of poetry than he had ever written. His eyes glistening with tears, he gazed reverentially at the venerable man, and said within himself that never was there an aspect so worthy of a prophet and a sage as that mild, sweet, thoughtful countenance, with the glory of white hair diffused about it. At a distance, but distinctly to be seen, high up in the golden light of the setting sun, appeared the Great Stone Face, with hoary mists around it, like the white hairs around the brow of Ernest. Its look of grand beneficence seemed to embrace the world.

At that moment, in sympathy with a thought which he was about to utter, the face of Ernest assumed a grandeur of expression, so imbued with benevolence, that the poet,[1] by an irresistible impulse, threw his arms aloft, and shouted, —

"Behold! Behold! Ernest is himself the likeness of the Great Stone Face!"

Then all the people looked, and saw that what the deep-sighted poet said was true. The prophecy was fulfilled. But Ernest, having finished what he had to say, took the poet's arm, and walked slowly

---

[1] That the poet should have been the one to discover the re semblance accords with the conception of the poet himself in this little apologue. Poetic insight is still separable from integrity of character, and it was quite possible for this poet to see the ideal beauty in another, while conscious of his own defect. The humility of Ernest, as the last word of the story, completes the certainty of the likeness.

homeward, still hoping that some wiser and better man than himself would by and by appear, bearing a resemblance to the GREAT STONE FACE.

III.

DROWNE'S WOODEN IMAGE.

[IN his preface to *The Marble Faun* Hawthorne speaks of the difficulty of reproducing American life in romance, but in the story of *Drowne's Wooden Image* he has within narrow limits achieved a more difficult task, that of translating a Greek myth into the Yankee vernacular, without impairing the native flavor. In the course of the story he laughingly refers to the myth of Pygmalion, the statuary of Cyprus, who shunned the society of women, but became so enamored of one of his own beautiful creations that he besought Venus to give her life. The same theme, with a wider and more subtle application, reappears in this little story, and it is interesting to see how Hawthorne has avoided the merely grotesque, and by the sincerity of the carver has given dignity to the illusion. The personages of the story appear in history. There was a Drowne, who was a carver, and whose work, as Hawthorne reminds us, was to be seen in Boston. He is known as Deacon Shem Drowne, and died in 1774. From several allusions in the story, the time may be made to be in King George II.'s reign, say about 1760. The poet, William Morris, has told the story of *Pygmalion and the Image* in *The Earthly Paradise.*]

ONE sunshiny morning, in the good old times of the town of Boston, a young carver in wood, well known by the name of Drowne, stood contemplating a large oaken log, which it was his purpose to convert into the figure-head of a vessel. And while he discussed within his own mind what sort of shape or similitude it were well to bestow upon this excellent piece of timber, there came into Drowne's workshop a certain Captain Hunnewell, owner and commander of the good brig called the Cynosure, which had just returned from her first voyage to Fayal.

" Ah ! that will do, Drowne, that will do ! " cried the jolly captain, tapping the log with his rattan. " I bespeak this very piece of oak for the figure-head of the Cynosure. She has shown herself the sweetest craft that ever floated, and I mean to decorate her prow with the handsomest image that the skill of man can cut out of timber. And, Drowne, you are the fellow to execute it."

" You give me more credit than I deserve, Captain Hunnewell," said the carver, modestly, yet as one conscious of eminence in his art. " But, for the sake of the good brig, I stand ready to do my best. And which of these designs do you prefer? Here," — pointing to a staring, half-length figure.

in a white wig and scarlet coat, — " here is an excellent model, the likeness of our gracious king.
Here is the valiant Admiral Vernon.[1]   Or, if you
prefer a female figure, what say you to Britannia
with the trident ? "

"All very fine, Drowne; all very fine," answered the mariner. " But as nothing like the
brig ever swam the ocean, so I am determined she
shall have such a figure-head as old Neptune never
saw in his life.   And what is more, as there is a
secret in the matter, you must pledge your credit
not to betray it."

" Certainly," said Drowne, marvelling, however,
what possible mystery there could be in reference
to an affair so open, of necessity, to the inspection
of all the world as the figure-head of a vessel.
" You may depend, Captain, on my being as secret
as the nature of the case will permit."

Captain Hunnewell then took Drowne by the
button, and communicated his wishes in so low a
tone that it would be unmannerly to repeat what
was evidently intended for the carver's private ear.
We shall, therefore, take the opportunity to give
the reader a few desirable particulars about Drowne
himself.

[1] Edward Vernon, 1684-1757, was a distinguished English
admiral. He saw a good deal of service in the West Indies, and
in 1739 took the town of Porto Bello; and as the affair made
much noise and there was a brisk trade between Boston and the
West Indies, we may guess that Drowne found Admiral Vernon
a popular model for figure-heads.   There was a tavern called
the Admiral Vernon on the lower corner of State Street and
Merchant's Row, Boston.

He was the first American who is known to have
attempted — in a very humble line, it is true —
that art in which we can now reckon so many
names already distinguished, or rising to distinction. From his earliest boyhood he had exhibited
a knack, — for it would be too proud a word to call
it genius, — a knack, therefore, for the imitation of
the human figure in whatever material came most
readily to hand. The snows of a New England
winter had often supplied him with a species of
marble as dazzlingly white, at least, as the Parian
or the Carrara, and if less durable, yet sufficiently
so to correspond with any claims to permanent existence possessed by the boy's frozen statues. Yet
they won admiration from maturer judges than his
school-fellows, and were, indeed, remarkably clever,
though destitute of the native warmth that might
have made the snow melt beneath his hand. As he
advanced in life, the young man adopted pine and
oak as eligible materials for the display of his skill,
which now began to bring him a return of solid silver as well as the empty praise that had been an
apt reward enough for his productions of evanes-
cent snow. He became noted for carving ornamental pump-heads, and wooden urns for gate-posts,
and decorations, more grotesque than fanciful, for
mantel-pieces. No apothecary would have deemed
himself in the way of obtaining custom, without
setting up a gilded mortar, if not a head of Galen
or Hippocrates, from the skilful hand of Drowne.

But the great scope of his business lay in the

manufacture of figure-heads for vessels. Whether it were the monarch himself, or some famous British admiral or general, or the governor of the province, or perchance the favorite daughter of the ship-owner, there the image stood above the prow, decked out in gorgeous colors, magnificently gilded, and staring the whole world out of countenance, as if from an innate consciousness of its own superiority. These specimens of native sculpture had crossed the sea in all directions, and been not ignobly noticed among the crowded shipping of the Thames, and wherever else the hardy mariners of New England had pushed their adventures. It must be confessed that a family likeness pervaded these respectable progeny of Drowne's skill; that the benign countenance of the king resembled those of his subjects, and that Miss Peggy Hobart, the merchant's daughter, bore a remarkable similitude to Britannia, Victory, and other ladies of the allegoric sisterhood; and, finally, that they all had a kind of wooden aspect, which proved an intimate relationship with the unshaped blocks of timber in the carver's workshop. But at least there was no inconsiderable skill of hand, nor a deficiency of any attribute to render them really works of art, except that deep quality, be it of soul or intellect, which bestows life upon the lifeless and warmth upon the cold, and which, had it been present, would have made Drowne's wooden image instinct with spirit.

The captain of the Cynosure had now finished his instructions.

"And, Drowne," said he, impressively, "you must lay aside all other business and set about this forthwith. And as to the price, only do the job in first-rate style, and you shall settle that point yourself."

"Very well, Captain," answered the carver, who looked grave and somewhat perplexed, yet had a sort of smile upon his visage; "depend upon it, I'll do my utmost to satisfy you."

From that moment the men of taste about Long Wharf and the Town Dock who were wont to show their love for the arts by frequent visits to Drowne's workshop, and admiration of his wooden images, began to be sensible of a mystery in the carver's conduct. Often he was absent in the daytime. Sometimes, as might be judged by gleams of light from the shop-windows, he was at work until a late hour of the evening; although neither knock nor voice, on such occasions, could gain admittance for a visitor, or elicit any word of response. Nothing remarkable, however, was observed in the shop at those hours when it was thrown open. A fine piece of timber, indeed, which Drowne was known to have reserved for some work of especial dignity, was seen to be gradually assuming shape. What shape it was destined ultimately to take was a problem to his friends and a point on which the carver himself preserved a rigid silence. But day after day, though Drowne was seldom noticed in the act of working upon it, this rude form began to be developed until it became evident to all observers that a female figure was growing into mimic life. At each new visit they beheld a larger pile of wooden chips and a nearer approximation to something beautiful. It seemed as if the hamadryad of the oak had sheltered herself from the unimaginative world within the heart of her native tree, and that it was only necessary to remove the strange shapelessness that had incrusted her, and reveal the grace and loveliness of a divinity. Imperfect as the design, the attitude, the costume, and especially the face of the image still remained, there was already an effect that drew the eye from the wooden cleverness of Drowne's earlier productions and fixed it upon the tantalizing mystery of this new project.

Copley,[1] the celebrated painter, then a young man and a resident of Boston, came one day to visit Drowne ; for he had recognized so much of moderate ability in the carver as to induce him, in the dearth of professional sympathy, to cultivate his acquaintance. On entering the shop the artist glanced at the inflexible image of king, commander, dame, and allegory that stood around, on the best of which might have been bestowed the questionable praise that it looked as if a living man had here been changed to wood, and that not only the physical, but the intellectual and spiritual part, partook of the stolid transformation. But in not a single instance did it seem as if the wood were imbibing the ethereal essence of humanity. What a wide distinction is here ! and how far would the

[1] John Singleton Copley was born in Boston in 1737.

slightest portion of the latter merit have outvalued the utmost degree of the former !

" My friend Drowne," said Copley, smiling to himself, but alluding to the mechanical and wooden cleverness that so invariably distinguished the images, " you are really a remarkable person ! I have seldom met with a man in your line of business that could do so much ; for one other touch might make this figure of General Wolfe,[1] for instance, a breathing and intelligent human creature."

" You would have me think that you are praising me highly, Mr. Copley," answered Drowne, turning his back upon Wolfe's image in apparent disgust. " But there has come a light into my mind. I know, what you know as well, that the one touch which you speak of as deficient is the only one that would be truly valuable, and that without it these works of mine are no better than worthless abortions. There is the same difference between them and the works of an inspired artist as between a sign-post daub and one of your best pictures."

" This is strange," cried Copley, looking him in the face, which now, as the painter fancied, had a singular depth of intelligence, though hitherto it had not given him greatly the advantage over his own family of wooden images. " What has come over you ? How is it that, possessing the idea which you have now uttered, you should produce only such works as these ? "

---

[1] General Wolfe, the hero of Quebec, was killed on the **Plains of Abraham**, September 13, 1759.

The carver smiled, but made no reply. Copley turned again to the images, conceiving that the sense of deficiency which Drowne had just expressed, and which is so rare in a merely mechanical character, must surely imply a genius, the tokens of which had heretofore been overlooked. But no; there was not a trace of it. He was about to withdraw when his eyes chanced to fall upon a half-developed figure which lay in a corner of the workshop, surrounded by scattered chips of oak. It arrested him at once.

"What is here? Who has done this?" he broke out, after contemplating it in speechless astonishment for an instant. "Here is the divine, the life-giving touch. What inspired hand is beckoning this wood to arise and live? Whose work is this?"

"No man's work," replied Drowne. "The figure lies within that block of oak, and it is my business to find it."

"Drowne," said the true artist, grasping the carver fervently by the hand, "you are a man of genius!"

As Copley departed, happening to glance backward from the threshold, he beheld Drowne bending over the half-created shape, and stretching forth his arms as if he would have embraced and drawn it to his heart; while, had such a miracle been possible, his countenance expressed passion enough to communicate warmth and sensibility to the lifeless oak.

"Strange enough!" said the artist to himself. "Who would have looked for a modern Pygmalion in the person of a Yankee mechanic!"

As yet, the image was but vague in its outward presentment; so that, as in the cloud-shapes around the western sun, the observer rather felt, or was led to imagine, than really saw what was intended by it. Day by day, however, the work assumed greater precision, and settled its irregular and misty outline into distincter grace and beauty. The general design was now obvious to the common eye. It was a female figure, in what appeared to be a foreign dress; the gown being laced over the bosom, and opening in front so as to disclose a skirt or petticoat, the folds and inequalities of which were admirably represented in the oaken substance. She wore a hat of singular gracefulness, and abundantly laden with flowers, such as never grew in the rude soil of New England, but which, with all their fanciful luxuriance, had a natural truth that it seemed impossible for the most fertile imagination to have attained without copying from real prototypes. There were several little appendages to this dress, such as a fan, a pair of earrings, a chain about the neck, a watch in the bosom, and a ring upon the finger, all of which would have been deemed beneath the dignity of sculpture. They were put on, however, with as much taste as a lovely woman might have shown in her attire, and could therefore have shocked none but a judgment spoiled by artistic rules.

The face was still imperfect; but gradually, by a magic touch, intelligence and sensibility brightened through the features, with all the effect of

light gleaming forth from within the solid oak.
The face became alive.   It was a beautiful, though
not precisely regular, and somewhat haughty aspect, but with a certain piquancy about the eyes
and mouth, which, of all expressions, would have
seemed the most impossible to throw over a wooden
countenance.   And now, so far as carving went,
this wonderful production was complete.

"Drowne," said Copley, who had hardly missed
a single day in his visits to the carver's workshop,
"if this work were in marble it would make you
famous at once ; nay, I would almost affirm that it
would make an era in the art.   It is as ideal as an
antique statue, and yet as real as any lovely woman whom one meets at a fireside or in the street.
But I trust you do not mean to desecrate this exquisite creature with paint, like those staring kings
and admirals yonder ? "

"Not paint her ! " exclaimed Captain Hunnewell, who stood by ; " not paint the figure-head of
the Cynosure !   And what sort of a figure should I
cut in a foreign port with such an unpainted oaken
stick as this over my prow !   She must, and she
shall, be painted to the life, from the topmost
flower in her hat down to the silver spangles on
her slippers."

"Mr. Copley," said Drowne, quietly, "I know
nothing of marble statuary, and nothing of the
sculptor's rules of art ; but of this wooden image,
this work of my hands, this creature of my heart,"
— and here his voice faltered and choked in a very

singular manner, — " of this — of her — I may say
that I know something. A wellspring of inward
wisdom gushed within me as I wrought upon the
oak with my whole strength, and soul, and faith.
Let others do what they may with marble, and
adopt what rules they choose. If I can produce
my desired effect by painted wood, those rules are
not for me, and I have a right to disregard them."

" The very spirit of genius," muttered Copley
to himself. " How otherwise should this carver feel
himself entitled to transcend all rules, and make
me ashamed of quoting them ? "

He looked earnestly at Drowne, and again saw
that expression of human love which, in a spiritual
sense, as the artist could not help imagining was the
secret of the life that had been breathed into this
block of wood.

The carver, still in the same secrecy that marked
all his operations upon this mysterious image, proceeded to paint the habiliments in their proper colors, and the countenance with nature's red and
white. When all was finished he threw open his
workshop, and admitted the towns-people to behold
what he had done. Most persons, at their first entrance, felt impelled to remove their hats, and pay
such reverence as was due to the richly dressed and
beautiful young lady who seemed to stand in a corner of the room, with oaken chips and shavings
scattered at her feet. Then came a sensation of
fear ; as if, not being actually human, yet so like
humanity, she must therefore be something preter

natural.   There was, in truth, an indefinable air
and expression that might reasonably induce the
query, Who and from what sphere this daughter of
the oak should be ?   The strange, rich flowers of
Eden on her head ; the complexion, so much deeper
and more brilliant than those of our native beauties ; the foreign, as it seemed, and fantastic garb,
yet not too fantastic to be worn decorously in the
street ; the delicately wrought embroidery of the
skirt ; the broad gold chain about her neck ; the curious ring upon her finger ; the fan, so exquisitely
sculptured in open-work, and painted to resemble
pearl and ebony ; where could Drowne, in his sober
walk of life, have beheld the vision here so match-
lessly embodied !   And then her face !   In the dark
eyes and around the voluptuous mouth there played
a look made up of pride, coquetry, and a gleam of
mirthfulness, which impressed Copley with the idea
that the image was secretly enjoying the perplexing
admiration of himself and other beholders.

" And will you," said he to the carver, " permit
this masterpiece to become the figure-head of a
vessel ?   Give the honest captain yonder figure of
Britannia, — it will answer his purpose far better,
— and send this fairy queen to England, where,
for aught I know, it may bring you a thousand
pounds."

" I have not wrought it for money," said
Drowne.

" What sort of a fellow is this ! " thought Copley.
" A Yankee, and throw away the chance of making

his fortune! He has gone mad; and thence has come this gleam of genius."

There was still further proof of Drowne's lunacy, if credit were due to the rumor that he had been seen kneeling at the feet of the oaken lady, and gazing with a lover's passionate ardor into the face that his own hands had created. The bigots of the day hinted that it would be no matter of surprise if an evil spirit were allowed to enter this beautiful form and seduce the carver to destruction.

The fame of the image spread far and wide. The inhabitants visited it so universally that after a few days of exhibition there was hardly an old man or a child who had not become minutely familiar with its aspect. Even had the story of Drowne's wooden image ended here, its celebrity might have been prolonged for many years by the reminiscences of those who looked upon it in their childhood, and saw nothing else so beautiful in after life. But the town was now astounded by an event the narrative of which has formed itself into one of the most singular legends that are yet to be met with in the traditionary chimney-corners of the New England metropolis, where old men and women sit dreaming of the past, and wag their heads at the dreamers of the present and the future.

One fine morning, just before the departure of the Cynosure on her second voyage to Fayal, the commander of that gallant vessel was seen to issue from his residence in Hanover Street. He was stylishly dressed in a blue broadcloth coat, with gold·

lace at the seams and button-holes, an embroidered
scarlet waistcoat, a triangular hat, with a loop and
broad binding of gold, and wore a silver-hilted
hanger at his side.   But the good captain might
have been arrayed in the robes of a prince or the
rags of a beggar, without in either case attracting
notice, while obscured by such a companion as now
leaned on his arm.   The people in the street
started, rubbed their eyes, and either leaped aside
from their path, or stood as if transfixed to wood or
marble in astonishment.

    " Do you see it ? — do you see it ? " cried one,
with tremulous eagerness.   " It is the very same ! "

    " The same ? " answered another, who had ar-
rived in town only the night before.   " Who do
you mean ?   I see only a sea-captain in his shore-
going clothes, and a young lady in a foreign habit,
with a bunch of beautiful flowers in her hat.   On
my word, she is as fair and bright a damsel as my
eyes have looked on this many a day ! "

    " Yes ; the same ! — the very same ! " repeated
the other.   " Drowne's wooden image has come to
life ! "

    Here was a miracle indeed !   Yet, illuminated by
the sunshine, or darkened by the alternate shade of
the houses, and with its garments fluttering lightly
in the morning breeze, there passed the image
along the street.   It was exactly and minutely the
shape, the garb, and the face which the towns-people had so recently thronged to see and admire.
Not a rich flower upon her head, not a single leaf,

but had had its prototype in Drowne's wooden workmanship, although now their fragile grace had become flexible, and was shaken by every footstep that the wearer made. The broad gold chain upon the neck was identical with the one represented on the image, and glistened with the motion imparted by the rise and fall of the bosom which it decorated. A real diamond sparkled on her finger. In her right hand she bore a pearl and ebony fan, which she flourished with a fantastic and bewitching coquetry that was likewise expressed in all her movements as well as in the style of her beauty and the attire that so well harmonized with it. The face, with its brilliant depth of complexion, had the same piquancy of mirthful mischief that was fixed upon the countenance of the image, but which was here varied and continually shifting, yet always essentially the same, like the sunny gleam upon a bubbling fountain. On the whole, there was something so airy and yet so real in the figure, and withal so perfectly did it represent Drowne's image, that people knew not whether to suppose the magic wood etherealized into a spirit or warmed and softened into an actual woman.

"One thing is certain," muttered a Puritan of the old stamp, "Drowne has sold himself to the Devil; and doubtless this gay Captain Hunnewell is a party to the bargain."

"And I," said a young man who overheard him, "would almost consent to be the third victim, for the liberty of saluting those lovely lips."

"And so would I," said Copley, the painter, "for the privilege of taking her picture."

The image, or the apparition, whichever it might be, still escorted by the bold captain, proceeded from Hanover Street through some of the cross lanes that make this portion of the town so intricate, to Ann Street, thence into Dock Square, and so downward to Drowne's shop, which stood just on the water's edge. The crowd still followed, gathering volume as it rolled along. Never had a modern miracle occurred in such broad daylight, nor in the presence of such a multitude of witnesses. The airy image, as if conscious that she was the object of the murmurs and disturbance that swelled behind her, appeared slightly vexed and flustered, yet still in a manner consistent with the light vivacity and sportive mischief that were written in her countenance. She was observed to flutter her fan with such vehement rapidity that the elaborate delicacy of its workmanship gave way, and it remained broken in her hand.

Arriving at Drowne's door, while the captain threw it open, the marvellous apparition paused an instant on the threshold, assuming the very attitude of the image, and casting over the crowd that glance of sunny coquetry which all remembered on the face of the oaken lady. She and her cavalier then disappeared.

"Ah!" murmured the crowd, drawing a deep breath, as with one vast pair of lungs.

"The world looks darker now that she has van ished," said some of the young men.

But the aged, whose recollections dated as far back as witch times, shook their heads, and hinted that our forefathers would have thought it a pious deed to burn the daughter of the oak with fire.

" If she be other than a bubble of the elements," exclaimed Copley, " I must look upon her face again."

He accordingly entered the shop ; and there, in her usual corner, stood the image, gazing at him, as it might seem, with the very same expression of mirthful mischief that had been the farewell look of the apparition when, but a moment before, she turned her face towards the crowd. The carver stood beside his creation, mending the beautiful fan, which by some accident was broken in her hand.[1] But there was no longer any motion in the lifelike image, nor any real woman in the workshop, nor even the witchcraft of a sunny shadow, that might have deluded people's eyes as it flitted along the street. Captain Hunnewell, too, had vanished. His hoarse, sea-breezy tones, however, were audible on the other side of a door that opened upon the water.

" Sit down in the stern sheets, my lady," said the gallant captain. " Come, bear a hand, you lubbers, and set us on board in the turning of a minute-glass."

And then was heard the stroke of oars.

" Drowne," said Copley, with a smile of intelligence, " you have been a truly fortunate man.

[1] A slight touch to keep in sight the mysterious affinity of lady and image.

What painter or statuary ever had such a subject! No wonder that she inspired a genius into you, and first created the artist who afterwards created her image."

Drowne looked at him with a visage that bore the traces of tears, but from which the light of imagination and sensibility, so recently illuminating it, had departed. He was again the mechanical carver that he had been known to be all his lifetime.

" I hardly understand what you mean, Mr. Copley," said he, putting his hand to his brow. " This image! Can it have been my work? Well, I have wrought it in a kind of dream; and now that I am broad awake I must set about finishing yonder figure of Admiral Vernon."

And forthwith he employed himself on the stolid countenance of one of his wooden progeny, and completed it in his own mechanical style, from which he was never known afterwards to deviate. He followed his business industriously for many years, acquired a competence, and in the latter part of his life attained to a dignified station in the church, being remembered in records and traditions as Deacon Drowne, the carver. One of his productions, an Indian chief, gilded all over, stood during the better part of a century on the cupola of the Province House, bedazzling the eyes of those who looked upward, like an angel of the sun. Another work of the good deacon's hand — a reduced likeness of his friend Captain Hunnewell, holding a telescope and quadrant — may be seen to this day, at the corner of Broad and State Streets, serving in the useful capacity of sign to the shop of a nautical instrument maker. We know not how to account for the inferiority of this quaint old figure as compared with the recorded excellence of the Oaken Lady, unless on the supposition that in every human spirit there is imagination, sensibility, creative power, genius, which, according to circumstances, may either be developed in this world, or shrouded in a mask of dulness until another state of being. To our friend Drowne there came a brief season of excitement, kindled by love. It rendered him a genius for that one occasion, but, quenched in disappointment, left him again the mechanical carver in wood, without the power even of appreciating the work that his own hands had wrought. Yet, who can doubt that the very highest state to which a human spirit can attain, in its loftiest aspirations, is its truest and most natural state, and that Drowne was more consistent with himself when he wrought the admirable figure of the mysterious lady, than when he perpetrated a whole progeny of blockheads?

There was a rumor in Boston, about this period, that a young Portuguese lady of rank, on some occasion of political or domestic disquietude, had fled from her home in Fayal and put herself under the protection of Captain Hunnewell, on board of whose vessel, and at whose residence, she was sheltered until a change of affairs. This fair stranger must have been the original of Drowne's Wooden Image.

6

IV.

HOWE'S MASQUERADE.

[THE second volume of *Twice-Told Tales* opens with four *Legends of the Province House*, of which *Howe's Masquerade* is the first. The introductory sketch of the Province House is included in it. The story was first published in *The United States Magazine and Democratic Review*, May, 1838, when the Province House was in the state described in the sketch. Nothing remains of it now but a portion of the exterior walls, and it is almost completely hemmed in by buildings. A history of the Province House and of its occupants will be found in Drake's *Old Landmarks and Historic Personages of Boston.* It would be an excellent study to expand the historic allusions contained in the procession of governors. Hawthorne has characterized these personages with great precision.]

ONE afternoon, last summer, while walking along Washington Street, my eye was attracted by a signboard protruding over a narrow archway, nearly opposite the Old South Church. The sign represented the front of a stately edifice, which was designated as the " OLD PROVINCE HOUSE, kept by Thomas Waite." I was glad to be thus reminded of a purpose, long entertained, of visiting and ram

bling over the mansion of the old royal governors
of Massachusetts ; and entering the arched passage, which penetrated through the middle of a
brick row of shops, a few steps transported me
from the busy heart of modern Boston into a small
and secluded court-yard. One side of this space
was occupied by the square front of the Province
House, three stories high, and surmounted by a cupola, on the top of which a gilded Indian was discernible, with his bow bent and his arrow on the
string, as if aiming at the weathercock on the spire
of the Old South. The figure has kept this attitude for seventy years or more, ever since good
Deacon Drowne, a cunning carver of wood, first
stationed him on his long sentinel's watch over the
city.

The Province House is constructed of brick,
which seems recently to have been overlaid with a
coat of light-colored paint. A flight of red freestone steps, fenced in by a balustrade of curiously
wrought iron, ascends from the court-yard to the
spacious porch, over which is a balcony, with an
iron balustrade of similar pattern and workmanship
to that beneath. These letters and figures — 16
P. S. 79 — are wrought into the iron-work of the
balcony, and probably express the date of the edifice, with the initials of its founder's name.[1] A
wide door with double leaves admitted me into the
hall or entry, on the right of which is the entrance
to the bar-room.

[1] Peter Sargeant, a Boston merchant, who came from London
in 1667, and was concerned in the overthrow of Andros.

It was in this apartment, I presume, that the ancient governors held their levees, with vice-regal pomp, surrounded by the military men, the councillors, the judges, and other officers of the crown, while all the loyalty of the province thronged to do them honor. But the room, in its present condition, cannot boast even of faded magnificence. The panelled wainscot is covered with dingy paint, and acquires a duskier hue from the deep shadow into which the Province House is thrown by the brick block that shuts it in from Washington Street. A ray of sunshine never visits this apartment any more than the glare of the festal torches which have been extinguished from the era of the Revolution. The most venerable and ornamental object is a chimney-piece set round with Dutch tiles of blue-figured china, representing scenes from Scripture; and, for aught I know, the lady of Pownall or Bernard may have sat beside this fireplace, and told her children the story of each blue tile. A bar in modern style, well replenished with decanters, bottles, cigar-boxes, and network bags of lemons, and provided with a beer-pump and a soda-fount, extends along one side of the room. At my entrance, an elderly person was smacking his lips, with a zest which satisfied me that the cellars of the Province House still hold good liquor, though doubtless of other vintages than were quaffed by the old governors. After sipping a glass of port sangaree, prepared by the skilful hands of Mr. Thomas Waite, I besought that worthy successor and rep-

resentative of so many historic personages to con
duct me over their time-honored mansion.

He readily complied; but, to confess the truth, I
was forced to draw strenuously upon my imagination, in order to find aught that was interesting in
a house which, without its historic associations,
would have seemed merely such a tavern as is usually favored by the custom of decent city boarders
and old-fashioned country gentlemen. The chambers, which were probably spacious in former times,
are now cut up by partitions, and subdivided into
little nooks, each affording scanty room for the
narrow bed and chair and dressing-table of a single
lodger. The great staircase, however, may be
termed, without much hyperbole, a feature of
grandeur and magnificence. It winds through the
midst of the house by flights of broad steps, each
flight terminating in a square landing-place, whence
the ascent is continued towards the cupola. A
carved balustrade, freshly painted in the lower
stories, but growing dingier as we ascend, borders
the staircase with its quaintly twisted and intertwined pillars, from top to bottom. Up these
stairs the military boots, or perchance the gouty
shoes, of many a governor have trodden, as the
wearers mounted to the cupola, which afforded
them so wide a view over their metropolis and the
surrounding country. The cupola is an octagon,
with several windows, and a door opening upon the
roof. From this station, as I pleased myself with
imagining, Gage may have beheld his disastrous

victory on Bunker Hill (unless one of the tri-
mountains intervened), and Howe have marked
the approaches of Washington's besieging army;
although the buildings, since erected in the vicinity,
have shut out almost every object, save the steeple
of the Old South, which seems almost within arm's
length.   Descending from the cupola, I paused in
the garret to observe the ponderous white-oak
framework, so much more massive than the frames
of modern houses, and thereby resembling an antique skeleton.   The brick walls, the materials of
which were imported from Holland, and the timbers of the mansion, are still as sound as ever; but
the floors and other interior parts being greatly decayed, it is contemplated to gut the whole, and
build a new house within the ancient frame and
brick-work.   Among other inconveniences of the
present edifice, mine host mentioned that any jar or
motion was apt to shake down the dust of ages out
of the ceiling of one chamber upon the floor of that
beneath it.

We stepped forth from the great front window
into the balcony, where, in old times, it was doubtless the custom of the king's representative to show
himself to a loyal populace, requiting their huzzas
and tossed-up hats with stately bendings of his dignified person.   In those days, the front of the Province House looked upon the street; and the whole
site now occupied by the brick range of stores, as
well as the present court-yard, was laid out in
grass-plats, overshadowed by trees and bordered by

a wrought-iron fence. Now, the old aristocratic edifice hides its time-worn visage behind an upstart modern building; at one of the back windows I observed some pretty tailoresses, sewing, and chat-ting, and laughing, with now and then a careless glance towards the balcony. Descending thence, we again entered the bar-room, where the elderly gentleman above mentioned, the smack of whose lips had spoken so favorably for Mr. Waite's good liquor, was still lounging in his chair. He seemed to be, if not a lodger, at least a familiar visitor of the house, who might be supposed to have his reg-ular score at the bar, his summer seat at the open window, and his prescriptive corner at the winter's fireside. Being of a sociable aspect, I ventured to address him with a remark, calculated to draw forth his historical reminiscences, if any such were in his mind; and it gratified me to discover, that, between memory and tradition, the old gentleman was really possessed of some very pleasant gossip about the Province House. The portion of his talk which chiefly interested me was the outline of the following legend. He professed to have re-ceived it at one or two removes from an eye-wit-ness; but this derivation, together with the lapse of time, must have afforded opportunities for many variations of the narrative; so that, despairing of literal and absolute truth, I have not scrupled to make such further changes as seemed conducive to the reader's profit and delight.

At one of the entertainments given at the Province House, during the latter part of the siege of Boston, there passed a scene which has never yet been satisfactorily explained. The officers of the British army, and the loyal gentry of the province, most of whom were collected within the beleaguered town, had been invited to a masked ball; for it was the policy of Sir William Howe to hide the distress and danger of the period, and the desperate aspect of the siege, under an ostentation of festivity. The spectacle of this evening, if the oldest members of the provincial court circle might be believed, was the most gay and gorgeous affair that had occurred in the annals of the government. The brilliantly lighted apartments were thronged with figures that seemed to have stepped from the dark canvas of historic portraits, or to have flitted forth from the magic pages of romance, or at least to have flown hither from one of the London theatres, without a change of garments. Steeled knights of the Conquest, bearded statesmen of Queen Elizabeth, and high-ruffled ladies of her court, were mingled with characters of comedy, such as a party-colored Merry Andrew, jingling his cap and bells; a Falstaff, almost as provocative of laughter as his prototype; and a Don Quixote, with a bean-pole for a lance and a potlid for a shield.

But the broadest merriment was excited by a group of figures ridiculously dressed in old regimentals, which seemed to have been purchased at ₰ military rag-fair, or pilfered from some receptacle of the cast-off clothes of both the French and British armies. Portions of their attire had probably been worn at the siege of Louisburg, and the coats of most recent cut might have been rent and tattered by sword, ball, or bayonet, as long ago as Wolfe's victory. One of these worthies — a tall, lank figure, brandishing a rusty sword of immense longitude — purported to be no less a personage than General George Washington ; and the other principal officers of the American army, such as Gates, Lee, Putnam, Schuyler, Ward, and Heath, were represented by similar scarecrows. An interview in the mock-heroic style, between the rebel warriors and the British commander-in-chief, was received with immense applause, which came loudest of all from the loyalists of the colony. There was one of the guests, however, who stood apart, eying these antics sternly and scornfully, at once with a frown and a bitter smile.

It was an old man, formerly of high station and great repute in the province, and who had been a very famous soldier in his day. Some surprise had been expressed, that a person of Colonel Joliffe's known whig principles, though now too old to take an active part in the contest, should have remained in Boston during the siege, and especially that he should consent to show himself in the mansion of Sir William Howe. But thither he had come, with a fair granddaughter under his arm ; and there, amid all the mirth and buffoonery, stood this stern old figure, the best sustained character in the mas-

querade, because so well representing the antique
spirit of his native land. The other guests affirmed
that Colonel Joliffe's black puritanical scowl threw
a shadow round about him; although in spite of his
sombre influence, their gayety continued to blaze
higher, like (an ominous comparison) the flickering
brilliancy of a lamp which has but a little while to
burn. Eleven strokes, full half an hour ago, had
pealed from the clock of the Old South, when
a rumor was circulated among the company that
some new spectacle or pageant was about to be exhibited, which should put a fitting close to the
splendid festivities of the night.

" What new jest has your Excellency in hand ? "
asked the Rev. Mather Byles, whose Presbyterian
scruples had not kept him from the entertainment.
" Trust me, sir, I have already laughed more than
beseems my cloth, at your Homeric confabulation
with yonder ragamuffin general of the rebels. One
other such fit of merriment, and I must throw off
my clerical wig and band."

" Not so, good Dr. Byles," answered Sir William
Howe ; " if mirth were a crime, you had never
gained your doctorate in divinity. As to this new
foolery, I know no more about it than yourself ;
perhaps not so much. Honestly now, Doctor, have
you not stirred up the sober brains of some of your
countrymen to enact a scene in our masquerade ? "

" Perhaps," slyly remarked the granddaughter
of Colonel Joliffe, whose high spirit had been stung
by many taunts against New England, — " perhaps

we are to have a mask of allegorical figures. Victory, with trophies from Lexington and Bunker
Hill, — Plenty, with her overflowing horn, to typ-
ify the present abundance in this good town, —
and Glory, with a wreath for his Excellency's
brow."

Sir William Howe smiled at words which he
would have answered with one of his darkest
frowns, had they been uttered by lips that wore a
beard. He was spared the necessity of a retort,
by a singular interruption. A sound of music was
heard without the house, as if proceeding from a
full band of military instruments stationed in the
street, playing, not such a festal strain as was suited
to the occasion, but a slow funeral march. The
drums appeared to be muffled, and the trumpets
poured forth a wailing breath, which at once hushed
the merriment of the auditors, filling all with wonder and some with apprehension. The idea occurred to many, that either the funeral procession of
some great personage had halted in front of the
Province House, or that a corpse, in a velvet-cov-
ered and gorgeously decorated coffin, was about to
be borne from the portal. After listening a moment, Sir William Howe called, in a stern voice,
to the leader of the musicians, who had hitherto
enlivened the entertainment with gay and light-
some melodies. The man was drum-major to one
of the British regiments.

" Dighton," demanded the general, " what means
this foolery? Bid your band silence that dead

march ; or, by my word, they shall have sufficient cause for their lugubrious strains ! Silence it, sirrah ! "

" Please your Honor," answered the drum-major, whose rubicund visage had lost all its color, " the fault is none of mine. I and my band are all here together; and I question whether there be a man of us that could play that march without book. I never heard it but once before, and that was at the funeral of his late Majesty, King George the Second."

" Well, well ! " said Sir William Howe, recovering his composure ; " it is the prelude to some masquerading antic. Let it pass."

A figure now presented itself, but, among the many fantastic masks that were dispersed through the apartments, none could tell precisely from whence it came. It was a man in an old-fashioned dress of black serge, and having the aspect of a steward, or principal domestic in the household of a nobleman, or great English landholder. This figure advanced to the outer door of the mansion, and throwing both its leaves wide open, withdrew a little to one side and looked back towards the grand staircase, as if expecting some person to descend. At the same time, the music in the street sounded a loud and doleful summons. The eyes of Sir William Howe and his guests being directed to the staircase, there appeared, on the uppermost landing-place that was discernible from the bottom, several personages descending towards the door

The foremost was a man of stern visage, wearing a steeple-crowned hat and a skullcap beneath it; a dark cloak, and huge wrinkled boots that came half-way up his legs. Under his arm was a rolled up banner, which seemed to be the banner of England, but strangely rent and torn; he had a sword in his right hand, and grasped a Bible in his left. The next figure was of milder aspect, yet full of dignity, wearing a broad ruff, over which descended a beard, a gown of wrought velvet, and a doublet and hose of black satin. He carried a roll of manuscript in his hand. Close behind these two came a young man of very striking countenance and demeanor, with deep thought and contemplation on his brow, and perhaps a flash of enthusiasm in his eye. His garb, like that of his predecessors, was of an antique fashion, and there was a stain of blood upon his ruff. In the same group with these were three or four others, all men of dignity and evident command, and bearing themselves like personages who were accustomed to the gaze of the multitude. It was the idea of the beholders, that these figures went to join the mysterious funeral that had halted in front of the Province House; yet that supposition seemed to be contradicted by the air of triumph with which they waved their hands, as they crossed the threshold and vanished through the portal.

"In the Devil's name, what is this?" muttered Sir William Howe to a gentleman beside him; "a procession of the regicide judges of King Charles the martyr?"

"These," said Colonel Joliffe, breaking silence almost for the first time that evening, — "these, if I interpret them aright, are the Puritan governors, — the rulers of the old, original democracy of Massachusetts. Endicott, with the banner from which he had torn the symbol of subjection,[1] and Winthrop, and Sir Henry Vane, and Dudley, Haynes, Bellingham, and Leverett."

"Why had that young man a stain of blood upon his ruff?" asked Miss Joliffe.

"Because, in after years," answered her grandfather, "he laid down the wisest head in England upon the block, for the principles of liberty."

"Will not your Excellency order out the guard?" whispered Lord Percy, who, with other British officers, had now assembled round the general. "There may be a plot under this mummery."

"Tush! we have nothing to fear," carelessly replied Sir William Howe. "There can be no worse treason in the matter than a jest, and that somewhat of the dullest. Even were it a sharp and bitter one, our best policy would be to laugh it off. See, here come more of these gentry."

Another group of characters had now partly descended the staircase. The first was a venerable and white-bearded patriarch, who cautiously felt his way downward with a staff. Treading hastily behind him, and stretching forth his gauntleted hand as if

[1] See Hawthorne's own story of *The Red Cross* in *Grandfather's Chair.*

to grasp the old man's shoulder, came a tall, soldier-like figure, equipped with a plumed cap of steel, a bright breastplate, and a long sword, which rattled against the stairs. Next was seen a stout man, dressed in rich and courtly attire, but not of courtly demeanor; his gait had the swinging motion of a seaman's walk; and chancing to stumble on the staircase, he suddenly grew wrathful, and was heard to mutter an oath. He was followed by a noble-looking personage in a curled wig, such as are represented in the portraits of Queen Anne's time and earlier; and the breast of his coat was decorated with an embroidered star. While advancing to the door, he bowed to the right hand and to the left, in a very gracious and insinuating style; but as he crossed the threshold, unlike the early Puritan governors, he seemed to wring his hands with sorrow.

"Prithee, play the part of a chorus, good Dr. Byles," said Sir William Howe. "What worthies are these?"

"If it please your Excellency, they lived somewhat before my day," answered the Doctor; "but doubtless our friend, the Colonel, has been hand in glove with them."

"Their living faces I never looked upon," said Colonel Joliffe, gravely; "although I have spoken face to face with many rulers of this land, and shall greet yet another with an old man's blessing, ere I die. But we talk of these figures. I take the venerable patriarch to be Bradstreet, the last of the Puritans, who was governor at ninety, or thereabouts. The next is Sir Edmund Andros, a tyrant, as any New England school-boy will tell you; and therefore the people cast him down from his high seat into a dungeon. Then comes Sir William Phipps, shepherd, cooper, sea-captain, and governor : may many of his countrymen rise as high, from as low an origin! Lastly, you saw the gracious Earl of Bellamont, who ruled us under King William."

" But what is the meaning of it all?" asked Lord Percy.

" Now, were I a rebel," said Miss Joliffe, half aloud, " I might fancy that the ghosts of these ancient governors had been summoned to form the funeral procession of royal authority in New England."

Several other figures were now seen at the turn of the staircase. The one in advance had a thoughtful, anxious, and somewhat crafty expression of face; and in spite of his loftiness of manner, which was evidently the result both of an ambitious spirit and of long continuance in high stations, he seemed not incapable of cringing to a greater than himself. A few steps behind came an officer in a scarlet and embroidered uniform, cut in a fashion old enough to have been worn by the Duke of Marlborough. His nose had a rubicund tinge, which, together with the twinkle of his eye, might have marked him as a lover of the wine-cup and good-fellowship; notwithstanding which tokens, he appeared ill at ease, and often glanced around him, as if apprehensive of some secret mischief. Next came a portly gentleman, wearing a coat of shaggy cloth, lined with silken velvet; he had sense, shrewdness, and humor in his face, and a folio volume under his arm; but his aspect was that of a man vexed and tormented beyond all patience and harassed almost to death. He went hastily down, and was followed by a dignified person, dressed in a purple velvet suit, with very rich embroidery; his demeanor would have possessed much stateliness, only that a grievous fit of the gout compelled him to hobble from stair to stair, with contortions of face and body. When Dr. Byles beheld this figure on the staircase, he shivered as with an ague, but continued to watch him steadfastly, until the gouty gentleman had reached the threshold, made a gesture of anguish and despair, and vanished into the outer gloom, whither the funeral music summoned him.

"Governor Belcher! — my old patron! — in his very shape and dress!" gasped Dr. Byles. "This is an awful mockery!"

"A tedious foolery, rather," said Sir William Howe, with an air of indifference. "But who were the three that preceded him?"

"Governor Dudley, a cunning politician, — yet his craft once brought him to a prison," replied Colonel Joliffe; "Governor Shute, formerly a colonel under Marlborough, and whom the people frightened out of the province; and learned Gov-

7

ernor Burnet, whom the Legislature tormented into
a mortal fever."

"Methinks they were miserable men, these
royal governors of Massachusetts," observed Miss
Joliffe. " Heavens, how dim the light grows ! "

It was certainly a fact that the large lamp which
illuminated the staircase now burned dim and dusk-
ily : so that several figures, which passed hastily
down the stairs and went forth from the porch, appeared rather like shadows than persons of fleshly
substance. Sir William Howe and his guests stood
at the doors of the contiguous apartments, watching the progress of this singular pageant, with various emotions of anger, contempt, or half-acknowl-
edged fear, but still with an anxious curiosity. The
shapes, which now seemed hastening to join the
mysterious procession, were recognized rather by
striking peculiarities of dress, or broad characteristics of manner, than by any perceptible resemblance of features to their prototypes. Their faces,
indeed, were invariably kept in deep shadow. But
Dr. Byles, and other gentlemen who had long been
familiar with the successive rulers of the province,
were heard to whisper the name of Shirley, of
Pownall, of Sir Francis Bernard, and of the well-
remembered Hutchinson ; thereby confessing that
the actors, whoever they might be, in this spectral
march of governors, had succeeded in putting on
some distant portraiture of the real personages.
As they vanished from the door, still did these
shadows toss their arms into the gloom of night,

with a dread expression of woe. Following the mimic representative of Hutchinson came a military figure, holding before his face the cocked hat which he had taken from his powdered head; but his epaulets and other insignia of rank were those of a general officer; and something in his mien reminded the beholder of one who had recently been master of the Province House, and chief of all the land.

"The shape of Gage, as true as in a looking-glass!" exclaimed Lord Percy, turning pale.

"No, surely," cried Miss Joliffe, laughing hysterically; "it could not be Gage, or Sir William would have greeted his old comrade in arms! Perhaps he will not suffer the next to pass unchallenged."

"Of that be assured, young lady," answered Sir William Howe, fixing his eyes, with a very marked expression, upon the immovable visage of her grandfather. "I have long enough delayed to pay the ceremonies of a host to these departing guests. The next that takes his leave shall receive due courtesy."

A wild and dreary burst of music came through the open door. It seemed as if the procession, which had been gradually filling up its ranks, were now about to move, and this loud peal of the wailing trumpets, and roll of the muffled drums, were a call to some loiterer to make haste. Many eyes, by an irresistible impulse, were turned upon Sir William Howe, as if it were he whom the dreary music summoned to the funeral of departed power.

" See! — here comes the last!" whispered Miss Joliffe, pointing her tremulous finger to the staircase.

A figure had come into view as if descending the stairs; although so dusky was the region whence it emerged, some of the spectators fancied that they had seen this human shape suddenly moulding itself amid the gloom. Downward the figure came, with a stately and martial tread, and reaching the lowest stair was observed to be a tall man, booted and wrapped in a military cloak, which was drawn up around the face so as to meet the flapped brim of a laced hat. The features, therefore, were completely hidden. But the British officers deemed that they had seen that military cloak before, and even recognized the frayed embroidery on the collar, as well as the gilded scabbard of a sword which protruded from the folds of the cloak, and glittered in a vivid gleam of light. Apart from these trifling particulars, there were characteristics of gait and bearing which impelled the wondering guests to glance from the shrouded figure to Sir William Howe, as if to satisfy themselves that their host had not suddenly vanished from the midst of them.

With a dark flush of wrath upon his brow, they saw the general draw his sword and advance to meet the figure in the cloak before the latter had stepped one pace upon the floor.

"Villain, unmuffle yourself!" cried he. "You pass no farther!"

The figure, without blenching a hair's-breadth from the sword which was pointed at his breast, made a solemn pause and lowered the cape of the cloak from about his face, yet not sufficiently for the spectators to catch a glimpse of it. But Sir William Howe had evidently seen enough. The sternness of his countenance gave place to a look of wild amazement, if not horror, while he recoiled several steps from the figure, and let fall his sword upon the floor. The martial shape again drew the cloak about his features and passed on; but reaching the threshold, with his back towards the spectators, he was seen to stamp his foot and shake his clinched hands in the air. It was afterwards affirmed that Sir William Howe had repeated that self-same gesture of rage and sorrow, when, for the last time, and as the last royal governor, he passed through the portal of the Province House.

"Hark! — the procession moves," said Miss Joliffe.

The music was dying away along the street, and its dismal strains were mingled with the knell of midnight from the steeple of the Old South, and with the roar of artillery, which announced that the beleaguering army of Washington had intrenched itself upon a nearer height than before. As the deep boom of the cannon smote upon his ear, Colonel Joliffe raised himself to the full height of his aged form, and smiled sternly on the British general.

" Would your Excellency inquire further into the mystery of the pageant ? " said he.

" Take care of your gray head ! " cried Sir William Howe, fiercely, though with a quivering lip. " It has stood too long on a traitor's shoulders ! "

" You must make haste to chop it off, then," calmly replied the Colonel ; " for a few hours longer, and not all the power of Sir William Howe, nor of his master, shall cause one of these gray hairs to fall. The empire of Britain, in this ancient province, is at its last gasp to-night ; almost while I speak it is a dead corpse ; and methinks the shadows of the old governors are fit mourners as its funeral ! "

With these words Colonel Joliffe threw on his cloak, and drawing his granddaughter's arm within his own, retired from the last festival that a British ruler ever held in the old province of Massachusetts Bay. It was supposed that the Colonel and the young lady possessed some secret intelligence in regard to the mysterious pageant of that night. However this might be, such knowledge has never become general. The actors in the scene have vanished into deeper obscurity than even that wild Indian band who scattered the cargoes of the tea-ships on the waves, and gained a place in history, yet left no names. But superstition, among other legends of this mansion, repeats the wondrous tale, that on the anniversary night of Britain's discomfiture, the ghosts of the ancient governors of Massachusetts still glide through the portal of the Province

House. And, last of all, comes a figure shrouded in a military cloak, tossing his clinched hands into the air, and stamping his iron-shod boots upon the broad freestone steps with a semblance of feverish despair, but without the sound of a foot-tramp.

WASHINGTON IRVING.

INTRODUCTION.

IRVING may be named as the first author in the
United States whose writings made a place for
themselves in general literature. Franklin, indeed, had preceded him with his autobiography,
but Franklin belongs rather to the colonial period.
It was under the influences of that time that his
mind and taste were formed, and there was a
marked difference between the Boston and Phila-
delphia of Franklin's youth and the New York of
Irving's time. Politics, commerce, and the rise of
industries were rapidly changing social relations
and manners, while the country was still dependent
on England for its higher literature. It had hardly
begun to find materials for literature in its own past
or in its aspects of nature, yet there was a very positive element in life which resented foreign inter-
ference. There were thus two currents crossing
each other ; the common life which was narrowly
American and the cultivated taste which was English, or imitative of England. Irving's first ventures,
in company with his brothers and Paulding, were

in the attempt to represent New York in literature
upon the model of contemporary or recent presen-
tations of London. "The town" in the minds of
these young writers was that portion of New York
society which might be construed into a miniature
reflection of London wit and amusement. His associates never advanced beyond this stage, but with
Washington Irving the sketches which he wrote
under the signature of *Jonathan Old Style* and in the
medley of *Salmagundi* were only the first experiments of a mind capable of larger things. After
five or six years of trifling with his pen, he wrote
and published, in 1809, *A History of New York, by
Diedrich Knickerbocker*, which he began in company
with his brother Peter as a mere *jeu d'esprit*, but
turned into a more determined work of humor, as
the capabilities of the subject disclosed themselves.
Grave historians had paid little attention to the
record of New York under the Dutch; Irving, who
saw the humorous contrast between the traditional
Dutch society of his day and the pushing new democracy, seized upon the early history and made
it the occasion for a good-natured burlesque. He
shocked the old families about him, but he amused
everybody else, and the book going to England,
made his name at once known to those who had
the making there of literary reputations.

Irving himself was born of a Scottish father and
English mother, who had come to this country only
twenty years before. He was but little removed,
therefore, from the traditions of Great Britain, and

his brothers and he carried on a trading business with the old country. His own tastes were not mercantile, and he was only silent partner in the house ; he wrote occasionally and was for a time the editor of a magazine, but his pleasure was chiefly in travel, good literature, and good society. It was while he was in England, in 1818, that the house in which he was a partner failed, and he was thrown on his own resources. Necessity gave the slight spur which was wanting to his inclination, and he began with deliberation the career of an author. He had found himself at home in England. His family origin and his taste for the best literature had made him English in his sympathies and tastes, and his residence and travels there, the society which he entered and the friends he made, confirmed him in English habits. Nevertheless he was sturdily American in his principles, he was strongly attached to New York and his American friends, and was always a looker-on in England. His foreign birth and education gave him significant advantages as an observer of English life, and he at once began the writing of those papers, stories, and sketches which appeared in the separate numbers of *The Sketch Book*, in *Bracebridge Hall*, and in *Tales of a Traveller*. They were chiefly drawn from material accumulated abroad, but an occasional American subject was taken. Irving instinctively felt that by the circumstances of the time and the bent of his genius he could pursue his calling more safely abroad than at home. He re-

mained in Europe seventeen years, sending home
his books for publication, and securing also the
profitable results of publication in London. During
that time, besides the books above named, he
wrote the *History of the Life and Voyages of Chris-
topher Columbus,* the *Voyages and Discoveries of the
Companions of Columbus, A Chronicle of the Conquest of Granada,* and *The Alhambra.* The Spanish material was obtained while residing in Spain,
whither he went at the suggestion of the American
minister to make translations of documents relating
to the voyages of Columbus which had recently
been collected. Irving's training and tastes led
him rather into the construction of popular narrative than into the work of a scientific historian, and,
with his strong American affections, he was quick
to see the interest and value which lay in the history of Spain as connected with America. He was
eminently a *raconteur,* very skilful and graceful in
the shaping of old material; his humor played
freely over the surface of his writing, and, with little power to create characters or plots, he had an
unfailing perception of the literary capabilities of
scenes and persons which came under his observation.

He came back to America in 1832 with an established reputation, and was welcomed enthusiastically by his friends and countrymen. He travelled into the new parts of America, and spent ten
years at home, industriously working at the material which had accumulated in his hands when

abroad, and been increased during his travels in the West. In this period he published *Legends of the Conquest of Spain; The Crayon Miscellany*, including his *Tour on the Prairies, Abbotsford and Newstead Abbey; Astoria;* a number of papers in the *Knickerbocker Magazine*, afterwards published under the title of *Wolfert's Roost;* and edited the *Adventures of Captain Bonneville, U. S. A., in the Rocky Mountains and the Far West.*

In 1842 he went back to Spain as American minister, holding the office for four years, when he returned to America, established himself at his home, Sunnyside on the banks of the Hudson, and remained there until his death in 1859. The fruits of this final period were *Mahomet and his Successors*, which, with a volume of posthumous publication, *Spanish Papers and other Miscellanies*, completed the series of Spanish and Moorish subjects which form a distinct part of his writings; *Oliver Goldsmith, a Biography;* and finally a *Life of Washington*, which occupied the closing years of his life, — years which were not free from physical suffering. In this book Irving embodied his strong admiration for the subject, whose name he bore and whose blessing he had received as a child; he employed, too, a pen which had been trained by its labors on the Spanish material, and, like that series, the work is marked by good taste, artistic sense of proportion, faithfulness, and candor rather than by the severer work of the historian. It is a popular and fair life of Washington, and account of the war for independence.

Irving's personal and literary history is recorded in *The Life and Letters of Washington Irving* by his nephew, Pierre M. Irving.   His death was the occasion of many affectionate and graceful eulogies and addresses, a number of which were gathered into *Irvingiana: a Memorial of Washington Irving.*

Rip Van Winkle and *Little Britain* are both from *The Sketch Book.*

I.

RIP VAN WINKLE.

A POSTHUMOUS WRITING OF DIEDRICH KNICKER-BOCKER.

[DIEDRICH KNICKERBOCKER was a humorous invention of Irving's, and his name was familiar to the public as the author of *A History of New York*. The *History* was published in 1809, but it was ten years more before the first number of *The Sketch Book of Geoffrey Crayon, Gent.*, was published. This number, which contained *Rip Van Winkle*, was, like succeeding numbers, written by Irving in England and sent home to America for publication. He laid the scene of the story in the Kaatskills, but he drew upon his imagination and the reports of others for the scenery, not visiting the spot until 1833. The story is not absolutely new; the fairy tale of *The Sleeping Beauty in the Wood* has the same theme; so has the story of Epimenides of Crete, who lived in the sixth or seventh century before Christ. He was said to have fallen asleep in a cave when a boy, and to have awaked at the end of fifty-seven years, his soul, meanwhile, having been growing in stature. There is the legend also of the Seven Sleepers of Ephesus, Christian mar-

tyrs who were walled into a cave to which they had
fled for refuge, and there were miraculously preserved for two centuries. Among the stories in
which the Harz Mountains of Germany are so prolific is one of Peter Klaus, a goatherd who was
accosted one day by a young man who silently
beckoned him to follow, and led him to a secluded
spot, where he found twelve knights playing, voice
less, at skittles. He saw a can of wine which
was very fragrant, and, drinking of it, was thrown
into a deep sleep, from which he did not wake for
twenty years. The story gives incidents of his
awaking and of the changes which he found in the
village to which he returned. This story, which
was published with others in 1800, may very likely
have been the immediate suggestion to Irving,
who has taken nearly the same framework. The
humorous additions which he has made, and the
grace with which he has invested the tale, have
caused his story to supplant earlier ones in the popular mind, so that Rip Van Winkle has passed into
familiar speech, and allusions to him are clearly
understood by thousands who have never read Irving's story. The recent dramatizing of the story,
though following the outline only, has done much
to fix the conception of the character. The story
appeals very directly to a common sentiment of
curiosity as to the future, which is not far removed
from what some have regarded as an instinct of
the human mind pointing to personal immortality.
The name Van Winkle was happily chosen by Irv-

ing, but not invented by him. The printer of the *Sketch Book*, for one, bore the name. The name of Knickerbocker, also, is among Dutch names, but Irving's use of it has made it representative. In *The Author's Apology*, which he prefixed to a new edition of the *History of New York*, he says : " I find its very name become a ' household word,' and used to give the home stamp to everything recommended for popular acceptation, such as Knickerbocker societies ; Knickerbocker insurance companies ; Knickerbocker steamboats ; Knickerbocker omnibuses ; Knickerbocker bread and Knickerbocker ice ; and . . . . New Yorkers of Dutch descent priding themselves upon being ' genuine Knickerbockers.' "]

> By Woden, God of Saxons,
> From whence comes Wensday, that is Wodensday.
> Truth is a thing that ever I will keep
> Unto thylke day in which I creep into
> My sepulchre.   CARTWRIGHT.[1]

THE following Tale was found among the papers of the late Diedrich Knickerbocker, an old gentleman of New York, who was very curious in the Dutch history of the province, and the manners of the descendants from its primitive settlers. His historical researches, however, did not lie so much among books as among men; for the former are lamentably scanty on his favorite topics; whereas he found the old burghers, and still more their wives, rich in that legendary lore so invaluable to true history. Whenever, therefore, he happened upon a genuine Dutch family, snugly shut up in its low-roofed farmhouse, under a spreading sycamore, he looked upon it as a little clasped

---

1 William Cartwright, 1611–1643, was a friend and disciple of Ben Jonson.

volume of black-letter, and studied it with the zeal of a book-worm.

The result of all these researches was a history of the province during the reign of the Dutch governors, which he published some years since. There have been various opinions as to the literary character of his work, and, to tell the truth, it is not a whit better than it should be. Its chief merit is its scrupulous accuracy, which indeed was a little questioned on its first appearance, but has since been completely established; and it is now admitted into all historical collections, as a book of unquestionable authority.

The old gentleman died shortly after the publication of his work, and now that he is dead and gone, it cannot do much harm to his memory [1] to say that his time might have been much better employed in weightier labors. He, however, was apt to ride his hobby his own way; and though it did now and then kick up the dust a little in the eyes of his neighbors, and grieve the spirit of some friends, for whom he felt the truest deference and affection; yet his errors and follies are remembered "more in sorrow than in anger," and it begins to be suspected that he never intended to injure or offend. But however his memory may be appreciated by critics, it is still held dear by many folk, whose good opinion is worth having; particularly by certain biscuit-bakers, who have gone so far as to imprint his likeness on their new-year cakes; [2] and have thus given him a chance for immor-

---

[1] *The History of New York* had given offence to many old New Yorkers because of its saucy treatment of names which were held in veneration as those of founders of families, and its general burlesque of Dutch character. Among the critics was a warm friend of Irving, Gulian C. Verplanck, who in a discourse before the New York Historical Society plainly said: "It is painful to see a mind as admirable for its exquisite perception of the beautiful, as it is for its quick sense of the ridiculous, wasting the richness of its fancy on an ungrateful theme, and its exuberant humor in a coarse caricature." Irving took the censure good-naturedly, and as he read Verplanck's words just as he was finishing the story of *Rip Van Winkle* he gåve them this playful notice in the introduction.

[2] An oblong seed-cake, still made in New York at New Year's time and of Dutch origin.

tality, almost equal to the being stamped on a Waterloo Medal, or a Queen Anne's Farthing.[1]

WHOEVER has made a voyage up the Hudson must remember the Kaatskill Mountains. They are a dismembered branch of the great Appalachian family, and are seen away to the west of the river, swelling up to a noble height, and lording it over the surrounding country. Every change of season, every change of weather, indeed, every hour of the day, produces some change in the magical hues and shapes of these mountains, and they are regarded by all the good wives, far and near, as perfect barometers. When the weather is fair and settled, they are clothed in blue and purple, and print their bold outlines on the clear evening sky; but, sometimes, when the rest of the landscape is cloudless, they will gather a hood of gray vapors about their summits, which, in the last rays of the setting sun, will glow and light up like a crown of glory.

At the foot of these fairy [2] mountains, the voyager may have descried the light smoke curling up from a village, whose shingle-roofs gleam among

[1] There was a popular story that only three farthings were struck in Queen Anne's reign; that two were in public keeping, and that the third was no one knew where, but that its lucky finder would be able to hold it at an enormous price. As a matter of fact there were eight coinings of farthings in the reign of Queen Anne, and numismatists do not set a high value on the piece.

[2] A light touch to help the reader into a proper spirit for receiving the tale.

the trees, just where the blue tints of the upland melt away into the fresh green of the nearer landscape. It is a little village of great antiquity, having been founded by some of the Dutch colonists in the early time of the province, just about the beginning of the government of the good Peter Stuyvesant,[1] (may he rest in peace !) and there were some of the houses of the original settlers standing within a few years, built of small yellow bricks brought from Holland, having latticed windows and gable fronts, surmounted with weather-cocks.

In that same village, and in one of these very houses (which, to tell the precise truth, was sadly time-worn and weather-beaten), there lived many years since, while the country was yet a province of Great Britain, a simple, good-natured fellow, of the name of Rip Van Winkle. He was a descendant of the Van Winkles who figured so gallantly in the chivalrous days of Peter Stuyvesant, and accompanied him to the siege of Fort Christina.[2] He inherited, however, but little of the martial character of his ancestors. I have observed that he was a simple, good-natured man ; he was, more-

---

[1] Stuyvesant was governor of New Netherlands from 1647 to 1664. He plays an important part in *Knickerbocker's History of New York*, as he did in actual life. Until quite recently a pear tree was shown on the Bowery, said to have been planted by him.

[2] The Van Winkles appear in the illustrious catalogue of heroes who accompanied Stuyvesant to Fort Christina, and were

" Brimful of wrath and cabbage."

See *History of New York*, book VI. chap. viii.

ɔver, a kind neighbor, and an obedient hen-pecked husband. Indeed, to the latter circumstance might be owing that meekness of spirit which gained him such universal popularity ; for those men are most apt to be obsequious and conciliating abroad, who are under the discipline of shrews at home. Their tempers, doubtless, are rendered pliant and malleable in the fiery furnace of domestic tribulation ; and a curtain lecture is worth all the sermons in the world for teaching the virtues of patience and long-suffering. A termagant wife may, therefore, in some respects, be considered a tolerable blessing ; and if so, Rip Van Winkle was thrice blessed.

Certain it is, that he was a great favorite among all the good wives of the village, who, as usual, with the amiable sex, took his part in all family squabbles ; and never failed, whenever they talked those matters over in their evening gossipings, to lay all the blame on Dame Van Winkle. The children of the village, too, would shout with joy whenever he approached. He assisted at their sports, made their playthings, taught them to fly kites and shoot marbles, and told them long stories of ghosts, witches, and Indians. Whenever he went dodging about the village, he was surrounded by a troop of them, hanging on his skirts, clambering on his back, and playing a thousand tricks on him with impunity ; and not a dog would bark at him throughout the neighborhood. .

The great error in Rip's composition was an insuperable aversion to all kinds of profitable labor

It could not be from the want of assiduity or perseverance; for he would sit on a wet rock, with a rod as long and heavy as a Tartar's lance, and fish all day without a murmur, even though he should not be encouraged by a single nibble. He would carry a fowling-piece on his shoulder for hours together, trudging through woods and swamps, and up hill and down dale, to shoot a few squirrels or wild pigeons. He would never refuse to assist a neighbor, even in the roughest toil, and was a foremost man at all country frolics for husking Indian corn, or building stone-fences; the women of the village, too, used to employ him to run their errands, and to do such little odd jobs as their less obliging husbands would not do for them. In a word, Rip was ready to attend to anybody's business but his own; but as to doing family duty, and keeping his farm in order, he found it impossible.

In fact, he declared it was of no use to work on his farm; it was the most pestilent little piece of ground in the whole country; everything about it went wrong, and would go wrong, in spite of him. His fences were continually falling to pieces; his cow would either go astray or get among the cabbages; weeds were sure to grow quicker in his fields than anywhere else; the rain always made a point of setting in just as he had some out-door work to do; so that though his patrimonial estate had dwindled away under his management, acre by acre, until there was little more left than a mere patch of Indian corn and potatoes, yet it was the worst conditioned farm in the neighborhood.

His children, too, were as ragged and wild as if they belonged to nobody. His son Rip, an urchin begotten in his own likeness, promised to inherit the habits, with the old clothes of his father. He was generally seen trooping like a colt at his mother's heels, equipped in a pair of his father's cast-off galligaskins, which he had much ado to hold up with one hand, as a fine lady does her train in bad weather.

Rip Van Winkle, however, was one of those happy mortals, of foolish, well-oiled dispositions, who take the world easy, eat white bread or brown, whichever can be got with least thought or trouble, and would rather starve on a penny than work for a pound. If left to himself, he would have whistled life away in perfect contentment; but his wife kept continually dinning in his ears about his idleness, his carelessness, and the ruin he was bringing on his family. Morning, noon, and night her tongue was incessantly going, and everything he said or did was sure to produce a torrent of household eloquence. Rip had but one way of replying to all lectures of the kind, and that, by frequent use, had grown into a habit. He shrugged his shoulders, shook his head, cast up his eyes, but said nothing. This, however, always provoked a fresh volley from his wife; so that he was fain to draw off his forces, and take to the outside of the house — the only side which, in truth, belongs to a hen-pecked husband.

Rip's sole domestic adherent was his dog Wolf,

who was as much hen-pecked as his master; for
Dame Van Winkle regarded them as companions
in idleness, and even looked upon Wolf with an
evil eye, as the cause of his master's going so often
astray. True it is, in all points of spirit befitting
an honorable dog, he was as courageous an animal
as ever scoured the woods — but what courage can
withstand the ever-during and all-besetting terrors
of a woman's tongue? The moment Wolf entered
the house his crest fell, his tail drooped to the
ground, or curled between his legs, he sneaked
about with a gallows air, casting many a sidelong
glance at Dame Van Winkle, and at the least flourish of a broomstick or ladle he would fly to the door
with yelping precipitation.

Times grew worse and worse with Rip Van
Winkle as years of matrimony rolled on; a tart
temper never mellows with age, and a sharp tongue
is the only edged tool that grows keener with constant use. For a long while he used to console
himself, when driven from home, by frequenting a
kind of perpetual club of the sages, philosophers,
and other idle personages of the village; which
held its sessions on a bench before a small inn,
designated by a rubicund portrait of His Majesty
George the Third. Here they used to sit in the
shade through a long lazy summer's day, talking
listlessly over village gossip, or telling endless
sleepy stories about nothing. But it would have
been worth any statesman's money to have heard
the profound discussions that sometimes took place,

when by chance an old newspaper fell into their hands from some passing traveller. How solemnly they would listen to the contents, as drawled out by Derrick Van Bummel, the school-master, a dapper learned little man, who was not to be daunted by the most gigantic word in the dictionary; and how sagely they would deliberate upon public events some months after they had taken place.

The opinions of this junto were completely controlled by Nicholas Vedder, a patriarch of the village, and landlord of the inn, at the door of which he took his seat from morning till night, just moving sufficiently to avoid the sun and keep in the shade of a large tree; so that the neighbors could tell the hour by his movements as accurately as by a sun-dial. It is true he was rarely heard to speak, but smoked his pipe incessantly. His adherents, however (for every great man has his adherents), perfectly understood him, and knew how to gather his opinions. When anything that was read or related displeased him, he was observed to smoke his pipe vehemently, and to send forth short, frequent, and angry puffs; but when pleased, he would inhale the smoke slowly and tranquilly, and emit it in light and placid clouds; and sometimes, taking the pipe from his mouth, and letting the fragrant vapor curl about his nose, would gravely nod his head in token of perfect approbation.

From even this stronghold the unlucky Rip was at length routed by his termagant wife, who would suddenly break in upon the tranquillity of the assemblage and call the members all to naught; nor was that august personage, Nicholas Vedder himself, sacred from the daring tongue of this terrible virago, who charged him outright with encouraging her husband in habits of idleness.

Poor Rip was at last reduced almost to despair; and his only alternative, to escape from the labor of the farm and clamor of his wife, was to take gun in hand and stroll away into the woods. Here he would sometimes seat himself at the foot of a tree, and share the contents of his wallet with Wolf, with whom he sympathized as a fellow-sufferer in persecution. " Poor Wolf," he would say, " thy mistress leads thee a dog's life of it; but never mind, my lad, whilst I live thou shalt never want a friend to stand by thee ! " Wolf would wag his tail, look wistfully in his master's face, and if dogs can feel pity I verily believe he reciprocated the sentiment with all his heart.

In a long ramble of the kind on a fine autumnal day, Rip had unconsciously scrambled to one of the highest parts of the Kaatskill Mountains. He was after his favorite sport of squirrel shooting, and the still solitudes had echoed and reëchoed with the reports of his gun. Panting and fatigued, he threw himself, late in the afternoon, on a green knoll, covered with mountain herbage, that crowned the brow of a precipice. From an opening between the trees he could overlook all the lower country for many a mile of rich woodland. He saw at a distance the lordly Hudson, far, far below him, moving on its silent but majestic course, with the reflection of a purple cloud, or the sail of a lagging bark, here and there sleeping on its glassy bosom, and at last losing itself in the blue highlands.

On the other side he looked down into a deep mountain glen, wild, lonely, and shagged, the bottom filled with fragments from the impending cliffs, and scarcely lighted by the reflected rays of the setting sun. For some time Rip lay musing on this scene ; evening was gradually advancing ; the mountains began to throw their long blue shadows over the valleys ; he saw that it would be dark long before he could reach the village, and he heaved a heavy sigh when he thought of encountering the terrors of Dame Van Winkle.

As he was about to descend, he heard a voice from a distance, hallooing, " Rip Van Winkle ! Rip Van Winkle ! " He looked round, but could see nothing but a crow winging its solitary flight across the mountain. He thought his fancy must have deceived him, and turned again to descend, when he heard the same cry ring through the still evening air : " Rip Van Winkle ! Rip Van Winkle ! "— at the same time Wolf bristled up his back, and giving a low growl, skulked to his master's side, looking fearfully down into the glen. Rip now felt a vague apprehension stealing over him ; he looked anxiously in the same direction, and perceived a strange figure slowly toiling up the rocks, and bending under the weight of something he carried on his back. He was surprised to see any human being

in this lonely and unfrequented place; but supposing it to be some one of the neighborhood in need
of his assistance, he hastened down to yield it.

On nearer approach he was still more surprised
at the singularity of the stranger's appearance. He
was a short, square-built old fellow, with thick bushy
hair, and a grizzled beard. His dress was of the
antique Dutch fashion — a cloth jerkin strapped
round the waist — several pair of breeches, the
outer one of ample volume, decorated with rows of
buttons down the sides, and bunches at the knees.
He bore on his shoulder a stout keg, that seemed
full of liquor, and made signs for Rip to approach
and assist him with the load. Though rather shy
and distrustful of this new acquaintance, Rip complied with his usual alacrity; and mutually relieving one another, they clambered up a narrow gully,
apparently the dry bed of a mountain torrent. As
they ascended, Rip every now and then heard long
rolling peals like distant thunder, that seemed to
issue out of a deep ravine, or rather cleft, between
lofty rocks, toward which their rugged path conducted. He paused for a moment, but supposing it
to be the muttering of one of those transient thun-
der-showers which often take place in mountain
heights, he proceeded. Passing through the ravine, they came to a hollow, like a small amphitheatre, surrounded by perpendicular precipices,
over the brinks of which impending trees shot their
branches, so that you only caught glimpses of the
azure sky and the bright evening cloud. During

the whole time Rip and his companion had labored on in silence; for though the former marvelled greatly what could be the object of carrying a keg of liquor up this wild mountain, yet there was something strange and incomprehensible about the unknown, that inspired awe and checked familiarity.

On entering the amphitheatre, new objects of wonder presented themselves. On a level spot in the centre was a company of odd-looking personages playing at nine-pins. They were dressed in a quaint outlandish fashion; some wore short doublets, others jerkins, with long knives in their belts, and most of them had enormous breeches of similar style with that of the guide's. Their visages, too, were peculiar; one had a large beard, broad face, and small piggish eyes; the face of another seemed to consist entirely of nose, and was surmounted by a white sugar-loaf hat, set off with a little red cock's tail. They all had beards, of various shapes and colors. There was one who seemed to be the commander. He was a stout old gentleman, with a weather-beaten countenance; he wore a laced doublet, broad belt and hanger, high crowned hat and feather, red stockings, and high-heeled shoes, with roses in them. The whole group reminded Rip of the figures in an old Flemish painting in the parlor of Dominie Van Shaick, the village parson, which had been brought over from Holland at the time of the settlement.

What seemed particularly odd to Rip was, that

though these folks were evidently amusing themselves, yet they maintained the gravest faces, the most mysterious silence, and were, withal, the most melancholy party of pleasure he had ever witnessed. Nothing interrupted the stillness of the scene but the noise of the balls, which, whenever they were rolled, echoed along the mountains like rumbling peals of thunder.

As Rip and his companion approached them, they suddenly desisted from their play, and stared at him with such fixed, statue-like gaze, and such strange, uncouth, lack-lustre countenances, that his heart turned within him, and his knees smote together. His companion now emptied the contents of the keg into large flagons, and made signs to him to wait upon the company. He obeyed with fear and trembling; they quaffed the liquor in profound silence, and then returned to their game.

By degrees Rip's awe and apprehension subsided. He even ventured, when no eye was fixed upon him, to taste the beverage, which he found had much of the flavor of excellent Hollands. He was naturally a thirsty soul, and was soon tempted to repeat the draught. One taste provoked another; and he reiterated his visits to the flagon so often that at length his senses were overpowered, his eyes swam in his head, his head gradually declined, and he fell into a deep sleep.

On waking, he found himself on the green knoll whence he had first seen the old man of the glen. He rubbed his eyes — it was a bright, sunny morning. The birds were hopping and twittering among the bushes, and the eagle was wheeling aloft, and breasting the pure mountain breeze. " Surely," thought Rip, " I have not slept here all night." He recalled the occurrences before he fell asleep. The strange man with a keg of liquor — the mountain ravine — the wild retreat among the rocks — the woe-begone party at nine-pins — the flagon — " Oh ! that flagon ! that wicked flagon ! " thought Rip — " what excuse shall I make to Dame Van Winkle ? "

He looked round for his gun, but in place of the clean, well-oiled fowling-piece, he found an old firelock lying by him, the barrel incrusted with rust, the lock falling off, and the stock worm-eaten. He now suspected that the grave roisters of the mountain had put a trick upon him, and, having dosed him with liquor, had robbed him of his gun. Wolf, too, had disappeared, but he might have strayed away after a squirrel or partridge. He whistled after him, and shouted his name, but all in vain; the echoes repeated his whistle and shout, but no dog was to be seen.

He determined to revisit the scene of the last evening's gambol, and if he met with any of the party, to demand his dog and gun. As he rose to walk, he found himself stiff in the joints, and wanting in his usual activity. " These mountain beds do not agree with me," thought Rip, " and if this frolic should lay me up with a fit of the rheumatism, I shall have a blessed time with Dame Van

Winkle." With some difficulty he got down into
the glen ; he found the gully up which he and his
companion had ascended the preceding evening ;
but to his astonishment a mountain stream was now
foaming down it, leaping from rock to rock, and
filling the glen with babbling murmurs. He, however, made shift to scramble up its sides, working
his toilsome way through thickets of birch, sassafras,
and witch-hazel, and sometimes tripped up or en-
tangled by the wild grapevines that twisted their
coils or tendrils from tree to tree, and spread a kind
of network in his path.

At length he reached to where the ravine had
opened through the cliffs to the amphitheatre ; but
no traces of such opening remained. The rocks
presented a high, impenetrable wall, over which the
torrent came tumbling in a sheet of feathery foam,
and fell into a broad, deep basin, black from the
shadows of the surrounding forest. Here, then,
poor Rip was brought to a stand. He again called
and whistled after his dog ; he was only answered
by the cawing of a flock of idle crows, sporting high
in air about a dry tree that overhung a sunny precipice ; and who, secure in their elevation, seemed
to look down and scoff at the poor man's perplex-
ities. What was to be done? the morning was
passing away, and Rip felt famished for want of his
breakfast. He grieved to give up his dog and gun ;
he dreaded to meet his wife ; but it would not do to
starve among the mountains. He shook his head,
shouldered the rusty firelock, and, with a heart full

of trouble and anxiety, turned his steps homeward.

As he approached the village he met a number
of people, but none whom he knew, which somewhat surprised him, for he had thought himself
acquainted with every one in the country round.
Their dress, too, was of a different fashion from
that to which he was accustomed. They all stared
at him with equal marks of surprise, and whenever
they cast their eyes upon him, invariably stroked
their chins. The constant recurrence of this gesture induced Rip, involuntarily, to do the same,
when, to his astonishment, he found his beard had
grown a foot long!

He had now entered the skirts of the village. A
troop of strange children ran at his heels, hooting
after him, and pointing at his gray beard. The
dogs, too, not one of which he recognized for an old
acquaintance, barked at him as he passed. The
very village was altered; it was larger and more
populous. There were rows of houses which he
had never seen before, and those which had been
his familiar haunts had disappeared. Strange
names were over the doors — strange faces at the
windows — everything was strange. His mind now
misgave him; he began to doubt whether both he
and the world around him were not bewitched.
Surely this was his native village, which he had
left but the day before. There stood the Kaatskill
Mountains — there ran the silver Hudson at a distance — there was every hill and dale precisely as

it had always been — Rip was sorely perplexed — " That flagon last night," thought he, " has addled my poor head sadly ! "

It was with some difficulty that he found the way to his own house, which he approached with silent awe, expecting every moment to hear the shrill voice of Dame Van Winkle. He found the house gone to decay — the roof fallen in, the windows shattered, and the doors off the hinges. A half-starved dog that looked like Wolf was skulking about it. Rip called him by name, but the cur snarled, showed his teeth, and passed on. This was an unkind cut indeed — " My very dog," sighed poor Rip, " has forgotten me ! "

He entered the house, which, to tell the truth, Dame Van Winkle had always kept in neat order. It was empty, forlorn, and apparently abandoned. This desolateness overcame all his connubial fears — he called loudly for his wife and children — the lonely chambers rang for a moment with his voice, and then again all was silence.

He now hurried forth, and hastened to his old resort, the village inn — but it, too, was gone. A large, rickety wooden building stood in its place, with great gaping windows, some of them broken and mended with old hats and petticoats, and over the door was painted, " The Union Hotel, by Jonathan Doolittle." Instead of the great tree that used to shelter the quiet little Dutch inn of yore, there now was reared a tall naked pole, with something on the top that looked like a red night-cap, and from it was fluttering a flag, on which was a singular assemblage of stars and stripes — all this was strange and incomprehensible. He recognized on the sign, however, the ruby face of King George, under which he had smoked so many a peaceful pipe; but even this was singularly metamorphosed. The red coat was changed for one of blue and buff, a sword was held in the hand instead of a sceptre, the head was decorated with a cocked hat, and underneath was painted in large characters, GENERAL WASHINGTON.

There was, as usual, a crowd of folk about the door, but none that Rip recollected. The very character of the people seemed changed. There was a busy, bustling, disputatious tone about it, instead of the accustomed phlegm and drowsy tranquillity. He looked in vain for the sage Nich. as Vedder, with his broad face, double chin, and fair long pipe, uttering clouds of tobacco-smoke instead of idle speeches; or Van Bummel, the school-master, doling forth the contents of an ancient newspaper. In place of these, a lean, bilious-looking fellow, with his pockets full of handbills, was haranguing vehemently about rights of citizens — elections — members of congress — liberty — Bunker's Hill — heroes of seventy - six — and other words, which were a perfect Babylonish jargon to the bewildered Van Winkle.

The appearance of Rip, with his long grizzled beard, his rusty fowling-piece, his uncouth dress, and an army of women and children at his heels,

soon attracted the attention of the tavern-politi-
cians. They crowded round him, eying him from
head to foot with great curiosity. The orator bustled up to him, and, drawing him partly aside, inquired " on which side he voted ? " Rip stared in
vacant stupidity. Another short but busy little
fellow pulled him by the arm, and, rising on tiptoe,
inquired in his ear, " Whether he was Federal or
Democrat ? " Rip was equally at a loss to comprehend the question; when a knowing, self-important old gentleman, in a sharp cocked hat, made
his way through the crowd, putting them to the
right and left with his elbows as he passed, and
planting himself before Van Winkle, with one arm
akimbo, the other resting on his cane, his keen eyes
and sharp hat penetrating, as it were, into his very
soul, demanded in an austere tone, " what brought
him to the election with a gun on his shoulder, and
a mob at his heels, and whether he meant to breed
a riot in the village ? " — " Alas ! gentlemen,"
cried Rip, somewhat dismayed, " I am a poor quiet
man, a native of the place, and a loyal subject of
the king, God bless him ! "

Here a general shout burst from the bystanders
— " A tory ! a tory ! a spy ! a refugee ! hustle him !
away with him ! " It was with great difficulty that
the self-important man in the cocked hat restored
order ; and, having assumed a tenfold austerity of
brow, demanded again of the unknown culprit,
what he came there for, and whom he was seeking ? The poor man humbly assured him that he

meant no harm, but merely came there in search of some of his neighbors, who used to keep about the tavern.

" Well — who are they ? — name them."

Rip bethought himself a moment, and inquired, " Where 's Nicholas Vedder ? "

There was a silence for a little while, when an old man replied, in a thin, piping voice. " Nicholas Vedder ! why, he is dead and gone these eighteen years ! There was a wooden tombstone in the churchyard that used to tell all about him, but that 's rotten and gone too."

" Where 's Brom Dutcher ? "

" Oh, he went off to the army in the beginning of the war ; some say he was killed at the storming of Stony Point [1] — others say he was drowned in a squall at the foot of Antony's Nose.[2] I don't know — he never came back again."

---

[1] On the Hudson. The place is famous for the daring assault made by Mad Anthony Wayne, July 15, 1779.

[2] A few miles above Stony Point is the promontory of Antony's Nose. If we are to believe Diedrich Knickerbocker, it was named after Antony Van Corlear, Stuyvesant's trumpeter. "It must be known, then, that the nose of Antony the Trumpeter was of a very lusty size, strutting boldly from his countenance like a mountain of Golconda. . . . . Now thus it happened, that bright and early in the morning the good Antony, having washed his burly visage, was leaning over the quarter railing of the galley, contemplating it in the glassy wave below. Just at this moment the illustrious sun, breaking in all his splendor from behind a high bluff of the highlands, did dart one of his most potent beams full upon the refulgent nose of the sounder of brass — the reflection of which shot straightway down, hissing hot, into the water and killed a mighty sturgeon

" Where 's Van Bummel, the school-master ? "

" He went off to the wars too, was a great militia general, and is now in Congress."

Rip's heart died away at hearing of these sad
changes in his home and friends, and finding himself thus alone in the world. Every answer puzzled him too, by treating of such enormous lapses
of time, and of matters which he could not understand : war — Congress — Stony Point ; — he had
no courage to ask after any more friends, but cried
out in despair, " Does nobody here know Rip Van
Winkle ? "

" Oh, Rip Van Winkle ! " exclaimed two or
three, " Oh, to be sure ! that 's Rip Van Winkle
yonder, leaning against the tree."

Rip looked, and beheld a precise counterpart of
himself, as he went up the mountain : apparently
as lazy, and certainly as ragged. The poor fellow
was now completely confounded. He doubted his
own identity, and whether he was himself or another man. In the midst of his bewilderment, the
man in the cocked hat demanded who he was, and
what was his name ?

" God knows," exclaimed he at his wit's end ;
" I 'm not myself — I 'm somebody else — that 's
me yonder — no — that 's somebody else got into

that was sporting beside the vessel ! . . . . When this aston-
ishing miracle came to be made known to Peter Stuyvesant he
. . . . marvelled exceedingly ; and as a monument thereof,
he gave the name of *Antony's Nose* to a stout promontory in the
neighborhood, and it has continued to be called Antony's Nose
ever since that time." *History of New York*, book VI. chap. 4.

my shoes — I was myself last night, but I fell asleep on the mountain, and they 've changed my gun, and everything 's changed, and I 'm changed, and I can't tell what 's my name, or who I am ! "

The bystanders began now to look at each other, nod, wink significantly, and tap their fingers against their foreheads. There was a whisper, also, about securing the gun, and keeping the old fellow from doing mischief, at the very suggestion of which the self-important man in the cocked hat retired with some precipitation. At this critical moment a fresh, comely woman pressed through the throng to get a peep at the gray-bearded man. She had a chubby child in her arms, which, frightened at his looks, began to cry. "Hush, Rip," cried she, "hush, you little fool; the old man won't hurt you." The name of the child, the air of the mother, the tone of her voice, all awakened a train of recollections in his mind. "What is your name, my good woman?" asked he.

"Judith Gardenier."

"And your father's name?"

"Ah, poor man, Rip Van Winkle was his name, but it 's twenty years since he went away from home with his gun, and never has been heard of since, — his dog came home without him; but whether he shot himself, or was carried away by the Indians, nobody can tell. I was then but a little girl."

Rip had but one question more to ask; and he put it with a faltering voice : —

"Where 's your mother ? "

" Oh, she too had died but a short time since ; she broke a blood-vessel in a fit of passion at a New England peddler."

There was a drop of comfort, at least, in this intelligence. The honest man could contain himself no longer. He caught his daughter and her child in his arms. " I am your father ! " cried he — " Young Rip Van Winkle once — old Rip Van Winkle now ! Does nobody know poor Rip Van Winkle ? "

All stood amazed, until an old woman tottering out from among the crowd, put her hand to her brow, and peering under it in his face for a moment, exclaimed, " Sure enough ! it is Rip Van Winkle — it is himself ! Welcome home again, old neighbor —Why, where have you been these twenty long years ? "

Rip's story was soon told, for the whole twenty years had been to him but as one night. The neighbors stared when they heard it ; some were seen to wink at each other, and put their tongues in their cheeks ; and the self-important man in the cocked hat, who, when the alarm was over, had returned to the field, screwed down the corners of his mouth, and shook his head — upon which there was a general shaking of the head throughout the assemblage.

It was determined, however, to take the opinion of old Peter Vanderdonk, who was seen slowly advancing up the road. He was a descendant of the historian of that name,[1] who wrote one of the

[1] Adrian Vanderdonk.

earliest accounts of the province. Peter was the most ancient inhabitant of the village, and well versed in all the wonderful events and traditions of the neighborhood. He recollected Rip at once, and corroborated his story in the most satisfactory manner. He assured the company that it was a fact, handed down from his ancestor the historian, that the Kaatskill Mountains had always been haunted by strange beings. That it was affirmed that the great Hendrick Hudson, the first discoverer of the river and country, kept a kind of vigil there every twenty years, with his crew of the Half-moon ; being permitted in this way to revisit the scenes of his enterprise, and keep a guardian eye upon the river, and the great city called by his name. That his father had once seen them in their old Dutch dresses playing at nine-pins in a hollow of the mountain ; and that he himself had heard, one summer afternoon, the sound of their balls, like distant peals of thunder.

To make a long story short, the company broke up, and returned to the more important concerns of the election. Rip's daughter took him home to live with her ; she had a snug, well-furnished house, and a stout, cheery farmer for a husband, whom Rip recollected for one of the urchins that used to climb upon his back. As to Rip's son and heir, who was the ditto of himself, seen leaning against the tree, he was employed to work on the farm ; but evinced an hereditary disposition to attend to anything else but his business.

Rip now resumed his old walks and habits; he soon found many of his former cronies, though all rather the worse for the wear and tear of time; and preferred making friends among the rising generation, with whom he soon grew into great favor.

Having nothing to do at home, and being arrived at that happy age when a man can be idle with impunity, he took his place once more on the bench at the inn door, and was reverenced as one of the patriarchs of the village, and a chronicle of the old times "before the war." It was some time before he could get into the regular track of gossip, or could be made to comprehend the strange events that had taken place during his torpor. How that there had been a revolutionary war — that the country had thrown off the yoke of old England — and that, instead of being a subject of his Majesty George the Third, he was now a free citizen of the United States. Rip, in fact, was no politician; the changes of states and empires made but little impression on him; but there was one species of despotism under which he had long groaned, and that was — petticoat government. Happily that was at an end; he had got his neck out of the yoke of matrimony, and could go in and out whenever he pleased, without dreading the tyranny of Dame Van Winkle. Whenever her name was mentioned, however, he shook his head, shrugged his shoulders, and cast up his eyes, which might pass either for an expression of resignation to his fate, or joy at his deliverance.

He used to tell his story to every stranger that arrived at Mr. Doolittle's hotel. He was observed, at first, to vary on some points every time he told it, which was, doubtless, owing to his having so recently awaked. It at last settled down precisely to the tale I have related, and not a man, woman, or child in the neighborhood but knew it by heart. Some always pretended to doubt the reality of it, and insisted that Rip had been out of his head, and that this was one point on which he always remained flighty. The old Dutch inhabitants, however, almost universally gave it full credit. Even to this day they never hear a thunder-storm of a summer afternoon about the Kaatskill, but they say Hendrick Hudson and his crew are at their game of nine-pins ; and it is a common wish of all henpecked husbands in the neighborhood, when life hangs heavy on their hands, that they might have a quieting draught out of Rip Van Winkle's flagon.

NOTE.

The foregoing Tale, one would suspect, had been suggested to Mr. Knickerbocker by a little German superstition about the Emperor Frederick *der Rothbart*,[1] and the Kypphaüser mountain; the subjoined note, however, which he had appended to the tale, shows that it is an absolute fact, narrated with his usual fidelity.

" The story of Rip Van Winkle may seem incredible to many,

[1] Frederick I. of Germany, 1121–1190, called Barbarossa *der Rothbart* (Redbeard, or Rufus), was fabled not to have died but to have gone into a long sleep, and that he would awake when Germany should need him The same legend was told by the Danes of their Holger.

but nevertheless I give it my full belief, for I know the vicinity of our old Dutch settlements to have been very subject to marvellous events and appearances. Indeed, I have heard many stranger stories than this, in the villages along the Hudson; all of which were too well authenticated to admit of a doubt. I have even talked with Rip Van Winkle myself, who, when last I saw him, was a very venerable old man, and so perfectly rational and consistent on every other point, that I think no conscientious person could refuse to take this into the bargain; nay, I have seen a certificate on the subject taken before a country justice and signed with a cross, in the justice's own handwriting. The story, therefore, is beyond the possibility of doubt.

" D. K."

POSTSCRIPT.

The following are travelling notes from a memorandum-book of Mr. Knickerbocker: —

The Kaatsberg, or Catskill Mountains, have always been a region full of fable. The Indians considered them the abode of spirits, who influenced the weather, spreading sunshine or clouds over the landscape, and sending good or bad hunting seasons. They were ruled by an old squaw spirit, said to be their mother. She dwelt on the highest peak of the Catskills, and had charge of the doors of day and night to open and shut them at the proper hour. She hung up the new moons in the skies, and cut up the old ones into stars. In times of drought, if properly propitiated, she would spin light summer clouds out of cobwebs and morning dew, and send them off from the crest of the mountain, flake after flake, like flakes of carded cotton, to float in the air; until, dissolved by the heat of the sun, they would fall in gentle showers, causing the grass to spring, the fruits to ripen, and the corn to grow an inch an hour. If displeased, however, she would brew up clouds black as ink, sitting in the midst of them like a bottle-bellied spider in the midst of its web; and when these clouds broke, woe betide the valleys!

In old times, say the Indian traditions, there was a kind of Manitou or Spirit, who kept about the wildest recesses of the Catskill Mountains, and took a mischievous pleasure in wreaking all kinds of evils and vexations upon the red men. Sometimes he would assume the form of a bear, a panther, or a deer, lead the bewildered hunter a weary chase throught angled forests and among ragged rocks; and then spring off with a loud ho! ho! leaving him aghast on the brink of a beetling precipice or raging torrent.

The favorite abode of this Manitou is still shown. It is a great rock or cliff on the loneliest part of the mountains, and, from the flowering vines which clamber about it, and the wild flowers which abound in its neighborhood, is known by the name of the Garden Rock. Near the foot of it is as mall lake, the haunt of the solitary bittern, with water-snakes basking in the sun on the leaves of the pond-lilies which lie on the surface. This place was held in great awe by the Indians, insomuch that the boldest hunter would not pursue his game within its precincts. Once upon a time, however, a hunter, who had lost his way, penetrated to the Garden Rock, where he beheld a number of gourds placed in the crotches of trees. One of these he seized and made off with it, but in the hurry of his retreat he let it fall among the rocks, when a great stream gushed forth, which washed him away and swept him down precipices, where he was dashed to pieces, and the stream made its way to the Hudson, and continues to flow to the present day; being the identical stream known by the name of the Kaaters-kill.

II.

LITTLE BRITAIN.

What I write is most true . . . . I have a whole booke of cases lying by me which if I should sette foorth, some grave auntients within the hearing of Bow bell) would be out of charity with me.

NASHE.

IN the centre of the great city of London lies a small neighborhood, consisting of a cluster of narrow streets and courts, of very venerable and debilitated houses, which goes by the name of LITTLE

BRITAIN. Christ Church School,[1] and St. Bartholomew's Hospital [2] bound it on the west ; Smithfield [3] and Long Lane on the north ; Aldersgate Street, like an arm of the sea, divides it from the eastern part of the city ; whilst the yawning gulf of Bull-and-Mouth Street separates it from Butcher Lane, and the regions of Newgate. Over this little territory, thus bounded and designated, the great dome of St. Paul's, swelling above the intervening houses of Paternoster Row, Amen Corner, and Ave Maria Lane, looks down with an air of motherly protection.

This quarter derives its appellation from having been, in ancient times, the residence of the Dukes of Brittany. As London increased, however, rank and fashion rolled off to the west, and trade, creeping on at their heels, took possession of their deserted abodes. For some time Little Britain became the great mart of learning, and was peopled by the busy and prolific race of booksellers ; these also gradually deserted it, and, emigrating beyond the great strait of Newgate Street, settled down in Paternoster Row and St. Paul's Churchyard, where

[1] More accurately Christ's Hospital, popularly known as The Blue Coat School, an old and famous school originally intended as a home for foundlings and fatherless children. Charles Lamb in *Essays of Elia* has some charming papers, *Recollections of Christ's Hospital* and *Christ's Hospital Five and Thirty Years Ago*.

[2] The earliest institution of the kind in London, founded in 1102.

[3] Famous as the scene of Wat Tyler's death, and of martyrdoms for religion under Henry VIII., Mary, and Elizabeth.

they continue to increase and multiply even at the present day.

But though thus falling into decline, Little Britain still bears traces of its former splendor. There are several houses ready to tumble down, the fronts of which are magnificently enriched with old oaken carvings of hideous faces, unknown birds, beasts, and fishes : and fruits and flowers which it would perplex a naturalist to classify. There are also, in Aldersgate Street, certain remains of what were once spacious and lordly family mansions, but which have in latter days been subdivided into several tenements. Here may often be found the family of a petty tradesman, with its trumpery furniture, burrowing among the relics of antiquated finery, in great, rambling, time-stained apartments, with fretted ceilings, gilded cornices, and enormous marble fireplaces. The lanes and courts also contain many smaller houses, not on so grand a scale, but, like your small ancient gentry, sturdily maintaining their claims to equal antiquity. These have their gable ends to the street ; great bow-windows, with diamond panes set in lead, grotesque carvings, and low arched door-ways.[1]

In this most venerable and sheltered little nest have I passed several quiet years of existence,[2] com-

---

[1] It is evident that the author of this interesting communication has included, in his general title of Little Britain, many of those little lanes and courts that belong immediately to Cloth Fair. — *Irving's Note.*

[2] It must be remembered that it is Geoffrey Crayon who is writing, and not Washington Irving.

fortably lodged in the second floor of one of the smallest but oldest edifices. My sitting-room is an old wainscoted chamber, with small panels, and set off with a miscellaneous array of furniture. I have a particular respect for three or four high-backed claw-footed chairs, covered with tarnished brocade, which bear the marks of having seen better days, and have doubtless figured in some of the old palaces of Little Britain. They seem to me to keep together, and to look down with sovereign contempt upon their leathern-bottomed neighbors : as I have seen decayed gentry carry a high head among the plebeian society with which they were reduced to associate. The whole front of my sitting-room is taken up with a bow-window, on the panes of which are recorded the names of previous occupants for many generations, mingled with scraps of very indifferent gentlemanlike poetry, written in characters which I can scarcely decipher, and which extol the charms of many a beauty of Little Britain, who has long, long since bloomed, faded, and passed away. As I am an idle personage, with no apparent occupation, and pay my bill regularly every week, I am looked upon as the only independent gentleman of the neighborhood.; and, being curious to learn the internal state of a community so apparently shut up within itself, I have managed to work my way into all the concerns and secrets of the place.

Little Britain may truly be called the heart's core of the city ; the stronghold of true John Bullism. It is a fragment of London as it was in its better days, with its antiquated folks and fashions. Here flourish in great preservation many of the holiday games and customs of yore. The inhabitants most religiously eat pancakes on Shrove Tuesday, hot-cross-buns on Good Friday, and roast goose at Michaelmas; they send love-letters on Valentine's Day, burn the pope on the fifth of November,[1] and kiss all the girls under the mistletoe at Christmas. Roast beef and plum-pudding are also held in superstitious veneration, and port and sherry maintain their grounds as the only true English wines; all others being considered vile, outlandish beverages.

Little Britain has its long catalogue of city wonders, which its inhabitants consider the wonders of the world; such as the great bell of St. Paul's, which sours all the beer when it tolls; the figures that strike the hours at St. Dunstan's clock; the Monument;[2] the lions in the Tower; and the wooden giants[3] in Guildhall. They still believe in dreams and fortune-telling, and an old woman that lives in Bull-and-Mouth Street makes a tolerable subsistence by detecting stolen goods, and promising the girls good husbands. They are apt to be rendered uncomfortable by comets and eclipses;

[1] The anniversary of the discovery of the Gunpowder Plot. Pope's Day, as it was called, was observed in New England until near the end of the last century.

[2] To commemorate the Great Fire of London, September 1666.

[3] Known as Gog and Magog.

and if a dog howls dolefully at night, it is looked upon as a sure sign of a death in the place. There are even many ghost stories current, particularly concerning the old mansion-houses ; in several of which it is said strange sights are sometimes seen. Lords and ladies, the former in full bottomed wigs, hanging sleeves, and swords, the latter in lappets, stays, hoops, and brocade, have been seen walking up and down the great waste chambers, on moonlight nights ; and are supposed to be the shades of the ancient proprietors in their court-dresses.

Little Britain has likewise its sages and great men. One of the most important of the former is a tall, dry old gentleman, of the name of Skryme, who keeps a small apothecary's shop. He has a cadaverous countenance, full of cavities and projections ; with a brown circle round each eye, like a pair of horned spectacles. He is much thought of by the old women, who consider him as a kind of conjuror, because he has two or three stuffed alligators hanging up in his shop, and several snakes in bottles. He is a great reader of almanacs and newspapers, and is much given to pore over alarming accounts of plots, conspiracies, fires, earthquakes, and volcanic eruptions ; which last phenomena he considers as signs of the times. He has always some dismal tale of the kind to deal out to his customers, with their doses ; and thus at the same time puts both soul and body into an uproar. He is a great believer in omens and predictions and has the prophecies of Robert Nixon [1] and Mother Shipton [2] by heart. No man can make so much out of an eclipse, or even an unusually dark day; and he shook the tail of the last comet over the heads of his customers and disciples until they were nearly frightened out of their wits. He has lately got hold of a popular legend or prophecy, on which he has been unusually eloquent. There has been a saying current among the ancient sibyls, who treasure up these things, that when the grasshopper on the top of the Exchange shook hands with the dragon on the top of Bow Church steeple, fearful events would take place. This strange conjunction, it seems, has as strangely come to pass. The same architect has been engaged lately on the repairs of the cupola of the Exchange, and the steeple of Bow Church ; and, fearful to relate, the dragon and the grasshopper actually lie, cheek by jole, in the yard of his workshop.

"Others," as Mr. Skryme is accustomed to say, "may go star-gazing, and look for conjunctions in the heavens, but here is a conjunction on the earth, near at home, and under our own eyes, which sur-passes all the signs and calculations of astrologers." Since these portentous weathercocks have thus laid

---

[1] Known as the Cheshire Idiot, a contemporary of Mother Shipton, and reckoned a poet. See *Memoirs of Extraordinary Popular Delusions*, by Charles Mackay, vol. i. pp. 196–201.

[2] A woman said to have been living in Yorkshire in the time of Henry VII., and to have had prophetic power. Many of her prophecies, in rhyme, are in the mouths of half-educated people in England to-day, and their fulfilment looked for.

their heads together, wonderful events had already
occurred. The good old king,[1] notwithstanding
that he had lived eighty-two years, had all at once
given up the ghost; another king had mounted the
throne; a royal duke had died suddenly [2] — another, in France, had been murdered; [3] there had
been radical meetings in all parts of the kingdom;
the bloody scenes at Manchester; [4] the great plot
in Cato Street; [5] — and, above all, the queen had
returned to England! [6]   All these sinister events

[1] George III., who died January 29, 1820, and was succeeded
by George IV.

[2] The Duke of Kent, who died in 1820.

[3] The Duke of Berri, second in succession to the crown, who
was assassinated in 1820.

[4] There had been a period of great suffering in England and a
chronic discontent at the existing order of things, when in August, 1819, an immense meeting, in opposition to the government, was held at Manchester. Troops were on the ground, and
in a sudden panic the magistrates ordered a charge which had a
frightful result.

[5] The Cato Street Conspiracy was a plot to murder all the
ministers of the crown at a cabinet dinner to be held February
23, 1820, to fire the barracks, and make an assault upon the Bank
of England and the Tower. It was the scheme of a few desperate men in the time of great popular discontent with the government.

[6] Caroline, queen of King George IV. She had gone to the
Continent in 1814, driven there by the persecution of her husband then Prince Regent. She returned in 1820 to vindicate
her rights, and all England was divided into two parties upon
the question of her innocency. A bill was introduced into Parlia-
ment for her deposition as queen and her divorce from the king,
but finally failed. Her acquittal was followed by immense popular rejoicings, but her own imprudence partly cooled the public
sympathy, and her death, in August, 1820, shortly after the
king's coronation, came in season to save her from further disaster.

are recounted by Mr. Skryme, with a mysterious look, and a dismal shake of the head ; and being taken with his drugs, and associated in the minds of his auditors with stuffed sea-monsters, bottled serpents, and his own visage, which is a title-page of tribulation, they have spread great gloom through the minds of the people of Little Britain. They shake their heads whenever they go by Bow Church, and observe, that they never expected any good to come of taking down that steeple, which in old times told nothing but glad tidings, as the history of Whittington and his Cat bears witness.

The rival oracle of Little Britain is a substantial cheesemonger, who lives in a fragment of one of the old family mansions, and is as magnificently lodged as a round-bellied mite in the midst of one of his own Cheshires. Indeed, he is a man of no little standing and importance ; and his renown extends through Huggin Lane, and Lad Lane, and even unto Aldermanbury. His opinion is very much taken in affairs of state, having read the Sunday papers for the last half century, together with the " Gentleman's Magazine," Rapin's " History of England," and the " Naval Chronicle." His head is stored with invaluable maxims which have borne the test of time and use for centuries. It is his firm opinion that " it is a moral impossible," so long as England is true to herself, that anything can shake her : and he has much to say on the subject of the national debt ; which, somehow or other, he proves to be a great national bulwark and blessing.

He passed the greater part of his life in the pur-
lieus of Little Britain, until of late years, when,
having become rich, and grown into the dignity of
a Sunday cane, he begins to take his pleasure and
see the world. He has therefore made several excursions to Hampstead, Highgate, and other neighboring towns, where he has passed whole afternoons
in looking back upon the metropolis through a
telescope, and endeavoring to descry the steeple of
St. Bartholomew's. Not a stage-coachman of Bull-
and-Mouth Street but touches his hat as he passes;
and he is considered quite a patron at the coach-
office of the Goose and Gridiron, St. Paul's Churchyard. His family have been very urgent for him
to make an expedition to Margate, but he has great
doubts of those new gimcracks, the steamboats, and
indeed thinks himself too advanced in life to undertake sea-voyages.

Little Britain has occasionally its factions and
divisions, and party spirit ran very high at one time
in consequence of two rival " Burial Societies "
being set up in the place. One held its meeting
at the Swan and Horse Shoe,[1] and was patronized

---

[1] It is just possible that this may have been The Swan and
Harp. " The Mitre was a celebrated music-house in London
House Yard at the northwest end of St. Paul's. When it ceased
to be a music-house the succeeding landlord, to ridicule its former destiny, chose for his sign a goose stroking the bars of a
gridiron with his foot (The *Goose and Gridiron*) in ridicule of
the Swan and Harp, a common sign for the early music-houses.
Such an origin does the *Tatler* give; but it may also be a vernacular reading of the coat of arms of the Company of Musicians, suspended probably at the door of the Mitre when it was a

by the cheesemonger; the other at the Cock and
Crown, under the auspices of the apothecary; it is
needless to say that the latter was the most flourishing. I have passed an evening or two at each, and
have acquired much valuable information, as to the
best mode of being buried, the comparative merits
of churchyards, together with divers hints on the
subject of patent-iron coffins. I have heard the
question discussed in all its bearings as to the le-
gality of prohibiting the latter on account of their
durability. The feuds occasioned by these societies
have happily died of late; but they were for a long
time prevailing themes of controversy, the people
of Little Britain being extremely solicitous of fu-
nereal honors and of lying comfortably in their
graves.

Besides these two funeral societies there is a third
of quite a different cast, which tends to throw the
sunshine of good-humor over the whole neighborhood. It meets once a week at a little old-fashioned
house, kept by a jolly publican of the name of
Wagstaff, and bearing for insignia a resplendent
half-moon, with a most seductive bunch of grapes.
The old edifice is covered with inscriptions to catch
the eye of the thirsty wayfarer, such as " Truman,
Hanbury, and Co.'s Entire," " Wine, Rum, and

music-house. These arms are, a swan with his wings expanded,
within a double tressure, counter, flory, argent. This double
tressure might have suggested a gridiron to unsophisticated pass-
ers-by." — *The History of Signboards,* by Jacob Larwood and
John Camden Hotten, pp. 445, 446.

Brandy Vaults," "Old Tom, Rum and Compounds,
etc." This indeed has been a temple of Bacchus
and Momus from time immemorial. It has always
been in the family of the Wagstaffs, so that its
history is tolerably preserved by the present landlord. It was much frequented by the gallants and
cavalieros of the reign of Elizabeth, and was looked
into now and then by the wits of Charles the
Second's day. But what Wagstaff principally
prides himself upon is, that Henry the Eighth, in
one of his nocturnal rambles, broke the head of one
of his ancestors with his famous walking-staff. This,
however, is considered as a rather dubious and vain-
glorious boast of the landlord.

The club which now holds its weekly sessions
here goes by the name of "The Roaring Lads of
Little Britain." They abound in old catches, glees,
and choice stories, that are traditional in the place,
and not to be met with in any other part of the
metropolis. There is a madcap undertaker who
is inimitable at a merry song; but the life of the
club, and indeed the prime wit of Little Britain, is
bully Wagstaff himself. His ancestors were all
wags before him, and he has inherited with the inn
a large stock of songs and jokes, which go with it
from generation to generation as heirlooms. He
is a dapper little fellow, with bandy legs and pot
belly, a red face, with a moist, merry eye, and a
little shock of gray hair behind. At the opening
of every club night he is called in to sing his
" Confession of Faith," which is the famous old

drinking trowl from "Gammer Gurton's Needle." [1]
He sings it, to be sure, with many variations, as he
received it from his father's lips ; for it has been a
standing favorite at the Half-Moon and Bunch of
Grapes ever since it was written : nay, he affirms
that his predecessors have often had the honor of
singing it before the nobility and gentry at Christmas mummeries, when Little Britain was in all its
glory.[2]

[1] *Gammer Gurton's Needle* is the name of a dramatic piece
by John Still, afterward Bishop of Bath and Wells, said to be
the second English comedy in point of time. It was written
about the time of Shakespeare's birth, and turns on the rustic
adventures of Gammer Gurton who lost her needle, — a very
precious piece of property in those days, — and found it finally
in the breeches of her man Hodge, where she had left it when at
her work.

[2] As mine host of the Half-Moon's Confession of Faith may
not be familiar to the majority of readers, and as it is a specimen
of the current songs of Little Britain, I subjoin it in its original
orthography. I would observe, that the whole club always join
in the chorus with a fearful thumping on the table and clattering
of pewter pots. W. I.

> "I cannot eate but lytle meate,
>   My stomacke is not good,
> But sure I thinke that I can drinke
>   With him that weares a hood.
> Though I go bare, take ye no care,
>   I nothing am a colde,
> I stuff my skyn so full within,
>   Of joly good ale and olde.
> *Chorus.* Backe and syde go bare, go bare,
>   Booth foote and hand go colde,
>   But belly, God send thee good ale ynoughe
>   Whether it be new or olde.

> "I have no rost, but a nut brawne toste,
>   And a crab laid in the fyre ;
> A little breade shall do me steade,
>   Much breade I not desyre.

It would do one's heart good to hear, on a club night, the shouts of merriment, the snatches of song, and now and then the choral bursts of half a dozen discordant voices, which issue from this jovial mansion. At such times the street is lined with listeners, who enjoy a delight equal to that of gazing into a confectioner's window, or snuffing up the steams of a cookshop.

There are two annual events which produce great stir and sensation in Little Britain; these are St. Bartholomew's Fair,[1] and the Lord Mayor's

> No frost nor snow, nor winde, I trowe,
>   Can hurte mee, if I wolde,
> I am so wrapt and throwly lapt
>   Of joly good ale and olde.
> *Chorus.* Backe and syde go bare, go bare, etc.
>
> " And Tyb my wife, that, as her lyfe,
>   Loveth well good ale to seeke,
> ˙ Full oft drynkes shee, tyll ye may see,
>   The teares run downe her cheeke.
> Then doth she trowle to me the bowle,
>   Even as a mault-worme sholde,
> And sayth, sweete harte, I took my parte
>   Of this joly good ale and olde.
> *Chorus.* Backe and syde go bare, go bare, etc.
>
> " Now let them drynke, tyll they nod and winke
>   Even as goode fellowes sholde doe,
> They shall not mysse to have the blisse,
>   Good ale doth bring men to ;
> And all poore soules that have scowred bowles
>   Or have them lustily trolde,
> God save the lyves of them and their wives,
>   Whether they be yonge or olde.
> *Chorus.* Backe and syde go bare, go bare," etc.

[1] A famous annual fair, so called because it was kept at Bartholomew Tide (St. Bartholomew's Day is August 24th), and held within the precinct of St. Bartholomew in Smithfield. It

Day. During the time of the fair, which is held in the adjoining regions of Smithfield, there is nothing going on but gossiping and gadding about. The late quiet streets of Little Britain are overrun with an irruption of strange figures and faces; every tavern is a scene of rout and revel. The fiddle and the song are heard from the tap-room, morning, noon, and night; and at each window may be seen some group of boon companions, with half-shut eyes, hats on one side, pipe in mouth, and tankard in hand, fondling, and prosing, and singing maudlin songs over their liquor. Even the sober decorum of private families, which I must say is rigidly kept up at other times among my neighbors, is no proof against this Saturnalia. There is no such thing as keeping maid-servants within doors. Their brains are absolutely set madding with Punch and the Puppet Show; the Flying Horses; Signior Polito;[1] the Fire-Eater; the celebrated Mr. Paap; and the Irish Giant. The children, too, lavish all their holiday money in toys and gilt gingerbread, and fill the house with the Lilliputian din of drums, trumpets, and penny whistles.

But the Lord Mayor's Day[2] is the great anni-

was for several centuries the great Cloth Fair of England. It became afterward a kind of Carnival, and finally degenerating into a public nuisance, died out of public notice.

[1] The showman of a menagerie of that day.

[2] On the 9th of November each year the mayor of London goes up to Westminster to be sworn into office. The pageant was once a striking and brilliant one, when it was significant of the political importance of the city of London. It is still kept up out is a mere mockery of its old splendor.

versary. The Lord Mayor is looked up to by the inhabitants of Little Britain as the greatest potentate upon earth; his gilt coach with six horses as the summit of human splendor; and his procession, with all the Sheriffs and Aldermen in his train, as the grandest of earthly pageants. How they exult in the idea that the King himself dare not enter the city without first knocking at the gate of Temple Bar, and asking permission of the Lord Mayor : for if he did, heaven and earth! there is no knowing what might be the consequence. The man in armor who rides before the Lord Mayor, and is the city champion, has orders to cut down everybody that offends against the dignity of the city; and then there is the little man with a velvet porringer on his head, who sits at the window of the state-coach, and holds the city sword, as long as a pike-staff — Odd's blood! If he once draws that sword, Majesty itself is not safe !

Under the protection of this mighty potentate, therefore, the good people of Little Britain sleep in peace. Temple Bar is an effectual barrier against all interior foes ; and as to foreign invasion, the Lord Mayor has but to throw himself into the Tower, call in the train-bands, and put the standing army of Beef-eaters [1] under arms, and he may bid defiance to the world !

[1] The yeomen of the Royal Guard who are attached to the service of the Tower are popularly called *Beef-eaters*, a corruption, we are told, of *buffetiers*, that is, personal attendants of the sovereign, who on high festivals were ranged near the royal side board or *buffet*.

Thus wrapped up in its own concerns, its own habits, and its own opinions, Little Britain has long flourished as a sound heart to this great fungous metropolis. I have pleased myself with considering it as a chosen spot, where the principles of sturdy John Bullism were garnered up, like seed corn, to renew the national character, when it had run to waste and degeneracy. I have rejoiced also in the general spirit of harmony that prevailed throughout it; for though there might now and then be a few clashes of opinion between the adherents of the cheesemonger and the apothecary, and an occasional feud between the burial societies, yet these were but transient clouds, and soon passed away. The neighbors met with good-will, parted with a shake of the hand, and never abused each other except behind their backs.

I could give rare descriptions of snug junketing parties at which I have been present; where we played at All-Fours, Pope-Joan, Tom-come-tickle-me, and other choice old games; and where we sometimes had a good old English country dance to the tune of Sir Roger de Coverley.[1] Once a year, also, the neighbors would gather together, and go on a gipsy party to Epping Forest.[2] It would

[1] In the time of Richard I. there was a Sir Roger of Calverley, after whom a tune was named which was long the air of a country dance, which by custom was invariably made the conclusion of balls. The name underwent the slight change into the form which it held in Addison's time, and he and Steele at Swift's suggestion used it as the name of the knight whose character and fortune constitute the most charming portion of *The Spectator*.

[2] A famous royal preserve, sixteen miles from London.

have done any man's heart good to see the merriment that took place here as we banqueted on the grass under the trees. How we made the woods ring with bursts of laughter at the songs of little Wagstaff and the merry undertaker! After dinner, too, the young folks would play at blind-man's-buff and hide and-seek; and it was amusing to see them tangled among the briers, and to hear a fine romping girl now and then squeak from among the bushes. The elder folks would gather round the cheesemonger and the apothecary, to hear them talk politics; for they generally brought out a newspaper in their pockets, to pass away time in the country. They would now and then, to be sure, get a little warm in argument; but their disputes were always adjusted by reference to a worthy old umbrella-maker, in a double chin, who, never exactly comprehending the subject, managed somehow or other to decide in favor of both parties.

All empires, however, says some philosopher or historian, are doomed to changes and revolutions. Luxury and innovation creep in; factions arise; and families now and then spring up, whose ambition and intrigues throw the whole system into confusion. Thus in latter days has the tranquillity of Little Britain been grievously disturbed, and its golden simplicity of manners threatened with total subversion by the aspiring family of a retired butcher.

The family of the Lambs had long been among

the most thriving and popular in the neighborhood; the Miss Lambs were the belles of Little Britain, and everybody was pleased when Old Lamb had made money enough to shut up shop, and put his name on a brass plate on his door. In an evil hour, however, one of the Miss Lambs had the honor of being a lady in attendance on the Lady Mayoress, at her grand annual ball, on which occasion she wore three towering ostrich feathers on her head. The family never got over it; they were immediately smitten with a passion for high life; set up a one-horse carriage, put a bit of gold lace round the errand boy's hat, and have been the talk and detestation of the whole neighborhood ever since. They could no longer be induced to play at Pope-Joan or blind-man's-buff; they could endure no dances but quadrilles, which nobody had ever heard of in Little Britain; and they took to reading novels, talking bad French, and playing upon the piano. Their brother, too, who had been articled to an attorney, set up for a dandy and a critic, characters hitherto unknown in these parts; and he confounded the worthy folks exceedingly by talking about Kean,[1] the opera, and the " Edinburgh Review."

What was still worse, the Lambs gave a grand ball, to which they neglected to invite any of their old neighbors; but they had a great deal of genteel company from Theobald's Road, Red-Lion Square,

[1] Edmund Kean, a celebrated English tragedian, who died in 1833.

and other parts towards the west. There were several beaux of their brother's acquaintance from Gray's Inn Lane and Hatton Garden; and not less than three Aldermen's ladies with their daughters. This was not to be forgotten or forgiven. All Little Britain was in an uproar with the smacking of whips, the lashing of miserable horses, and the rattling and the jingling of hackney coaches. The gossips of the neighborhood might be seen popping their nightcaps out at every window, watching the crazy vehicles rumble by; and there was a knot of virulent old cronies, that kept a lookout from a house just opposite the retired butcher's, and scanned and criticised every one that knocked at the door.

This dance was a cause of almost open war, and the whole neighborhood declared they would have nothing more to say to the Lambs. It is true that Mrs. Lamb, when she had no engagements with her quality acquaintance, would give little humdrum tea-junketings to some of her old cronies, "quite," as she would say, "in a friendly way;" and it is equally true that her invitations were always accepted, in spite of all previous vows to the contrary. Nay, the good ladies would sit and be delighted with the music of the Miss Lambs, who would condescend to strum an Irish melody for them on the piano; and they would listen with wonderful interest to Mrs. Lamb's anecdotes of Alderman Plunket's family, of Portsokenward, and the Miss Timberlakes, the rich heiresses of Crutched-Friars; but then they relieved their consciences, and averted the reproaches of their confederates, by canvassing at the next gossiping convocation everything that had passed, and pulling the Lambs and their rout all to pieces.

The only one of the family that could not be made fashionable was the retired butcher himself. Honest Lamb, in spite of the meekness of his name, was a rough, hearty old fellow, with the voice of a lion, a head of black hair like a shoe-brush, and a broad face mottled like his own beef. It was in vain that the daughters always spoke of him as " the old gentleman," addressed him as " papa," in tones of infinite softness, and endeavored to coax him into a dressing-gown and slippers, and other gentlemanly habits. Do what they might, there was no keeping down the butcher. His sturdy nature would break through all their glozings. He had a hearty vulgar good-humor that was irrepressible. His very jokes made his sensitive daughters shudder; and he persisted in wearing his blue cotton coat of a morning, dining at two o'clock, and having a " bit of sausage with his tea."

He was doomed, however, to share the unpopularity of his family. He found his old comrades gradually growing cold and civil to him ; no longer laughing at his jokes ; and now and then throwing out a fling at " some people," and a hint about " quality binding." This both nettled and perplexed the honest butcher ; and his wife and daughters, with the consummate policy of the shrewder sex, taking advantage of the circumstance, at length prevailed upon him to give up his afternoon's pipe and tankard at Wagstaff's ; to sit after dinner by himself, and take his pint of port — a liquor he detested — and to nod in his chair in solitary and dismal gentility.

The Miss Lambs might now be seen flaunting along the streets in French bonnets, with unknown beaux ; and talking and laughing so loud that it distressed the nerves of every good lady within hearing. They even went so far as to attempt patronage, and actually induced a French dancing-master to set up in the neighborhood ; but the worthy folks of Little Britain took fire at it, and did so persecute the poor Gaul that he was fain to pack up fiddle and dancing-pumps, and decamp with such precipitation that he absolutely forgot to pay for his lodgings.

I had flattered myself, at first, with the idea that all this fiery indignation on the part of the community was merely the overflowing of their zeal for good old English manners, and their horror of innovation ; and I applauded the silent contempt they were so vociferous in expressing, for upstart pride, French fashions, and the Miss Lambs. But I grieve to say that I soon perceived the infection had taken hold ; and that my neighbors, after condemning, were beginning to follow their example. I overheard my landlady importuning her husband to let their daughters have one quarter at French and music, and that they might take a few lessons

11

in quadrille. I even saw, in the course of a few Sundays, no less than five French bonnets, precisely like those of the Miss Lambs, parading about Little Britain.

I still had my hopes that all this folly would gradually die away; that the Lambs might move out of the neighborhood; might die, or might run away with attorneys' apprentices; and that quiet and simplicity might be again restored to the community. But unluckily a rival power arose. An opulent oilman died, and left a widow with a large jointure and a family of buxom daughters. The young ladies had long been repining in secret at the parsimony of a prudent father, which kept down all their elegant aspirings. Their ambition, being now no longer restrained, broke out into a blaze, and they openly took the field against the family of the butcher. It is true that the Lambs, having had the first start, had naturally an advantage of them in the fashionable career. They could speak a little bad French, play the piano, dance quadrilles, and had formed high acquaintances; but the Trotters were not to be distanced. When the Lambs appeared with two feathers in their hats, the Miss Trotters mounted four, and of twice as fine colors. If the Lambs gave a dance, the Trotters were sure not to be behindhand: and though they might not boast of as good company, yet they had double the number, and were twice as merry.

The whole community has at length divided itself into fashionable factions, under the banners of these two families. The old games of Pope-Joan and Tom-come-tickle-me are entirely discarded; there is no such thing as getting up an honest country dance; and on my attempting to kiss a young lady under the mistletoe last Christmas, I was indignantly repulsed; the Miss Lambs having pronounced it "shocking vulgar." Bitter rivalry has also broken out as to the most fashionable part of Little Britain; the Lambs standing up for the dignity of Cross-Keys Square, and the Trotters for the vicinity of St. Bartholomew's.

Thus is this little territory torn by factions and internal dissensions, like the great empire whose name it bears; and what will be the result would puzzle the apothecary himself, with all his talent at prognostics, to determine; though I apprehend that it will terminate in the total downfall of genuine John Bullism.

The immediate effects are extremely unpleasant to me. Being a single man, and, as I observed before, rather an idle good-for-nothing personage, I have been considered the only gentleman by profession in the place. I stand therefore in high favor with both parties, and have to hear all their cabinet councils and mutual backbitings. As I am too civil not to agree with the ladies on all occasions, I have committed myself most horribly with both parties, by abusing their opponents. I might manage to reconcile this to my conscience, which is a truly accommodating one, but I cannot to my apprehension — if the Lambs and Trotters ever come to a reconciliation, and compare notes, I am ruined !

I have determined, therefore, to beat a retreat in time, and am actually looking out for some other nest in this great city, where old English manners are still kept up ; where French is neither eaten, drunk, danced, nor spoken ; and where there are no fashionable families of retired tradesmen.   This found, I will, like a veteran rat, hasten away before I have an old house about my ears ; bid a long, though a sorrowful, adieu to my present abode, and leave the rival factions of the Lambs and the Trotters to divide the distracted empire of LITTLE BRITAIN.

HENRY WADSWORTH LONGFELLOW.

INTRODUCTION.

WITH a single exception the prose writings of Longfellow all belong to that period of his life which was connected with his early travels in Europe and the beginning of his professional career as a teacher of modern literature. In 1833 he published a translation of a paper on *Ancient French Romances* by Paulin Paris, and an *Essay on the Moral and Devotional Poetry of Spain.* A little later appeared *Outre-Mer.* Between the publication of *Outre-Mer* and *Hyperion*, which appeared in 1839, he contributed those papers to periodicals which are included in the third volume of his collected prose works under the title of *Drift-Wood*, papers on *Frithiof's Saga,* Hawthorne's *Twice-Told Tales, The Great Metropolis, Anglo-Saxon Literature,* and *Paris in the Seventeenth Century.* A period of six years includes these writings, and it was not until it closed that he began the publication of original verse, his poetic work before this having been in the form of translation from the French and Spanish. His prose writings thus precede, in time, his poetry, and they are intimately connected with his personal experience and observation as a traveller and student. He came back from Europe freighted with memories of the Old World, and at once began pouring from a full cup the generous wine of foreign vineyards. Within the shelter of academic life, and under the impulse of a catholic zeal for literature, he eagerly offered the treasures of art, legend, and history, which had been made his own by the appropriating power of an appreciative taste, and he inclosed most of his work within forms of literary art which served to give continuity without involution. Thus *Outre-Mer* is a record of travel, continuous in its geographical outline, but separated from ordinary itineraries by noting less the personal accidents of the traveller than the poetic and romantic scenes which, whether in the present or the past, marked the journey and transformed it into the pilgrimage of a devotee to art. In *Hyperion* a more deliberate romance is intended, but the lights and shades of the story are heightened or deepened by the passages of travel and study, which form the background from which the human figures are relieved. It is interesting to observe how, as the writer was more withdrawn from the actual Europe of his eyes, he used the Europe of his memory and imagination to wait upon the movements of a profounder study, the adventures of a human soul. These two books and the occasional critical papers, are characterized by a strong consciousness of literary art. Life seems always to suggest a book or a picture, and nature is always viewed in its immediate relation to form and color. There is a singular discovery of the Old World, and while European writers, like Châteaubriand for example, were turning to America for new and unworn images, Longfellow, reflecting the awaking desire for the enduring forms of art which his countrymen were showing, eagerly disclosed the treasures to which the owners seemed almost indifferent. It is difficult to measure the influence which his broad, catholic taste and his refined choice of subjects have had upon American culture through the medium of these works, and that large body of his poetry which draws an inspiration from foreign life. In one of his prose works he makes a character say, in answer to a demand for a national literature : —

" Nationality is a good thing to a certain extent, but universality is better. All that is best in the great poets of· all countries is not what is national in them, but what is universal. Their roots are in their native soil ; but their branches wave in the unpatriotic air, that speaks the same language unto all men, and their leaves shine with the illimitable light that pervades all lands. Let us throw all the windows open ; let us admit the light and air on all sides ; that we may look toward the four corners of the heavens, and not always in the same direction." [1] It is this universality of interest which rendered the poet so open to the best which

[1] *Kavanagh*, xx.

older life and literature could afford, and he frankly
reflected it in his writings. " As the blood of all
nations," he continues, " is mingling with our own,
so will their thoughts and feelings finally mingle in
our literature. We shall draw from the Germans
tenderness ; from the Spaniards passion ; from the
French vivacity, to mingle more and more with our
English solid sense. And this will give us universality so much to be desired."

Ten years elapsed after the publication of *Hyperion* before another, and his latest, prose work
appeared. During that period many of his well
known shorter poems had been issued and followed
by *The Spanish Student* and *Evangeline.* Two
years after the publication of this his best known
work, appeared *Kavanagh, a Tale,* in 1849. It is
a prose idyll, the scene laid in a New England, pre-
sumably Maine, village, and the story gently reflecting the life of a few typical characters. The style
is simpler than in his previous prose, and the positive presence of the old world life has given place
to a faint odor of the same which pervades the atmosphere of the book. The stormy passions of
life are merely hinted at in the story, while the
more pensive graces and romantic aspirations are
made to form the tints of the picture. The plot
is only sketched, for it is in the sentiment of the
characters that the author, and consequently the
reader, has his real interest. The student of literature sees some traces in it of the influence of
Jean Paul Richter. It is less studied and less con-

scious, but its material is quite as distinctly pure sentiment.

With *Kavanagh* prose has been left behind, and indeed after this the poet has trod with firmer step, and with a more marked individuality. That is to say, and the lesson is a valuable one to students, so far he had been forming his work upon models already created and had been advancing as a student in literature while yet using creative power. The long apprenticeship which he had been serving to great masters was drawing to a close, and he was to stand forth more distinctly as himself a master. There are few examples in literature, none certainly in our own, so instructive of the power which comes from admiration of great work, and an imitation which is not servile but fresh, enthusiastic, and with constant reference to new creation. The consummate mastery of poetic form which displays itself in the sonnets, especially in Mr. Longfellow's recent work, may be traced back step by step to the patient, untiring study of the earlier days. With equal truth it may be said that the final exclusion of prose from his composition is the result of the gradual perfection of higher forms of art and the withdrawal of his attention from the mere rescript of material to the creation of self-contained art. The attentive reader will discover how closely *Kavanagh* borders upon the poetic in form, for it is careless of the details which give richness to prose romance, and careful only of the essential facts in which poetry and prose alike are concerned.

The form of *Hyperion* and *Kavanagh* renders it inexpedient to select detached scenes from them. The two chapters which follow are both from *Outre-Mer.*

I.

THE VALLEY OF THE LOIRE.

Je ne conçois qu'une manière de voyager plus agréable que d'aller à cheval ; c'est d'aller à pied. On part à son moment, on s'arrête à sa vo-
'lonté, on fait tant et si peu d'exercise qu'on veut.

Quand on ne veut qu'arriver, on peut courir en chaise de poste ; mais quand on veut voyager, il faut aller à pied.

ROUSSEAU.

IN the beautiful month of October, I made a foot excursion along the banks of the Loire, from Or-léans to Tours. This luxuriant region is justly called the garden of France. From Orléans to Blois the whole valley of the Loire is one contin-ued vineyard. The bright green foliage of the vine spreads, like the undulations of the sea, over all the landscape, with here and there a silver flash of the river, a sequestered hamlet, or the towers of an old château, to enliven and variegate the scene. The vintage had already commenced. The peas-antry were busy in the fields, — the song that cheered their labor was on the breeze, and the heavy wagon tottered by laden with the clusters of the vine. Everything around me wore that happy look which makes the heart glad. In the morning I arose with the lark ; and at night I slept where sunset overtook me. The healthy exercise of foot-travelling, the pure, bracing air of autumn, and the cheerful aspect of the whole landscape about me gave fresh elasticity to a mind not over-burdened with care, and made me forget not only the fatigue of walking, but also the consciousness of being alone.

My first day's journey brought me at evening to a village, whose name I have forgotten, situated about eight leagues from Orléans. It is a small, obscure hamlet, not mentioned in the guide-book, and stands upon the precipitous banks of a deep ravine, through which a noisy brook leaps down to turn the ponderous wheel of a thatch-roofed mill. The village inn stands upon the highway; but the village itself is not visible to the traveller as he passes. It is completely hidden in the lap of a wooded valley, and so embowered in trees that not a roof nor a chimney peeps out to betray its hiding-place. It is like the nest of a ground-swallow, which the passing footstep almost treads upon, and yet it is not seen. I passed by without suspecting that a village was near; and the little inn had a look so uninviting that I did not even enter it.

After proceeding a mile or two farther I perceived, upon my left, a village spire rising over the vineyards. Towards this I directed my footsteps; but it seemed to recede as I advanced, and at last quite disappeared. It was evidently many miles distant; and as the path I followed descended from the highway, it had gradually sunk beneath a swell of the vine-clad landscape. I now found myself in the midst of an extensive vineyard. It was just sunset; and the last golden rays lingered on the rich and mellow scenery around me. The peasantry were still busy at their task; and the occasional bark of a dog, and the distant sound of an evening bell, gave fresh romance to the scene. The reality of many a daydream of childhood, of many a poetic revery of youth, was before me. I stood at sunset amid the luxuriant vineyards of France!

The first person I met was a poor old woman, a little bowed down with age, gathering grapes into a large basket. She was dressed like the poorest class of peasantry, and pursued her solitary task alone, heedless of the cheerful gossip and the merry laugh which came from a band of more youthful vintagers at a short distance from her. She was so intently engaged in her work, that she did not perceive my approach until I bade her good evening. On hearing my voice, she looked up from her labor, and returned the salutation; and, on my asking her if there were a tavern or a farm-house in the neighborhood where I could pass the night, she showed me the pathway through the vineyard that led to the village, and then added, with a look of curiosity, —

"You must be a stranger, sir, in these parts."

"Yes; my home is very far from here."

"How far?"

"More than a thousand leagues."

The old woman looked incredulous.

"I came from a distant land beyond the sea."

"More than a thousand leagues!" at length repeated she; "and why have you come so far from home?"

"To travel, — to see how you live in this country."

"Have you no relations in your own?"

"Yes; I have both brothers and sisters, a father and " —

"And a mother?"

"Thank Heaven, I have."

"And did you leave *her*?"

Here the old woman gave me a piercing look of reproof; shook her head mournfully, and, with a deep sigh, as if some painful recollections had been awakened in her bosom, turned again to her solitary task. I felt rebuked; for there is something almost prophetic in the admonitions of the old. The eye of age looks meekly into my heart! the voice of age echoes mournfully through it! the hoary head and palsied hand of age plead irresistibly for its sympathies! I venerate old age; and I love not the man who can look without emotion upon the sunset of life, when the dusk of evening begins to gather over the watery eye, and the shadows of twilight grow broader and deeper upon the understanding!

I pursued the pathway which led towards the village, and the next person I encountered was an old man, stretched lazily beneath the vines upon a little strip of turf, at a point where four paths met, forming a crossway in the vineyard. He was clad in a coarse garb of gray, with a pair of long gai-

ters or spatterdashes. Beside him lay a blue cloth
cap, a staff, and an old weather-beaten knapsack.
I saw at once that he was a foot-traveller like myself, and therefore, without more ado, entered into
conversation with him. From his language, and
the peculiar manner in which he now and then
wiped his upper lip with the back of his hand, as if
in search of the mustache which was no longer
there, I judged that he had been a soldier. In this
opinion I was not mistaken. He had served under
Napoleon, and had followed the imperial eagle
across the Alps, and the Pyrenees, and the burning
sands of Egypt. Like every *vieille moustache*, he
spake with enthusiasm of the Little Corporal, and
cursed the English, the Germans, the Spanish, and
every other race on earth, except the Great Nation,
— his own.

"I like," said he, "after a long day's march, to
lie down in this way upon the grass, and enjoy the
cool of the evening. It reminds me of the bivouacs
of other days, and of old friends who are now up
there."

Here he pointed with his finger to the sky.

"They have reached the last *étape* before me, in
the long march. But I shall go soon. We shall
all meet again at the last roll-call. *Sacré nom
de* —— ! There 's a tear ! "

He wiped it away with his sleeve.

Here our colloquy was interrupted by the approach of a group of vintagers, who were returning
homeward from their labor. To this party I joined

myself, and invited the old soldier to do the same; but he shook his head.

" I thank you; my pathway lies in a different direction."

" But there is no other village near, and the sun has already set."

" No matter, I am used to sleeping on the ground. Good night."

I left the old man to his meditations, and walked on in company with the vintagers. Following a well-trodden pathway through the vineyards, we soon descended the valley's slope, and I suddenly found myself in the bosom of one of those little hamlets from which the laborer rises to his toil as the sky-lark to his song. My companions wished me a good night, as each entered his own thatch-roofed cottage, and a little girl led me out to the very inn which an hour or two before I had disdained to enter.

When I awoke in the morning a brilliant autumnal sun was shining in at my window. The merry song of birds mingled sweetly with the sound of rustling leaves and the gurgle of the brook. The vintagers were going forth to their toil; the wine-press was busy in the shade, and the clatter of the mill kept time to the miller's song. I loitered about the village with a feeling of calm delight. I was unwilling to leave the seclusion of this seques-tered hamlet; but at length, with reluctant step, I took the cross-road through the vineyard, and in a moment the little village had sunk again, as if by enchantment, into the bosom of the earth.

I breakfasted at the town of Mer ; and, leaving
the high-road to Blois on the right, passed down to
the banks of the Loire, through a long, broad
avenue of poplars and sycamores. I crossed the
river in a boat, and in the after part of the day I
found myself before the high and massive walls of
the château of Chambord. This château is one of
the finest specimens of the ancient Gothic castle to
be found in Europe. The little river Cosson fills
its deep and ample moat, and above it the huge
towers and heavy battlements rise in stern and solemn grandeur, moss-grown with age, and blackened
by the storms of three centuries. Within, all is
mournful and deserted. The grass has overgrown
the pavement of the courtyard, and the rude sculpture upon the walls is broken and defaced. From
the courtyard I entered the central tower, and, as-
cending the principal staircase, went out upon the
battlements. I seemed to have stepped back into
the precincts of the feudal ages ; and, as I passed
along through echoing corridors, and vast, deserted
halls, stripped of their furniture, and mouldering
silently away, the distant past came back upon me ;
and the times when the clang of. arms, and the
tramp of mail-clad men, and the sounds of music
and revelry and wassail echoed along those high-
vaulted and solitary chambers !

My third day's journey brought me to the ancient city of Blois, the chief town of the depart-
ment of Loire-et-Cher. This city is celebrated for
the purity with which even the lower classes of its

12

inhabitants speak their native tongue. It rises precipitously from the northern bank of the Loire; and many of its streets are so steep as to be almost impassable for carriages. On the brow of the hill, overlooking the roofs of the city, and commanding a fine view of the Loire and its noble bridge, and the surrounding country, sprinkled with cottages and châteaux, runs an ample terrace, planted with trees, and laid out as a public walk. The view from this terrace is one of the most beautiful in France. But what most strikes the eye of the traveler at Blois is an old, though still unfinished, castle. Its huge parapets of hewn stone stand upon either side of the street; but they have walled up the wide gateway, from which the colossal drawbridge was to have sprung high in air, connecting together the main towers of the building, and the two hills upon whose slope its foundations stand. The aspect of this vast pile is gloomy and desolate. It seems as if the strong hand of the builder had been arrested in the midst of his task by the stronger hand of death; and the unfinished fabric stands a lasting monument both of the power and weakness .of man, — of his vast desires, his sanguine hopes, his ambitious purposes, — and of the unlooked-for conclusion, where all these desires, and hopes, and purposes are so often arrested. There is also at Blois another ancient château, to which some historic interest is attached, as being the scene of the massacre of the Duke of Guise.[1]

[1] Blois was the place of meeting of the States General in 1588,

On the following day, I left Blois for Amboise ; and, after walking several leagues along the dusty highway, crossed the river in a boat to the little village of Moines, which lies amid luxuriant vineyards upon the southern bank of the Loire. From Moines to Amboise the road is truly delightful. The rich lowland scenery, by the margin of the river, is verdant even in October ; and occasionally the landscape is diversified with the picturesque cottages of the vintagers, cut in the rock along the roadside, and overhung by the thick foliage of the vines above them.

At Amboise I took a cross-road, which led me to the romantic borders of the Cher and the château of Chenonceau. This beautiful château, as well as that of Chambord, was built by the gay and munificent Francis the First. One is a specimen of strong and massive architecture, — a dwelling for a warrior ; but the other is of a lighter and more graceful construction, and was destined for those soft languishments of passion with which the fascinating Diane de Poitiers had filled the bosom of that voluptuous monarch.

The château of Chenonceau is built upon arches across the river Cher, whose waters are made to supply the deep moat at each extremity. There is a spacious courtyard in front, from which a drawbridge conducts to the outer hall of the castle.

and it was on December 23d of that year that Henry III. caused the murder of the Duke of Guise, an event which grew out of the violence of the religious wars of France.

There the armor of Francis the First still hangs upon the wall, — his shield, and helm, and lance, — as if the chivalrous prince had just exchanged them for the silken robes of the drawing-room. From this hall a door opens into a long gallery, extending the whole length of the building, across the Cher. The walls of the gallery are hung with the faded portraits of the long line of the descendants of Hugh Capet; and the windows, looking up and down the stream, command a fine reach of pleasant river scenery. This is said to be the only château in France in which the ancient furniture of its original age is preserved. In one part of the building you are shown the bed-chamber of Diane de Poitiers, with its antique chairs covered with faded damask and embroidery, her bed, and a portrait of the royal favorite hanging over the mantelpiece. In another you see the apartment of the infamous Catherine de' Medici; a venerable armchair and an autograph letter of Henry the Fourth; and in an old laboratory, among broken crucibles, and neckless retorts, and drums, and trumpets, and skins of wild beasts, and other ancient lumber, of various kinds, are to be seen the bed-posts of Francis the First! Doubtless the naked walls and the vast solitary chambers of an old and desolate château inspire a feeling of greater solemnity and awe; but when the antique furniture of the olden time remains, — the faded tapestry on the walls, and the arm-chair by the fireside, — the effect upon the mind is more magical and delightful. The old

inhabitants of the place, long gathered to their
fathers, though living still in history, seem to have
left their halls for the chase or the tournament;
and as the heavy door swings upon its reluctant
hinge, one almost expects to see the gallant princes
and courtly dames enter those halls again, and
sweep in stately procession along the silent corridors.

Rapt in such fancies as these, and gazing on the
beauties of this noble edifice, and the soft scenery
around it, I lingered, unwilling to depart, till the
rays of the setting sun, streaming through the dusty
windows, admonished me that the day was drawing
rapidly to a close. I sallied forth from the southern gate of the château, and, crossing the broken
drawbridge, pursued a pathway along the bank of
the river, still gazing back upon those towering
walls, now bathed in the rich glow of sunset, till a
turn in the road and a clump of woodland at length
shut them out from my sight.

A short time after candle-lighting I reached the
little tavern of the Boule d'Or, a few leagues from
Tours, where I passed the night. The following
morning was lowering and sad. A veil of mist
hung over the landscape, and ever and anon a
heavy shower burst from the overburdened clouds,
that were driven by before a high and piercing
wind. This unpropitious state of the weather de-
tained me until noon, when a cabriolet for Tours
drove up ; and taking a seat within it, I left the
hostess of the Boule d'Or in the middle of a long

story about a rich countess, who always alighted
there when she passed that way. We drove lei-
surely along through a beautiful country, till at
length we came to the brow of a steep hill, which
commands a fine view of the city of Tours and its
delightful environs. But the scene was shrouded
by the heavy drifting mist, through which I could
trace but indistinctly the graceful sweep of the
Loire, and the spires and roofs of the city far below me.

The city of Tours and the delicious plain in
which it lies have been too often described by other
travellers to render a new description, from so list-
less a pen as mine, either necessary or desirable.
After a sojourn of two cloudy and melancholy days,
I set out on my return to Paris, by the way of
Vendôme and Chartres. I stopped a few hours at
the former place, to examine the ruins of a château
built by Jeanne d'Albret, mother of Henry the
Fourth. It stands upon the summit of a high and
precipitous hill, and almost overhangs the town beneath. The French Revolution has completed the
ruin that time had already begun ; and nothing now
remains but a broken and crumbling bastion, and
here and there a solitary tower dropping slowly to
decay. In one of these is the grave of Jeanne
d'Albret. A marble entablature in the wall above
contains the inscription, which is nearly effaced,
though enough still remains to tell the curious traveller that there lies buried the mother of the " Bon
Henri." To this is added a prayer that the repose
of the dead may be respected.

Here ended my foot excursion. The object of my journey was accomplished; and, delighted with this short ramble through the valley of the Loire, I took my seat in the diligence for Paris, and on the following day was again swallowed up in the crowds of the metropolis, like a drop in the bosom of the sea.

II.

THE JOURNEY INTO SPAIN.

A l'issue de l'yver que le joly temps de primavère commence, et qu'on voit arbres verdoyer, fleurs espanouir, et qu'on oit les oisillons chanter en toute joie et doulceur, tant que les verts bocages reten-tissent de leurs sons et que cœurs tristes pensifs y dolens s'en esjouis-sent, s'émeuvent à delaisser deuil et toute tristesse, et se parforcent à valoir mieux.

LA PLAISANTE HISTOIRE DE GUERIN DE MONGLAVE.

SOFT-BREATHING Spring! how many pleasant thoughts, how many delightful recollections, does thy name awaken in the mind of a traveller! Whether he has followed thee by the banks of the Loire or the Guadalquiver, or traced thy footsteps slowly climbing the sunny slope of Alp or Apennine, the thought of thee shall summon up sweet visions of the past, and thy golden sunshine and soft vapory atmosphere become a portion of his day-dreams and of him. Sweet images of thee, and scenes that have oft inspired the poet's song, shall mingle in his recollections of the past. The

shooting of the tender leaf, — the sweetness and
elasticity of the air, — the blue sky, — the fleet-
drifting cloud, — and the flocks of wild fowl wheeling in long-drawn phalanx through the air, and
screaming from their dizzy height, — all these shall
pass like a dream before his imagination,

> " And gently o'er his memory come at times
> A glimpse of joys that had their birth in thee,
> Like a brief strain of some forgotten tune."

It was at the opening of this delightful season of
the year that I passed through the South of France,
and took the road of St. Jean de Luz for the Spanish frontier. I left Bordeaux amid all the noise
and gayety of the last scene of Carnival. The
streets and public walks of the city were full of
merry groups in masks, — at every corner crowds
were listening to the discordant music of the
wandering ballad-singer ; and grotesque figures,
mounted on high stilts, and dressed in the garb of
the peasants of the Landes of Gascony, were stalk-
ing up and down like so many long-legged cranes ;
others were amusing themselves with the tricks
and grimaces of little monkeys, disguised like little
men, bowing to the ladies, and figuring away in red
coats and ruffles ; and here and there a band of
chimney-sweeps were staring in stupid wonder at
the miracles of a showman's box. In a word, all
was so full of mirth and merrimake, that even beg-
gary seemed to have forgotten that it was wretched,
and gloried in the ragged masquerade of one poor
holiday.

To this scene of noise and gayety succeeded the silence and solitude of the Landes of Gascony. The road from Bordeaux to Bayonne winds along through immense pine forests and sandy plains, spotted here and there with a dingy little hovel, and the silence is interrupted only by the dismal hollow roar of the wind among the melancholy and majestic pines. Occasionally, however, the way is enlivened by a market-town or a straggling village; and I still recollect the feelings of delight which I experienced, when, just after sunset, we passed through the romantic town of Roquefort, built upon the sides of the green valley of the Douze, which has scooped out a verdant hollow for it to nestle in, amid those barren tracts of sand.

On leaving Bayonne the scene assumes a character of greater beauty and sublimity. To the vast forests of the Landes of Gascony succeeds a scene of picturesque beauty, delightful to the traveller's eye. Before him rise the snowy Pyrenees, — a long line of undulating hills, —

> "Bounded afar by peak aspiring bold,
> Like giant capped with helm of burnished gold."

To the left, as far as the eye can reach, stretch the delicious valleys of the Nive and Adour; and to the right the sea flashes along the pebbly margin of its silver beach, forming a thousand little bays and inlets, or comes tumbling in among the cliffs of a rock-bound coast, and beats against its massive barriers with a distant, hollow, continual roar.

Should these pages meet the eye of any solitary

traveller who is journeying into Spain by the road I here speak of, I would advise him to travel from Bayonne to St. Jean de Luz on horseback. At the gate of Bayonne he will find a steed ready caparisoned for him, with a dark-eyed Basque girl for his companion and guide, who is to sit beside him upon the same horse. This style of travelling is, I believe, peculiar to the Basque provinces ; at all events, I have seen it nowhere else. The saddle is constructed with a large frame-work extending on each side, and covered with cushions ; and the traveller and his guide, being placed on the opposite extremities, serve as a balance to each other. We overtook many travellers mounted in this way, and I could not help thinking it a mode of travelling far preferable to being cooped up in a diligence. The Basque girls are generally beautiful ; and there was one of these merry guides we met upon the road to Bidart whose image haunts me still. She had large and expressive black eyes, teeth like pearls, a rich and sunburnt complexion, and hair of a glossy blackness, parted on the forehead, and falling down behind in a large braid, so long as almost to touch the ground with the little ribbon that confined it at the end. She wore the common dress of the peasantry of the South of France, and a large gypsy straw hat was thrown back over her shoulder, and tied by a ribbon about her neck. There was hardly a dusty traveller in the coach who did not envy her companion the seat he occupied beside her.

Just at nightfall we entered the town of St. Jean ne Luz, and dashed down its narrow streets at full gallop. The little madcap postilion cracked his knotted whip incessantly, and the sound echoed back from the high dingy walls like the report of a pistol. The coach-wheels nearly touched the houses on each side of us ; the idlers in the street jumped right and left to save themselves ; window-shutters flew open in all directions ; a thousand heads popped out from cellar and upper story ; " *Sacr-r-ré mâtin !* " shouted the postilion, — and we rattled on like an earthquake.

St. Jean de Luz is a smoky little fishing town, situated on the low grounds at the mouth of the Nivelle, and a bridge connects it with the faubourg of Sibourne, which stands on the opposite bank of the river. I had no time, however, to note the peculiarities of the place, for I was whirled out of it with the same speed and confusion with which I had been whirled in, and I can only recollect the sweep of the road across the Nivelle, — the church of Sibourne by the water's edge, — the narrow streets, — the smoky-looking houses with red window-shutters, and " a very ancient and fish-like smell."

I passed by moonlight the little river Bidasoa, which forms the boundary between France and Spain ; and when the morning broke, found myself far up among the mountains of San Salvador, the most westerly links of the great Pyrenean chain. The mountains around me were neither rugged nor precipitous, but they rose one above another in a long, majestic swell, and the trace of the plough-share was occasionally visible to their summits. They seemed entirely destitute of trees; and as the season of vegetation had not yet commenced, their huge outlines lay black, and barren, and desolate against the sky. But it was a glorious morning, and the sun rose up into a cloudless heaven, and poured a flood of gorgeous splendor over the mountain landscape, as if proud of the realm he shone upon. The scene was enlivened by the dashing of a swollen mountain-brook, whose course we followed for miles down the valley, as it leaped onward to its journey's end, now breaking into a white cascade, and now foaming and chafing beneath a rustic bridge. Now and then we drove through a dilapidated town, with a group of idlers at every corner, wrapped in tattered brown cloaks, and smoking their little paper cigars in the sun; then would succeed a desolate tract of country, cheered only by the tinkle of a mule-bell, or the song of a muleteer; then we would meet a solitary traveller mounted on horseback, and wrapped in the ample folds of his cloak, with a gun hanging at the pommel of his saddle. Occasionally, too, among the bleak, inhospitable hills, we passed a rude little chapel, with a cluster of ruined cottages around it; and whenever our carriage stopped at the relay, or loitered slowly up the hillside, a crowd of children would gather around us, with little images and crucifixes for sale, curiously ornamented with ribbons and bits of tawdry finery.

A day's journey from the frontier brought us to Vitoria, where the diligence stopped for the night. I spent the scanty remnant of daylight in rambling about the streets of the city, with no other guide than the whim of the moment. Now I plunged down a dark and narrow alley, now emerged into a wide street or a spacious market-place, and now aroused the drowsy echoes of a church or cloister with the sound of my intruding footsteps. But descriptions of churches and public squares are dull and tedious matters for those readers who are in search of amusement, and not of instruction ; and if any one has accompanied me thus far on my fatiguing journey towards the Spanish capital, I will readily excuse him from the toil of an evening ramble through the streets of Vitoria.

On the following morning we left the town, long before daybreak, and during our forenoon's journey the postilion drew up at an inn, on the southern slope of the Sierra de San Lorenzo, in the province of Old Castile. The house was an old, dilapidated tenement, built of rough stone, and coarsely plastered upon the outside. The tiled roof had long been the sport of wind and rain, the motley coat of plaster was broken and time-worn, and the whole building sadly out of repair ; though the fanciful mouldings under the eaves, and the curiously carved wood-work that supported the little balcony over the principal entrance, spoke of better days gone by. The whole building reminded me of a dilapidated Spanish Don, down at the heel and out at elbows, but with here and there a remnant of former magnificence peeping through the loopholes of his tattered cloak.

A wide gateway ushered the traveller into the interior of the building, and conducted him to a low-roofed apartment, paved with round stones, and serving both as a courtyard and a stable. It seemed to be a neutral ground for man and beast, — a little republic, where horse and rider had common privileges, and mule and muleteer lay cheek by jowl. In one corner a poor jackass was patiently devouring a bundle of musty straw, — in another, its master lay sound asleep, with his saddle-cloth for a pillow; here a group of muleteers were quarrelling over a pack of dirty cards, — and there the village barber, with a self-important air, stood laving the Alcalde's chin from the helmet of Mambrino. On the wall, a little taper glimmered feebly before an image of St. Anthony; directly opposite these a leathern wine-bottle hung by the neck from a pair of ox-horns; and the pavement below was covered with a curious medley of boxes, and bags, and cloaks, and pack-saddles, and sacks of grain, and skins of wine, and all kinds of lumber.

A small door upon the right led us into the inn-kitchen. It was a room about ten feet square, and literally all chimney; for the hearth was in the centre of the floor, and the walls sloped upward in the form of a long, narrow pyramid, with an opening at the top for the escape of the smoke. Quite round this little room ran a row of benches, upon which sat one or two grave personages smoking paper cigars. Upon the hearth blazed a handful of fagots, whose bright flame danced merrily among a motley congregation of pots and kettles, and a long wreath of smoke wound lazily up through the huge tunnel of the roof above. The walls were black with soot, and ornamented with sundry legs of bacon and festoons of sausages ; and as there were no windows in this dingy abode, the only light which cheered the darkness within, came flickering from the fire upon the hearth, and the smoky sunbeams that peeped down the long-necked chimney.

I had not been long seated by the fire, when the tinkling of mule-bells, the clatter of hoofs, and the hoarse voice of a muleteer in the outer apartment, announced the arrival of new guests. A few moments afterward the kitchen-door opened, and a person entered, whose appearance strongly arrested my attention. It was a tall, athletic figure, with the majestic carriage of a grandee, and a dark, sunburnt countenance, that indicated an age of about fifty years. His dress was singular, and such as I had not before seen. He wore a round hat with wide, flapping brim, from beneath which his long, black hair hung in curls upon his shoulders ; a .eather jerkin, with cloth sleeves, descended to his hips ; around his waist was closely buckled a leather belt, with a cartouch-box on one side ; a pair of loose trousers of black serge hung in ample folds to the knees, around which they were closely gathered by embroidered garters of blue silk; and black broadcloth leggins, buttoned close to the calves, and strapped over a pair of brown leather shoes, completed the singular dress of the stranger. He doffed his hat as he entered, and, saluting the company with a " *Dios guarde á Ustedes, caballeros* " (God guard you, Gentlemen), took a seat by the fire, and entered into conversation with those around him.

As my curiosity was not a little excited by the peculiar dress of this person, I inquired of a travelling companion, who sat at my elbow, who and what this new-comer was. From him I learned that he was a muleteer of the Maragatería, — a name given to a cluster of small towns which lie in the mountainous country between Astorga and Villafranca, in the western corner of the kingdom of Leon.

" Nearly every province in Spain," said he, " has its peculiar costume, as you will see, when you have advanced farther into our country. For instance, the Catalonians wear crimson caps, hanging down upon the shoulder like a sack; wide pantaloons of green velvet, long enough in the waistband to cover the whole breast; and a little strip of a jacket, made of the same material, and so short as to bring the pocket directly under the armpit. The Valencians, on the contrary, go almost naked: a linen shirt, white linen trousers, reaching no lower than the knees, and a pair of coarse leather sandals complete their simple garb ; it is only in mid-winter that they indulge in the luxury of a jacket. The most beautiful and expensive costume, however, is that of Andalusia; it consists of a velvet jacket, faced with rich and various-colored embroidery, and covered with tassels and silken cord; a waistcoat of some gay color; a silken handkerchief round the neck, and a crimson sash round the waist; breeches that button down each side; gaiters and shoes of white leather; and a handkerchief of bright-colored silk wound about the head like a turban, and surmounted by a velvet cap or a little round hat, with a wide band, and an abundance of silken loops and tassels. The Old Castilians are more grave in their attire: they wear a leather breastplate instead of a jacket, breeches and leggins, and a montera cap. This fellow is a Maragato; and in the villages of the Maragatería the costume varies a little from the rest of Leon and Castile."

"If he is indeed a Maragato," said I, jestingly, "who knows but he may be a descendant of the muleteer who behaved so naughtily at Cacabelos, as related in the second chapter of the veracious history of Gil Blas de Santillana?"

"*¿ Quien sabe?*"[1] was the reply. "Notwithstanding the pride which even the meanest Castilian feels in counting over a long line of good-for-nothing ancestors, the science of genealogy has become of late a very intricate study in Spain."

[1] In Spanish use an inverted interrogation mark also precedes a question.

Here our conversation was cut short by the *Mayoral* of the diligence, who came to tell us that mules were waiting ; and before many hours had elapsed we were scrambling through the square of the ancient city of Burgos. On the morrow we crossed the river Duero and the Guadarrama Mountains, and early in the afternoon entered the " Heróica Villa," of Madrid, by the Puerta de Fuencarral.

JOHN GREENLEAF WHITTIER.

THE circumstances attending the production of
most of Whittier's prose writings have not
been favorable to sustained composition. Much of
his work has been in the form of contributions to
journals which he has edited, and the two volumes
which now constitute his collected prose writings
have been gathered from these occasional papers,
the only extended work being in *Leaves from Mar-
garet Smith's Journal*, an imitative work, suggested,
no doubt, by the successful *Lady Willoughby's Diary*.
In that work he has given a picture of the New
England of the last quarter of the seventeenth century, when a heroic life had become somewhat hardened by prosperity and authority into intolerance,
and the superstitious alloy of religious life had
become prominent by the decline of a living faith.
Himself of Quaker descent and belief, he has touched
kindly but firmly the changing life of the day which
culminated in the witchcraft delusion and displayed
itself in the persecution of the Quakers. Yet the
best life of the day, whether Puritan or Quaker, is
reproduced in the book, and the changing elements

of a transition period are all clearly presented. The studied and imitative form of the book prevents it from enjoying a wide popularity, but the genuineness of the spirit, and the graceful style in which the Puritan maiden's diary is preserved render it one of the best mediums for approaching a difficult period of New England history. The reader will find it interesting to compare with it the historical record of Robert Pike, presented in *The New Puritan*,[1] a sketch of the character by James S. Pike.

The subjects which are prominent in Whittier's verse appear also in his prose. The superstitions of New England were treated of by him in a small volume which has not been kept in print, *The Supernaturalism of New England;* the heroic lives of men and women content to be true to duty and God, and gaining their distinction often by their patience under suffering, are reproduced in a series of papers entitled *Old Portraits and Modern Sketches;* the homely beauty of a life of toil is recorded in the papers which make up the little volume, *The Stranger in Lowell*, which was published in 1845 and has since been merged, in part, in the second volume of his prose works, which bears the general title of *Literary Recreations and Miscellanies.* He was engaged at this time in the conduct of a paper in Lowell, and the life about him suggested occasional essays upon

[1] *The New Puritan.* New England two hundred years ago. Some account of the life of Robert Pike, the Puritan who defended the Quakers, resisted clerical domination, and opposed the witchcraft persecution. By James S. Pike. New York, Harper and Brothers, 1879.

topics free from political feeling. Two of the papers then published are here given, and they serve in part to illustrate his interest in life and history, for an unfailing attribute of his writing, whether in prose or verse, has been his sympathy with homely forms of life about him ; and the interest which he has shown in that part of history which deals with the relations of the Indian to the white man may be referred in part to his traditional Quaker principle, in part to his instinctive championship of the weak and wronged. In his prefatory note to *Literary Recreations and Miscellanies* he speaks lightly of his work, which, as there given, was rather a relief from severer tasks than itself serious and deliberate, but the spirit which pervades all his writings, whether in prose or in verse, is the same, and the recreations of a man of serious and simple purpose rarely fail to disclose his character and temper. The absence of mere moods in Whittier's writings is a singular testimony to the elevation of his common thought, and the simplicity of his aims in literature appears quite as significantly in his desultory prose as in his more deliberate poetry. At no time does the reader seem to pass out of the presence of an earnest man into that of a professional *littérateur ;* the carelessness of literary fame which Whittier has shown may be referred to the sincerity of his devotion to that which literature effects, and he has written and sung out of a heart very much in earnest to offer some help, or out of the pleasure of his work. The careful student of his writings will always value most the integrity of his life.

I.

YANKEE GYPSIES.

" Here 's to budgets, packs, and wallets;
Here 's to all the wandering train."
BURNS.[1]

I CONFESS it, I am keenly sensitive to " skyey influences." [2] I profess no indifference to the movements of that capricious old gentleman known as the clerk of the weather. I cannot conceal my interest in the behavior of that patriarchal bird whose wooden similitude gyrates on the church spire. Winter proper is well enough. Let the thermometer go to zero if it will; so much the better, if thereby the very winds are frozen and unable to flap their stiff wings. Sounds of bells in the keen air, clear, musical, heart-inspiring; quick tripping of fair moccasined feet on glittering ice pavements; bright eyes glancing above the uplifted muff like a sultana's behind the folds of her *yashmak;* [3] school-boys coasting down street like mad Greenlanders;

---

[1] From the closing air in *The Jolly Beggars*, a cantata.

[2]   " A breath thou art
Servile to al. the skyey influences,
That dost this habitation, where thou keep'st,
Hourly afflict."
      Shakspere: *Measure for Measure*, act III. scene 1.

[3] " She turns and turns again, and carefully glances around

the cold brilliance of oblique sunbeams flashing
back from wide surfaces of glittering snow, or blazing upon ice jewelry of tree and roof. There is
nothing in all this to complain of. A storm of
summer has its redeeming sublimities, — its slow,
upheaving mountains of cloud glooming in the western horizon like new-created volcanoes, veined with
fire, shattered by exploding thunders. Even the
wild gales of the equinox have their varieties, —
sounds of wind-shaken woods and waters, creak and
clatter of sign and casement, hurricane puffs, and
down-rushing rain-spouts. But this dull, dark autumn day of thaw and rain, when the very clouds
seem too spiritless and languid to storm outright
or take themselves out of the way of fair weather;
wet beneath and above, reminding one of that rayless atmosphere of Dante's Third Circle, where the
infernal Priessnitz[1] administers his hydropathic torment, —

> "A heavy, cursed, and relentless drench, —
> The land it soaks is putrid ; "

or rather, as everything animate and inanimate, is

her on all sides, to see that she is safe from the eyes of Mussul-
mans, and then suddenly withdrawing the yashmak she shines
upon your heart and soul with all the pomp and might of her
beauty." Kinglake's *Eothen*, chap. iii. In a note to *Yashmak*
Kinglake explains that it is not a mere semi-transparent veil,
but thoroughly conceals all the features except the eyes : it is
withdrawn by being pulled down.

[1] Vincenz Priessnitz was the originator of the water-cure.
After experimenting upon himself and his neighbors he took up
the profession of hydropathy and established baths at his native
place, Gräfenberg in Silesia, in 1829. He died in 1851.

seething in warm mist, suggesting the idea that Nature, grown old and rheumatic, is trying the efficacy of a Thomsonian steam-box[1] on a grand scale; no sounds save the heavy plash of muddy feet on the pavements; the monotonous, melancholy drip from trees and roofs; the distressful gurgling of water-ducts, swallowing the dirty amal·gam of the gutters; a dim, leaden-colored horizon of only a few yards in diameter, shutting down about one, beyond which nothing is visible save in faint line or dark projection; the ghost of a church spire or the eidolon of a chimney-pot. He who can extract pleasurable emotions from the alembic of such a day has a trick of alchemy with which I am wholly unacquainted.

Hark! a rap at my door. Welcome anybody just now. One gains nothing by attempting to shut out the sprites of the weather. They come in at the keyhole; they peer through the dripping panes; they insinuate themselves through the crevices of the casement, or plump down chimney astride of the rain-drops.

I rise and throw open the door. A tall, shambling, loose-jointed figure; a pinched, shrewd face, sun-brown and wind-dried; small, quick-winking black eyes. There he stands, the water dripping from his pulpy hat and ragged elbows.

[1] Dr. Samuel Thomson, a New Hampshire physician, advocated the use of the steam bath as a restorer of the system when diseased. He died in 1843 and left behind an autobiography (*Life and Medical Discoveries*) which contains a record of the persecutions he underwent.

I speak to him ; but he returns no answer. With a dumb show of misery, quite touching, he hands me a soiled piece of parchment, whereon I read what purports to be a melancholy account of ship-wreck and disaster, to the particular detriment, loss, and damnification of one Pietro Frugoni, who is, in consequence, sorely in want of the alms of all char-itable Christian persons, and who is, in short, the bearer of this veracious document, duly certified and indorsed by an Italian consul in one of our Atlantic cities, of a high-sounding, but to Yankee organs unpronounceable, name.

Here commences a struggle. Every man, the Mahometans tell us, has two attendant angels, — the good one on his right shoulder, the bad on his left. " Give," says Benevolence, as with some difficulty I fish up a small coin from the depths of my pocket. " Not a cent," says selfish Prudence ; and I drop it from my fingers. " Think," says the good angel, " of the poor stranger in a strange land, just escaped from the terrors of the sea-storm, in which his little property has perished, thrown half-naked and helpless on our shores, ignorant of our language, and unable to find employment suited to his capacity." " A vile impostor ! " replies the left-hand sentinel. " His paper, purchased from one of those ready-writers in New York who man-ufacture beggar-credentials at the low price of one dollar per copy, with earthquakes, fires, or ship-wrecks, to suit customers."

Amidst this confusion of tongues I take another

survey of my visitant. Ha! a light dawns upon me. That shrewd, old face, with its sharp, winking eyes, is no stranger to me. Pietro Frugoni, I have seen thee before. *Sì, signor,* that face of thine has looked at me over a dirty white neckcloth, with the corners of that cunning mouth drawn downwards, and those small eyes turned up in sanctimonious gravity, while thou wast offering to a crowd of half-grown boys an extemporaneous exhortation in the capacity of a travelling preacher. Have I not seen it peering out from under a blanket, as that of a poor Penobscot Indian, who had lost the use of his hands while trapping on the Madawaska? Is it not the face of the forlorn father of six small children, whom the " marcury doctors " had " pisened " and crippled? Did it not belong to that down-East unfortunate who had been out to the " Genesee country "[1] and got the " fevern-nager," and whose hand shook so pitifully when held out to receive my poor gift? The same, under all disguises, — Stephen Leathers, of Barrington, — him, and none other! Let me conjure him into his own likeness : —

" Well, Stephen, what news from old Barrington ? "

---

[1] The *Genesee Country* is the name by which the western part of New York, bordering on Lakes Ontario and Erie, was known, when, at the close of the last and beginning of this century, it was to people on the Atlantic coast the Great West. In 1792 communication was opened by a road with the Pennsylvania settlements, but the early settlers were almost all from New England.

" Oh, well, I thought I knew ye," he answers, not
the least disconcerted. " How do you do? and
how 's your folks? All well, I hope. I took this
'ere paper, you see, to help a poor furriner, who
could n't make himself understood any more than
a wild goose. I thought I 'd just start him for'ard
a little. It seemed a marcy to do it."

Well and shiftily answered, thou ragged Proteus.
One cannot be angry with such a fellow. I will
just inquire into the present state of his Gospel
mission and about the condition of his tribe on the
Penobscot; and it may be not amiss to congratu-
late him on the success of the steam-doctors in
sweating the " pisen " of the regular faculty out of
him. But he evidently has no wish to enter into
idle conversation. Intent upon his benevolent errand he is already clattering down stairs. Involuntarily I glance out of the window just in season
to catch a single glimpse of him ere he is swallowed up in the mist.

He has gone; and, knave as he is, I can hardly
help exclaiming, " Luck go with him!" He has
broken in upon the sombre train of my thoughts
and called up before me pleasant and grateful recollections. The old farm-house nestling in its valley;
hills stretching off to the south and green meadows
to the east; the small stream which came noisily
down its ravine, washing the old garden-wall and
softly lapping on fallen stones and mossy roots of
beeches and hemlocks; the tall sentinel poplars at
the gateway; the oak-forest, sweeping unbroken to

the northern horizon ; the grass-grown carriage-path,
with its rude and crazy bridge, — the dear old landscape of the boyhood lies outstretched before me
like a daguerreotype from that picture within which
I have borne with me in all my wanderings. I am
a boy again, once more conscious of the feeling,
half terror, half exultation, with which I used to an-
nounce the approach of this very vagabond and his
" kindred after the flesh."

The advent of wandering beggars, or " old stragglers," as we were wont to call them, was an event
of no ordinary interest in the generally monotonous
quietude of our farm-life. Many of them were well
known ; they had their periodical revolutions and
transits ; we would calculate them like eclipses or
new moons. Some were sturdy knaves, fat and
saucy ; and, whenever they ascertained that the
" men folks " were absent, would order provisions
and cider like men who expected to pay for them,
seating themselves at the hearth or table with the
air of Falstaff, — " Shall I not take mine ease in
mine own inn ? " Others, poor, pale, patient, like
Sterne's monk,[1] came creeping up to the door, hat
in hand, standing there in their gray wretchedness
with a look of heartbreak and forlornness which
was never without its effect on our juvenile sensibilities. At times, however, we experienced a slight
revulsion of feeling when even these humblest children of sorrow somewhat petulantly rejected our

[1] Whom he met at Calais, as described in his *Sentimental
Journey.*

proffered bread and cheese, and demanded instead a glass of cider. Whatever the temperance society might in such cases have done, it was not in our hearts to refuse the poor creatures a draught of their favorite beverage ; and was n't it a satisfaction to see their sad, melancholy faces light up as we handed them the full pitcher, and, on receiving it back empty from their brown, wrinkled hands, to hear them, half breathless from their long, delicious draught, thanking us for the favor, as " dear, good children " ! Not unfrequently these wandering tests of our benevolence made their appearance in interesting groups of man, woman, and child, picturesque in their squalidness, and manifesting a maudlin affection which would have done honor to the revellers at Poosie-Nansie's, immortal in the cantata of Burns.[1] I remember some who were evidently the victims of monomania, — haunted and hunted by some dark thought, — possessed by a fixed idea. One, a black-eyed, wild-haired woman, with a whole tragedy of sin, shame, and suffering written in her countenance, used often to visit us, warm herself by our winter fire, and supply herself with a stock of cakes and cold meat; but was never

[1] The *cantata* is *The Jolly Beggars*, from which the motto, heading this sketch was taken. *Poosie-Nansie* was the keeper of a tavern in Mauchline, which was the favorite resort of the lame sailors, maimed soldiers, travelling ballad-singers, and all such loose companions as hang about the skirts of society. The cantata has for its theme the rivalry of a "pigmy scraper with his fiddle " and a strolling tinker for a beggar woman : hence the *maudlin affection.*

known to answer a question or to ask one. She never smiled; the cold, stony look of her eye never changed; a silent, impassive face, frozen rigid by some great wrong or sin. We used to look with awe upon the "still woman," and think of the demoniac of Scripture who had a " dumb spirit."

One — I think I see him now, grim, gaunt, and ghastly, working his slow way up to our door — used to gather herbs by the wayside and call himself doctor. He was bearded like a he-goat, and used to counterfeit lameness; yet, when he supposed himself alone, would travel on lustily, as if walking for a wager. At length, as if in punishment of his deceit, he met with an accident in his rambles and became lame in earnest, hobbling ever after with difficulty on his gnarled crutches. Another used to go stooping, like Bunyan's pilgrim, under a pack made of an old bed-sacking, stuffed out into most plethoric dimensions, tottering on a pair of small, meagre legs, and peering out with his wild, hairy face from under his burden like a big-bodied spider. That "man with the pack" always inspired me with awe and reverence. Huge, almost sublime, in its tense rotundity, the father of all packs, never laid aside and never opened, what might there not be within it? With what flesh-creeping curiosity I used to walk round about it at a safe distance, half expecting to see its striped covering stirred by the motions of a mysterious life, or that some evil monster would leap out of it, like robbers from Ali Baba's jars or armed men from the Trojan horse!

There was another class of peripatetic philosophers — half pedler, half mendicant — who were
in the habit of visiting us. One, we recollect, a
lame, unshaven, sinister-eyed, unwholesome fellow,
with his basket of old newspapers and pamphlets,
and his tattered blue umbrella, serving rather as a
walking-staff than as a protection from the rain.
He told us on one occasion, in answer to our in-
quiring into the cause of his lameness, that when a
young man he was employed on the farm of the
chief magistrate of a neighboring State; where, as
his ill luck would have it, the governor's handsome
daughter fell in love with him. He was caught one
day in the young lady's room by her father; whereupon the irascible old gentleman pitched him un-
ceremoniously out of the window, laming him for
life, on a brick pavement below, like Vulcan on
the rocks of Lemnos.[1] As for the lady, he assured
us "she took on dreadfully about it." "Did she
die?" we inquired, anxiously. There was a cunning twinkle in the old rogue's eye as he responded,
" Well, no, she did n't. She got married."

Twice a year, usually in the spring and autumn,
we were honored with a call from Jonathan Plummer, maker of verses, pedler and poet, physician
and parson, — a Yankee troubadour, — first and
last minstrel of the valley of the Merrimac, encir-
cled, to my wondering young eyes, with the very
nimbus of immortality. He brought with him pins,

[1] It was upon the Isle of Lemnos that Vulcan was flung by
Jupiter, according to the myth, for attempting to aid his mother
Juno.

needles, tape, and cotton-thread for my mother
jack-knives, razors, and soap for my father; and
verses of his own composing, coarsely printed and
illustrated with rude wood-cuts, for the delectation
of the younger branches of the family. No love-
sick youth could drown himself, no deserted maiden
bewail the moon, no rogue mount the gallows, without fitting memorial in Plummer's verses. Earthquakes, fires, fevers, and shipwrecks he regarded as
personal favors from Providence, furnishing the
raw material of song and ballad. Welcome to us
in our country seclusion, as Autolycus to the clown
in " Winter's Tale," [1] we listened with infinite satisfaction to his reading of his own verses, or to his
ready improvisation upon some domestic incident
or topic suggested by his auditors. When once
fairly over the difficulties at the outset of a new
subject his rhymes flowed freely, " as if he had
eaten ballads, and all men's ears grew to his tunes."
His productions answered, as nearly as I can remember, to Shakspere's description of a proper
ballad, — " doleful matter merrily set down, or a
very pleasant theme sung lamentably." He was
scrupulously conscientious, devout, inclined to theological disquisitions, and withal mighty in Scripture.
He was thoroughly independent; flattered nobody,
cared for nobody, trusted nobody. When invited

[1] "He could never come better," says the clown in Shakspere's *The Winter's Tale*, when Autolycus, the pedler, is announced; "he shall come in. I love a ballad but even too
well, if it be doleful matter merrily set down, or a very pleasant
thing indeed and sung lamentably." Act IV. scene 4.

to sit down at our dinner-table he invariably took the precaution to place his basket of valuables between his legs for safe keeping. "Never mind thy basket, Jonathan," said my father; "we shan't steal thy verses." "I'm not sure of that," returned the suspicious guest. "It is written, 'Trust ye not in any brother.'"

Thou, too, O Parson B., — with thy pale student's brow and rubicund nose, with thy rusty and tattered black coat overswept by white, flowing locks, with thy professional white neckcloth scrupulously preserved when even a shirt to thy back was problematical, — art by no means to be overlooked in the muster-roll of vagrant gentlemen possessing the *entrée* of our farm-house. Well do we remember with what grave and dignified courtesy he used to step over its threshold, saluting its inmates with the same air of gracious condescension and patronage with which in better days he had delighted the hearts of his parishioners. Poor old man! He had once been the admired and almost worshipped minister of the largest church in the town where he afterwards found support in the winter season, as a pauper. He had early fallen into intemperate habits; and at the age of threescore and ten, when I remember him, he was only sober when he lacked the means of being otherwise. Drunk or sober, however, he never altogether forgot the proprieties of his profession; he was always grave, decorous, and gentlemanly; he held fast the form of sound words, and the weak-

14

ness of the flesh abated nothing of the rigor of his
stringent theology. He had been a favorite pupil
of the learned and astute Emmons,[1] and was to the
last a sturdy defender of the peculiar dogmas of his
school. The last time we saw him he was holding
a meeting in our district school-house, with a vagabond pedler for deacon and travelling companion.
The tie which united the ill-assorted couple was
doubtless the same which endeared Tam O'Shanter to the souter :[2] —

"They had been fou for weeks thegither."

He took for his text the first seven verses of the
concluding chapter of Ecclesiastes, furnishing in
himself its fitting illustration. The evil days had
come ; the keepers of the house trembled ; the
windows of life were darkened. A few months
later the silver cord was loosened, the golden bowl
was broken, and between the poor old man and
the temptations which beset him fell the thick curtains of the grave.

One day we had a call from a "pawky auld
carle "[3] of a wandering Scotchman. To him I owe

[1] Nathaniel Emmons was a New England theologian of marked
character and power, who for seventy years was connected with
a church in that part of Wrentham, Mass., now called Franklin.
He exercised considerable influence over the religious thought
of New England, and is still read by theologians. He died in
1840, in his ninety-sixth year.

[2] Souter (or cobbler) Johnny, in Burns's poetic tale of *Tam
O'Shanter*, had been *fou'* or *full* of drink with Tam for weeks
together.

[3] From the first line of *The Gaberlunzie Man*, attributed to
King James V. of Scotland, —

"The pawky auld carle came o'er the lee."

my first introduction to the songs of Burns. After eating his bread and cheese and drinking his mug of cider he gave us Bonny Doon, Highland Mary, and Auld Lang Syne. He had a rich, full voice, and entered heartily into the spirit of his lyrics. I have since listened to the same melodies from the lips of Dempster [1] (than whom the Scottish bard has had no sweeter or truer interpreter), but the skilful performance of the artist lacked the novel charm of the gaberlunzie's singing in the old farmhouse kitchen. Another wanderer made us acquainted with the humorous old ballad of "Our gude man cam hame at e'en." He applied for supper and lodging, and the next morning was set at work splitting stones in the pasture. While thus engaged the village doctor came riding along the highway on his fine, spirited horse, and stopped to talk with my father. The fellow eyed the animal attentively, as if familiar with all his good points, and hummed over a stanza of the old poem : —

> "Our gude man cam hame at e'en,
>   And hame cam he ;
> And there he saw a saddle horse
>   Where nae horse should be.

The original like Whittier's was a sly old fellow, as an English phrase would translate the Scottish. *The Gaberlunzie Man* is given in Percy's *Reliques of Ancient Poetry* and in Child's *English and Scottish Ballads*, viii. 98.

[1] William R. Dempster, a Scottish vocalist who had recently sung in America, and whose music to Burns's song " A man 's a man for a that " was very popular.

'How cam this horse here?
    How can it be?
  How cam this horse here
      Without the leave of me?'
'A horse?' quo she.
'Ay, a horse,' quo he.
'Ye auld fool, ye blind fool, —
    And blinder might ye be, —
'T is naething but a milking cow
    My mamma sent to me.'
'A milch cow?' quo he.
'Ay, a milch cow,' quo she.
'Weel, far hae I ridden,
    And muckle hae I seen;
  But milking cows wi' saddles on
    Saw I never nane.'"[1]

That very night the rascal decamped, taking
with him the doctor's horse, and was never after
heard of.

Often, in the gray of the morning, we used to see
one or more "gaberlunzie men," pack on shoulder
and staff in hand, emerging from the barn or other
outbuildings where they had passed the night. I
was once sent to the barn to fodder the cattle late
in the evening, and, climbing into the mow to pitch
down hay for that purpose, I was startled by the
sudden apparition of a man rising up before me,
just discernible in the dim moonlight streaming
through the seams of the boards. I made a rapid
retreat down the ladder; and was only reassured
by hearing the object of my terror calling after me,
and recognizing his voice as that of a harmless old

---

[1] The whole of this song may be found in Herd's *Ancient
and Modern Scottish Songs*, ii. 172.

pilgrim whom I had known before. Our farm-
house was situated in a lonely valley, half surrounded with woods, with no neighbors in sight.
One dark, cloudy night, when our parents chanced
to be absent, we were sitting with our aged grandmother in the fading light of the kitchen fire, working ourselves into a very satisfactory state of excitement and terror by recounting to each other all
the dismal stories we could remember of ghosts,
witches, haunted houses, and robbers, when we were
suddenly startled by a loud rap at the door. A
stripling of fourteen, I was very naturally regarded
as the head of the household ; so, with many mis-
givings, I advanced to the door, which I slowly
opened, holding the candle tremulously above my
head and peering out into the darkness. The feeble glimmer played upon the apparition of a gigantic horseman, mounted on a steed of a size worthy
of such a rider — colossal, motionless, like images
cut out of the solid night. The strange visitant
gruffly saluted me ; and, after making several ineffectual efforts to urge his horse in at the door, dis-
mounted and followed me into the room, evidently
enjoying the terror which his huge presence excited.
Announcing himself as the great Indian doctor,
he drew himself up before the fire, stretched his
arms, clinched his fists, struck his broad chest, and
invited our attention to what he called his " mortal
frame." He demanded in succession all kinds of
intoxicating liquors ; and on being assured that we
had none to give him, he grew angry, threatened

to swallow my younger brother alive, and, seizing
me by the hair of my head as the angel did the
prophet at Babylon,[1] led me about from room to
room. After an ineffectual search, in the course
of which he mistook a jug of oil for one of brandy,
and, contrary to my explanations and remonstrances,
insisted upon swallowing a portion of its contents,
he released me, fell to crying and sobbing, and
confessed that he was so drunk already that his
horse was ashamed of him. After bemoaning and
pitying himself to his satisfaction he wiped his
eyes, and sat down by the side of my grandmother,
giving her to understand that he was very much
pleased with her appearance ; adding, that if agreeable to her, he should like the privilege of paying
his addresses to her. While vainly endeavoring to
make the excellent old lady comprehend his very
flattering proposition, he was interrupted by the
return of my father, who, at once understanding
the matter, turned him out of doors without cere-
mony.

On one occasion, a few years ago, on my return
from the field at evening, I was told that a for-
eigner had asked for lodgings during the night, but
that, influenced by his dark, repulsive appearance,
my mother had very reluctantly refused his re-
quest. I found her by no means satisfied with
her decision. " What if a son of mine was in a
strange land ? " she inquired, self-reproachfully
Greatly to her relief, I volunteered to go in pursuit

[1] See Ezekiel viii. 3.

of the wanderer, and, taking a cross-path over the
fields, soon overtook him. He had just been rejected at the house of our nearest neighbor, and
was standing in a state of dubious perplexity in the
street. His looks quite justified my mother's sus-
picions. He was an olive-complexioned, black-
bearded Italian, with an eye like a live coal, such a
face as perchance looks out on the traveller in the
passes of the Abruzzi,[1] — one of those bandit
visages which Salvator [2] has painted. With some
difficulty I gave him to understand my errand, when
he overwhelmed me with thanks, and joyfully followed me back. He took his seat with us at the
supper-table ; and, when we were all gathered
around the hearth that cold autumnal evening, he
told us, partly by words and partly by gestures,
the story of his life and misfortunes, amused us
with descriptions of the grape-gatherings and festivals of his sunny clime, edified my mother with a
recipe for making bread of chestnuts; and in the
morning, when, after breakfast, his dark sullen
face lighted up and his fierce eye moistened with
grateful emotion as in his own silvery Tuscan ac-
cent he poured out his thanks, we marvelled at the
fears which had so nearly closed our door against
him ; and, as he departed, we all felt that he had left
with us the blessing of the poor.

[1] Provinces into which the old kingdom of Naples was divided.

[2] Salvator Rosa was a Neapolitan by birth, and was said to
have been himself a bandit in his youth; his landscapes often
contain figures drawn from the wild life of the region.

It was not often that, as in the above instance,
my mother's prudence got the better of her charity.
The regular "old stragglers" regarded her as an
unfailing friend; and the sight of her plain cap was
to them an assurance of forthcoming creature-com-
forts.   There was indeed a tribe of lazy strollers,
having their place of rendezvous in the town of
Barrington, New Hampshire, whose low vices had
placed them beyond even the pale of her benevolence.   They were not unconscious of their evil
reputation ; and experience had taught them the
necessity of concealing, under well-contrived disguises, their true character.   They came to us in
all shapes and with all appearances save the true
one, with most miserable stories of mishap and
sickness and all " the ills which flesh is heir to."
It was particularly vexatious to discover, when too
late, that our sympathies and charities had been
expended upon such graceless vagabonds as the
" Barrington beggars."   An old withered hag,
known by the appellation of Hopping Pat, — the
wise woman of her tribe, — was in the habit of
visiting us, with her hopeful grandson, who had
" a gift for preaching " as well as for many other
things not exactly compatible with holy orders.
He sometimes brought with him a tame crow, a
shrewd, knavish-looking bird, who, when in the humor for it, could talk like Barnaby Rudge's raven.
He used to say he could " do nothin' at exhortin'
without a white handkercher on his neck and money
in his pocket," — a fact going far to confirm the

opinions of the Bishop of Exeter and the Puseyites generally, that there can be no priest without tithes and surplice.

These people have for several generations lived distinct from the great mass of the community, like the gypsies of Europe, whom in many respects they closely resemble. They have the same settled aversion to labor and the same disposition to avail themselves of the fruits of the industry of others. They love a wild, out-of-door life, sing songs, tell fortunes, and have an instinctive hatred of " missionaries and cold water." It has been said — I know not upon what grounds — that their ancestors were indeed a veritable importation of English gypsyhood ; but if so, they have undoubtedly lost a good deal of the picturesque charm of its unhoused and free condition. I very much fear that my friend Mary Russell Mitford, — sweetest of England's rural painters, — who has a poet's eye for the fine points in gypsy character, would scarcely allow their claims to fraternity with her own vagrant friends, whose camp-fires welcomed her to her new home at Swallowfield.[1]

" The proper study of mankind is man ; " and, according to my view, no phase of our common humanity is altogether unworthy of investigation. Acting upon this belief two or three summers ago, when making, in company with my sister, a little excursion into the hill-country of New Hampshire, I turned my horse's head towards Barrington for

[1] See in Miss Mitford's *Our Village.*

the purpose of seeing these semi-civilized strollers
in their own home, and returning, once for all, their
numerous visits. Taking leave of our hospitable
cousins in old Lee with about as much solemnity as
we may suppose Major Laing [1] parted with his
friends when he set out in search of desert-girdled
Timbuctoo, we drove several miles over a rough
road, passed the Devil's Den unmolested, crossed a
fretful little streamlet noisily working its way into
a valley, where it turned a lonely, half-ruinous mill,
and climbing a steep hill beyond, saw before us a
wide, sandy level, skirted on the west and north by
low, scraggy hills, and dotted here and there with
dwarf pitch-pines. In the centre of this desolate
region were some twenty or thirty small dwellings,
grouped together as irregularly as a Hottentot
kraal. Unfenced, unguarded, open to all comers
and goers, stood that city of the beggars, — no wall
or paling between the ragged cabins to remind one
of the jealous distinctions of property. The great
idea of its founders seemed visible in its unappro-
priated freedom. Was not the whole round world
their own? and should they haggle about bounda-
ries and title-deeds? For them, on distant plains,

[1] Alexander Gordon Laing was a major in the British army
who served on the west coast of Africa and made journeys
into the interior in the attempt to establish commercial relations
with the natives, and especially to discover the sources of the
Niger. He was treacherously murdered in 1826 by the guard
that was attending him on his return from Timbuctoo to the
coast. His travels excited great interest in their day in Eng-
and and America.

ripened golden harvests; for them, in far-off work-
shops, busy hands were toiling ; for them, if they
had but the grace to note it, the broad earth put on
her garniture of beauty, and over them hung the
silent mystery of heaven and its stars. That comfortable philosophy which modern transcendentalism
has but dimly shadowed forth, — that poetic agra-
rianism, which gives all to each and each to all, —
is the real life of this city of unwork. To each of
its dingy dwellers might be not unaptly applied the
language of one who, I trust, will pardon me for
quoting her beautiful poem in this connection : —

> " Other hands may grasp the field and forest,
>   Proud proprietors in pomp may shine,
>   .   .   .   .
>   Thou art wealthier, — all the world is thine." [1]

But look ! the clouds are breaking. " Fair
weather cometh out of the north." The wind has
blown away the mists; on the gilded spire of John
Street glimmers a beam of sunshine ; and there is
the sky again, hard, blue, and cold in its eternal
purity, not a whit the worse for the storm. In the
beautiful present the past is no longer needed.
Reverently and gratefully let its volume be laid
aside ; and when again the shadows of the outward
world fall upon the spirit may I not lack a good
angel to remind me of its solace, even if he comes
in the shape of a Barrington beggar.

---

[1] From a poem, *Why Thus Longing?* by Mrs. Harriet Wins-
low Sewall, preserved in Whittier's *Songs of Three Centuries.*

II.

THE BOY CAPTIVES.

AN INCIDENT OF THE INDIAN WAR OF 1695.

THE township of Haverhill, even as late as the close of the seventeenth century, was a frontier settlement, occupying an advanced position in the great wilderness, which, unbroken by the clearing of a white man, extended from the Merrimac River to the French villages on the St. François. A tract of twelve miles on the river and three or four northwardly was occupied by scattered settlers, while in the centre of the town a compact village had grown up. In the immediate vicinity there were but few Indians, and these generally peaceful and inoffensive. On the breaking out of the Narragansett War,[1] the inhabitants had erected fortifications, and taken other measures for defence ; but, with the possible exception of one man who was found slain in the woods in 1676, none of the inhabitants were molested ; and it was not until about the year 1689 that the safety of the settlement was seriously threatened. Three persons were killed in that year. In 1690 six garrisons were established in different parts of the town, with a small

[1] The "Narragansett War" was a name applied to that part of King Philip's War which resulted from the defection of the powerful tribe of Narragansetts, formerly allies of the English, to the standard of the Indian chief.

company of soldiers attached to each. Two of these houses are still standing. They were built of brick, two stories high, with a single outside door, so small and narrow that but one person could enter at a time; the windows few, and only about two and a half feet long by eighteen inches wide, with thick diamond glass secured with lead, and crossed inside with bars of iron. The basement had but two rooms, and the chamber was entered by a ladder instead of stairs; so that the inmates, if driven thither, could cut off communication with the rooms below. Many private houses were strengthened and fortified. We remember one familiar to our boyhood, — a venerable old building of wood, with brick between the weather-boards and ceiling, with a massive balustrade over the door, constructed of oak timber and plank, with holes through the latter for firing upon assailants. The door opened upon a stone-paved hall, or entry, leading into the huge single room of the basement, which was lighted by two small windows, the ceiling black with the smoke of a century and a half; a huge fireplace, calculated for eight-feet wood, occupying one entire side; while, overhead, suspended from the timbers, or on shelves fastened to them, were household stores, farming utensils, fishing-rods, guns, bunches of herbs gathered perhaps a century ago, strings of dried apples and pumpkins, links of mottled sausages, spareribs, and flitches of bacon; the fire-light of an evening dimly revealing the checked woollen coverlet of the bed in one far-off corner, while in another —

"The pewter plates on the dresser
Caught and reflected the flame as shields of armies the sunshine." [1]

Tradition has preserved many incidents of life
in the garrisons. In times of unusual peril the
settlers generally resorted at night to the fortified
houses, taking thither their flocks and herds and
such household valuables as were most likely to
strike the fancy or minister to the comfort or vanity of the heathen marauders. False alarms were
frequent. The smoke of a distant fire, the bark of
a dog in the deep woods, a stump or bush, taking
in the uncertain light of stars and moon the appearance of a man, were sufficient to spread alarm
through the entire settlement and to cause the
armed men of the garrison to pass whole nights in
sleepless watching. It is said that at Haselton's
garrison-house the sentinel on duty saw, as he
thought, an Indian inside of the paling which surrounded the building, and apparently seeking to
gain an entrance. He promptly raised his musket
and fired at the intruder, alarming thereby the
entire garrison. The women and children left their
beds, and the men seized their guns and commenced firing on the suspicious object; but it
seemed to bear a charmed life, and remained unharmed. As the morning dawned, however, the
mystery was solved by the discovery of a black
quilted petticoat hanging on the clothes'-line, completely riddled with balls.

[1] Longfellow's *Evangeline*, vv. 205, 206.

As a matter of course, under circumstances of perpetual alarm and frequent peril, the duty of cultivating their fields, and gathering their harvests, and working at their mechanical avocations, was dangerous and difficult to the settlers. One instance will serve as an illustration. At the garrison-house of Thomas Dustin, the husband of the far-famed Mary Dustin (who, while a captive of the Indians, and maddened by the murder of her infant child, killed and scalped, with the assistance of a young boy, the entire band of her captors, ten in number), the business of brick-making was carried on. The pits where the clay was found were only a few rods from the house; yet no man ventured to bring the clay to the yard within the inclosure, without the attendance of a file of soldiers. An anecdote relating to this garrison has been handed down to the present time. Among its inmates were two young cousins, Joseph and Mary Whittaker; the latter a merry, handsome girl, relieving the tedium of garrison-duty with her light-hearted mirthfulness and —

"Making a sunshine in that shady place." [1]

Joseph, in the intervals of his labors in the double capacity of brick-maker and man-at-arms, was assiduous in his attentions to his fair cousin,

[1] " Her angel's face
As the great eye of heaven shyned bright,
And made a sunshine in the shadie place;
Did never mortal eye behold such heavenly grace."
Spenser: *The Faery Queene*, bk. I. canto iii. st. 4

who was not inclined to encourage him. Growing
desperate, he threatened one evening to throw himself into the garrison well. His threat only called
forth the laughter of his mistress; and, bidding her
farewell, he proceeded to put it in execution. On
reaching the well he stumbled over a log; whereupon, animated by a happy idea, he dropped the
wood into the water instead of himself, and, hiding
behind the curb, awaited the result. Mary, who
had been listening at the door, and who had not
believed her lover capable of so rash an act, heard
the sudden plunge of the wooden Joseph. She ran
to the well, and, leaning over the curb and peering
down the dark opening, cried out, in tones of anguish and remorse, " O Joseph, if you 're in the
land of the living, I 'll have you ! " " I 'll take ye
at your word," answered Joseph, springing up from
his hiding-place and avenging himself for her coy-
ness and coldness by a hearty embrace.

Our own paternal ancestor, owing to religious
scruples in the matter of taking arms even for defence of life and property, refused to leave his un-
defended house and enter the garrison. The Indians frequently came to his house; and the family
more than once in the night heard them whispering
under the windows, and saw them put their copper
faces to the glass to take a view of the apartments.
Strange as it may seem, they never offered any in-
jury or insult to the inmates.

In 1695 the township was many times molested
by Indians, and several persons were killed and

wounded. Early in the fall a small party made
their appearance in the northerly part of the town,
where, finding two boys at work in an open field,
they managed to surprise and capture them, and,
without committing further violence, retreated
through the woods to their homes on the shore of
Lake Winnipiseogee. Isaac Bradley, aged fifteen,
was a small but active and vigorous boy; his companion in captivity, Joseph Whittaker, was only
eleven, yet quite as large in size, and heavier in his
movements. After a hard and painful journey they
arrived at the lake, and were placed in an Indian
family, consisting of a man and squaw and two or
three children. Here they soon acquired a sufficient knowledge of the Indian tongue to enable
them to learn from the conversation carried on in
their presence that it was designed to take them to
Canada in the spring. This discovery was a painful one. Canada, the land of Papist priests and
bloody Indians, was the especial terror of the New
England settlers, and the anathema maranatha [1] of
Puritan pulpits. Thither the Indians usually hurried their captives, where they compelled them to
work in their villages or sold them to the French
planters. Escape from thence through a deep
wilderness, and across lakes, and mountains, and

---

[1] *Anathema maranatha* occurs at the close of St. Paul's first
epistle to the Corinthians, and in the English version is made to
appear as a composite phrase. It has so passed into common
use, *maranatha* being taken as intensifying the curse contained
in *anathema*. The words are properly to be divided, *maranatha*
signifying "The Lord cometh."

almost impassable rivers, without food or guide, was regarded as an impossibility. The poor boys, terrified by the prospect of being carried still farther from their home and friends, began to dream of escaping from their masters before they started for Canada. It was now winter; it would have been little short of madness to have chosen for flight that season of bitter cold and deep snows. Owing to exposure and want of proper food and clothing, Isaac, the eldest of the boys, was seized with a violent fever, from which he slowly recovered in the course of the winter. His Indian mistress was as kind to him as her circumstances permitted, — procuring medicinal herbs and roots for her patient, and tenderly watching over him in the long winter nights. Spring came at length; the snows melted; and the ice was broken up on the lake. The Indians began to make preparations for journeying to Canada; and Isaac, who had during his sickness devised a plan of escape, saw that the time of putting it in execution had come. On the evening before he was to make the attempt he for the first time informed his younger companion of his design, and told him, if he intended to accompany him, he must be awake at the time appointed. The boys lay down as usual in the wigwam in the midst of the family. Joseph soon fell asleep; but Isaac, fully sensible of the danger and difficulty of the enterprise before him, lay awake, watchful for his opportunity. About midnight he rose, cautiously stepping over the sleeping forms of the family, and

securing, as he went, his Indian master's flint, steel,
and tinder, and a small quantity of dry moose-meat
and corn-bread. He then carefully awakened his
companion, who, starting up, forgetful of the cause
of his disturbance, asked aloud, " What do you
want ? " The savages began to stir ; and Isaac,
trembling with fear of detection, lay down again
and pretended to be asleep. After waiting a while
he again rose, satisfied, from the heavy breathing
of the Indians, that they were all sleeping ; and
fearing to awaken Joseph a second time, lest he
should again hazard all by his thoughtlessness, he
crept softly out of the wigwam. He had proceeded
but a few rods when he heard footsteps behind him ;
and, supposing himself pursued, he hurried into the
woods, casting a glance backward. What was his
joy to see his young companion running after him !
They hastened on in a southerly direction as nearly
as they could determine, hoping to reach their distant home. When daylight appeared they found a
large hollow log, into which they crept for concealment, wisely judging that they would be hotly pursued by their Indian captors.

Their sagacity was by no means at fault. The
Indians, missing their prisoners in the morning,
started off in pursuit with their dogs. As the
young boys lay in the log they could hear the
whistle of the Indians and the barking of dogs
upon their track. It was a trying moment ; and
even the stout heart of the elder boy sank within
him as the dogs came up to the log and set up a

loud bark of discovery. But his presence of mind
saved him. He spoke in a low tone to the dogs,
who, recognizing his familiar voice, wagged their
tails with delight, and ceased barking. He then
threw to them the morsel of moose-meat he had
taken from the wigwam. While the dogs were
thus diverted, the Indians made their appearance.
The boys heard the light, stealthy sound of their
moccasins on the leaves. They passed close to
the log; and the dogs, having devoured their
moose-meat, trotted after their masters. Through
a crevice in the log the boys looked after them,
and saw them disappear in the thick woods. They
remained in their covert until night, when they
started again on their long journey, taking a new
route to avoid the Indians. At daybreak they
again concealed themselves, but travelled the next
night and day without resting. By this time they
had consumed all the bread which they had taken,
and were fainting from hunger and weariness.
Just at the close of the third day they were provi-
dentially enabled to kill a pigeon and a small tortoise, a part of which they ate raw, not daring to
make a fire, which might attract the watchful eyes
of savages. On the sixth day they struck upon an
old Indian path, and, following it until night, came
suddenly upon a camp of the enemy. Deep in the
heart of the forest, under the shelter of a ridge
of land heavily timbered, a great fire of logs and
brushwood was burning; and around it the Indians sat, eating their moose-meat and smoking their
pipes.

The poor fugitives, starving, weary, and chilled by the cold spring blasts, gazed down upon the ample fire, and the savory meats which the squaws were cooking by it, but felt no temptation to purchase warmth and food by surrendering themselves to captivity. Death in the forest seemed preferable. They turned and fled back upon their track, expecting every moment to hear the yells of pursuers. The morning found them seated on the bank of a small stream, their feet torn and bleeding, and their bodies emaciated. The elder, as a last effort, made search for roots, and fortunately discovered a few ground-nuts (*glycine apios*), which served to refresh in some degree himself and his still weaker companion. As they stood together by the stream, hesitating and almost despairing, it occurred to Isaac that the rivulet might lead to a larger stream of water, and that to the sea and the white settlements near it; and he resolved to follow it. They again began their painful march; the day passed, and the night once more overtook them. When the eighth morning dawned, the younger of the boys found himself unable to rise from his bed of leaves. Isaac endeavored to encourage him, dug roots, and procured water for him; but the poor lad was utterly exhausted. He had no longer heart or hope. The elder boy laid him on leaves and dry grass at the foot of a tree, and with a heavy heart bade him farewell. Alone he slowly and painfully proceeded down the stream, now greatly increased in size by tributary rivulets. On the top of a hill he climbed with difficulty into a tree, and saw in the distance what seemed to be a clearing and a newly-raised frame building. Hopeful and rejoicing, he turned back to his young companion, told him what he had seen, and, after chafing his limbs awhile, got him upon his feet. Sometimes supporting him, and at others carrying him on his back, the heroic boy staggered towards the clearing. On reaching it he found it deserted, and was obliged to continue his journey. Towards night signs of civilization began to appear, — the heavy, continuous roar of water was heard; and, presently emerging from the forest, he saw a great river dashing in white foam down precipitous rocks, and on its bank the gray walls of a huge stone building, with flankers, palisades, and moat, over which the British flag was flying. This was the famous Saco Fort, built by Governor Phips,[1] two years before, just below the falls of the Saco River. The soldiers of the garrison gave the poor fellows a kindly welcome. Joseph, who was scarcely alive, lay for a long time sick in the fort; but Isaac soon regained his strength, and set out for his home in Haverhill, which he had the good fortune to arrive at in safety.

Amidst the stirring excitements of the present day, when every thrill of the electric wire conveys

---

[1] An interesting account of Sir William Phips will be found in Parkman's *Frontenac and New France under Louis XIV.* Hawthorne also tells his romantic story in *Fanshawe and Other Pieces.*

a new subject for thought or action to a generation as eager as the ancient Athenians for some new thing, simple legends of the past like that which we have transcribed have undoubtedly lost in a great degree their interest. The lore of the fireside is becoming obsolete, and with the octogenarian few who still linger among us, will perish the unwritten history of border life in New England.

OLIVER WENDELL HOLMES.

IN the early years of Dr. Holmes's career his
literary reputation rested on verse which seemed
the playful pastime of a professional man. To
students in medicine indeed, he was known as a
keen writer, and his published papers upon professional topics showed how valuable was his literary skill in presenting subjects of a scientific
nature. To the general public, however, his prose
was known chiefly through the medium of the popular lecture, and the impression was easily created
that he was a witty and humorous writer with a
turn for satire. It was not until he delivered the
as yet unpublished lectures on the *English Poets of
the Nineteenth Century* before the Lowell Institute
in Boston, in 1852, that the wider range of his
thought and the penetration of his poetic insight
were recognized. Five or six years later a better
occasion came, and in the first number of *The Atlantic Monthly* was begun a series of prose writings,
which under various names gave a new and important place in literature to the author. The first of

the series was *The Autocrat of the Breakfast-Table*, the last, *The Poet at the Breakfast-Table*, and in this the writer distinctly says what the observant reader of the series will be pretty sure to discover for himself: "I have unburdened myself in this book, and in some other pages, of what I was born to say. Many things that I have said in my riper days have been aching in my soul since I was a mere child. I say aching, because they conflicted with many of my inherited beliefs, or rather traditions. I did not know then that two strains of blood were striving in me for the mastery — two! twenty, perhaps — twenty thousand, for aught I know — but represented to me by two — paternal and maternal. But I do know this: I have struck a good many chords, first and last, in the consciousness of other people. I confess to a tender feeling for my little brood of thoughts. When they have been welcomed and praised, it has pleased me; and if at any time they have been rudely handled and despitefully treated, it has cost me a little worry. I don't despise reputation, and I should like to be remembered as having said something worth lasting well enough to last."

This passage briefly presents three very noticeable characteristics of Dr. Holmes's prose as contained in the series of *Atlantic* papers and stories. They give the mature thought of the writer, held back through many years for want of an adequate occasion, and ripened in his mind during this enforced silence; they illustrate the effect upon his thought of his professional studies, which predisposed him to treat of the natural history of man, and to import into his analysis of the invisible organism of life the terms and methods employed in the science of the visible anatomy and physiology ; and finally they are warm with a sympathy for men and women, and singularly felicitous in their expression of many of the indistinct and half-understood experiences of life. For their form it may be said that the impression produced upon the reader of the *Autocrat* series which was finally gathered into a volume, is of a growth rather than of a premeditated artistic completeness. The first suggestion is found in the two papers under the title of *The Autocrat of the Breakfast-Table*, published in *The New England Magazine* for November, 1831, and January, 1832. These were written by Dr. Holmes shortly after his graduation from college and before he entered on his medical studies. They consist of brief, epigrammatic observations upon various topics, the desultory talk of a person engrossing conversation at a table. The form is monologue with scarcely more than a hint at interruptions, and no attempt at characterizing the speaker or his listeners. Twenty-five years later, when *The Atlantic Monthly* was founded, the author remembering the fancy resumed it, and under the same title began a series of papers which at once had great favor and grew, possibly, beyond the writer's original intention. Twenty-five years had not dulled the wit and gayety of the exuberant young author; rather, they had ripened the early fruit and imparted a richness of flavor which greatly increased the value. The maturity was seen not only in the wider reach and deeper tone of the talk, but in the humanizing of the scheme. Out of the talk at the breakfast-table one began to distinguish characters and faces in the persons about the board, and before the *Autocrat* was completed, there had appeared a series of portraits, vivid and full of interest. Two characters meanwhile were hinted at by the author rather than described or very palpably introduced, the Professor and the Poet. It is not difficult to see that these are thin disguises for the author himself, who, in the versatility of his nature, appeals to the reader now as a brilliant philosopher, now as a man of science, now as a seer and poet. *The Professor at the Breakfast-Table* followed, and there was a still stronger dramatic power disclosed; some of the former characters remained and others of even more positive individuality were added; a romance was inwoven and something like a plot sketched, so that while the talk still went on and eddied about graver subjects than before, the book which grew out of the papers had more distinctly the form of a series of sketches from life. It was followed by two novels, *Elsie Venner* and *The Guardian Angel.* The talks at the breakfast-table had often gravitated toward the deep themes of destiny and human freedom; the novels wrought the same subjects in dramatic form, and action interpreted the thought, while still

there flowed on the wonderful, apparently inex-
haustible stream of wit, tenderness, passion, and
human sympathy. Once more, fourteen years after
the appearance of the first of the series, came *The
Poet at the Breakfast-Table.* A new group of characters, with slight reminders of former ones, occupied the pages, again talk and romance blended,
and playfulness, satire, sentiment, wise reflection,
and sturdy indignation followed in quick succession.

The Breakfast-Table series forms a group, independent of the intercalated novels, and, with its
frequent poems, may be taken as an artistic whole.
It is hardly too much to say that it makes a new
contribution to the forms of literary art.   The elasticity of the scheme rendered possible a comprehen-
siveness of material ; the exuberance of the author's
fancy and the fullness of his thought gave a richness
to the fabric ; the poetic sense of fitness kept the
whole within just bounds.   Moreover, the personality of the author was vividly present in all parts.
There are few examples of literature in the first
person so successful as this.

It is from *The Poet at the Breakfast-Table* that
the following episode is taken.

THE GAMBREL-ROOFED HOUSE AND ITS OUTLOOK.

A PANORAMA, WITH SIDE-SHOWS.

My birthplace, the home of my childhood and earlier and later boyhood, has within a few months passed out of the ownership of my family into the hands of that venerable Alma Mater who seems to have renewed her youth, and has certainly re-painted her dormitories. In truth, when I last revisited that familiar scene and looked upon the *flammantia mœnia*[2] of the old halls, " Massachu-setts" with the dummy clock-dial,[3] " Harvard " with the garrulous belfry,[4] little " Holden "[5] with the

[1] "Know old Cambridge? Hope you do. —
    Born there ? Don't say so ! I was too.
    (Born in a house with a gambrel-roof, —
    Standing still, if you must have proof. —
    'Gambrel? — Gambrel ?' — Let me beg
    You 'll look at a horse's hinder leg, —
    First great angle above the hoof, —
    That 's the gambrel; hence gambrel-roof.)"
Parson Turell's Legacy in *The Autocrat of the Breakfast-Table.*
[2] Flame-red walls.
[3] Early views of Massachusetts show the clock in apparent activity.
[4] Harvard Hall holds in its belfry tower the college bell.
[5] Holden Chapel was built in 1744, and on the pediment front-ing the Common may be seen the arms of the Holden family of England, with whose gift the chapel was built. It has long been devoted to other uses.

sculptured unpunishable cherubs over its portal, and the rest of my early brick-and-mortar acquaintances,[1] I could not help saying to myself that I had lived to see the peaceable establishment of the Red Republic of Letters.

Many of the things I shall put down I have no doubt told before in a fragmentary way, how many I cannot be quite sure, as I do not very often read my own prose works. But when a man dies a great deal is said of him which has often been said in other forms, and now this dear old house is dead to me in one sense, and I want to gather up my recollections and wind a string of narrative round them, tying them up like a nosegay for the last tribute : the same blossoms in it I have often laid on its threshold while it was still living for me.

We Americans are all cuckoos, — we make our homes in the nests of other birds. I have read somewhere that the lineal descendants of the man who carted off the body of William Rufus, with Walter Tyrrel's arrow sticking in it, have driven a cart (not absolutely the same one, I suppose) in the New Forest from that day to this. I don't quite understand Mr. Ruskin's saying (if he said it) that he could n't get along in a country where there were no castles, but I do think we lose a great deal in living where there are so few permanent homes. You will see how much I parted with which was

---

[1] " There, in red brick, which softening time defies,
    Stand square and stiff the Muses' factories."
    An Indian Summer Reverie, by J. R. Lowell

not reckoned in the price paid for the old homestead.

I shall say many things which an uncharitable
reader might find fault with as personal. I should
not dare to call myself a poet if I did not ; for if
there is anything that gives one a title to that
name, it is that his inner nature is naked and is not
ashamed. But there are many such things I shall
put in words, not because they are personal, but
because they are human, and are born of just such
experiences as those who hear or read what I say
are like to have had in greater or less measure. I
find myself so much like other people that I often
wonder at the coincidence. It was only the other
day that I sent out a copy of verses [1] about my
great-grandmother's picture, and I was surprised to
find how many other people had portraits of their
great-grandmothers or other progenitors, about
which they felt as I did about mine, and for whom
I had spoken, thinking I was speaking for myself
only. And so I am not afraid to talk very freely
with you, my precious reader or listener. You too,
Beloved, were born somewhere and remember your
birthplace or your early home ; for you some house
is haunted by recollections ; to some roof you have
bid farewell. Your hand is upon mine, then, as I
guide my pen. Your heart frames the responses
to the litany of my remembrance. For myself it
is a tribute of affection I am rendering, and I
should put it on record for my own satisfaction,
were there none to read or to listen.

[1] See *Dorothy Q., a Family Portrait.*

I hope you will not say that I have built a pil
lared portico of introduction to a humble structure
of narrative. For when you look at the old gam-
brel-roofed house, you will see an unpretending
mansion, such as very possibly you were born in
yourself, or at any rate such a place of residence
as your minister or some of your well-to-do country
cousins find good enough, but not at all too grand
for them. We have stately old Colonial palaces [1]
in our ancient village, now a city, and a thriving
one, — square-fronted edifices that stand back from
the vulgar highway, with folded arms, as it were;
social fortresses of the time when the twilight lustre
of the throne reached as far as our half-cleared
settlement, with a glacis before them in the shape
of a long broad gravel-walk, so that in King
George's time they looked as formidable to any
but the silk-stocking gentry as Gibraltar or Ehren-
breitstein to a visitor without the password. We
forget all this in the kindly welcome they give us
to-day; for some of them are still standing and
doubly famous, as we all know. But the gambrel-
roofed house, though stately enough for college
dignitaries and scholarly clergymen, was not one
of those old tory, Episcopal-church-goer's strong-
holds. One of its doors opens directly upon the
green, always called the Common; the other, facing

[1] Such as what was known as the Bishop's Palace, the houses
on Brattle Street occupied in Colonial days by Brattle, the Vas-
sals, Oliver, Ruggles, Lee, Sewall, and others. Most of the
occupants were tories and Church of England men, and the prin-
cipa. line of mansions went by the name of Church Row.

the south, a few steps from it, over a paved foot-
walk, on the other side of which is the miniature
front yard, bordered with lilacs and syringas. The
honest mansion makes no pretensions. Accessible, companionable, holding its hand out to all,
comfortable, respectable, and even in its way dignified, but not imposing, not a house for his Majesty's
Counsellor, or the Right Reverend successor of
Him who had not where to lay his head, for something like a hundred and fifty years it has stood in
its lot, and seen the generations of men come and
go like the leaves of the forest. I passed some
pleasant hours, a few years since, in the Registry
of Deeds and the Town Records, looking up the
history of the old house. How those dear friends
of mine, the antiquarians, for whose grave councils
I compose my features on the too rare Thursdays [1]
when I am at liberty to meet them, in whose human herbarium the leaves and blossoms of past
generations are so carefully spread out and pressed
and laid away, would listen to an expansion of the
following brief details into an Historical Memoir!

The estate was the third lot of the eighth
" Squadron " (whatever that might be), and in the
year 1707 was allotted in the distribution of undi-
vided lands to " Mr. ffox," the Reverend Jabez
Fox, of Woburn, it may be supposed, as it passed
from his heirs to the first Jonathan Hastings; from
him to his son, the long-remembered College Steward; from him in the year 1792 to the Reverend

[1] The day of meeting of the Massachusetts Historical Society.

16

Eliphalet Pearson, Professor of Hebrew and other Oriental languages in Harvard College, whose large personality swam into my ken when I was looking forward to my teens; from him to the progenitors of my unborn self.

I wonder if there are any such beings nowadays as the great Eliphalet, with his large features and conversational *basso profundo*, seemed to me.[1] His very name had something elephantine about it, and it seemed to me that the house shook from cellar to garret at his foot-fall. Some have pretended that he had Olympian aspirations, and wanted to sit in the seat of Jove and bear the academic thunderbolt and the ægis inscribed *Christo et Ecclesiæ.* It is a common weakness enough to wish to find one's self in an empty saddle; Cotton Mather was miserable all his days, I am afraid, after that entry in his Diary: "This Day Dr. Sewall was chosen President, *for his Piety.*"

There is no doubt that the men of the older generation look bigger and more formidable to the boys whose eyes are turned up at their venerable countenances than the race which succeeds them, to the same boys grown older. Everything *is* twice as large, measured on a three-year-old's three-foot scale as on a thirty-year-old's six-foot scale; but age magnifies and aggravates persons out of due proportion. Old people are a kind of monsters to little folks; mild manifestations of the terrible, it

[1] See Dr. Holmes's reference to the *great Eliphalet*, in his poem, *The School-Boy,* vv. 256–262.

may be, but still, with their white locks and ridged
and grooved features, which those horrid little eyes
exhaust of their details, like so many microscopes,
not exactly what human beings ought to be. The
middle-aged and young men have left comparatively
faint impressions in my memory, but how grandly
the procession of the old clergymen who filled our
pulpit from time to time, and passed the day under
our roof, marches before my closed eyes! At their
head the most venerable David Osgood, the majestic minister of Medford, with massive front and
shaggy overshadowing eyebrows; following in the
train, mild-eyed John Foster of Brighton, with the
lambent aurora of a smile about his pleasant mouth,
which not even the "Sabbath" could subdue to the
true Levitical aspect; and bulky Charles Stearns
of Lincoln, author of "The Ladies' Philosophy of
Love. A Poem. 1797." (how I stared at him!
he was the first living person ever pointed out to
me as a poet); and Thaddeus Mason Harris [1] of
Dorchester (the same who, a poor youth, trudging
along, staff in hand, being then in a stress of sore
need, found all at once that somewhat was adher-
ing to the end of his stick, which somewhat proved

[1] "I remember in my boyhood the little quaint old man, bent
almost incredibly, but still wearing a hale aspect, who used to
haunt the alcoves of the old library in Harvard Hall. It was
rumored among us that he had once been appointed private sec-
retary to Washington, but had resigned from illness; and it was
known that he was arranging and indexing for Mr. Sparks the
one hundred and thirty-two manuscript volumes of Washington's correspondence." T. W. Higginson: *Memoir of Thaddeus William Harris* (son of T. M. H.).

to be a gold ring of price, bearing the words, " God speed thee, Friend! "), already in decadence as I remember him, with head slanting forward and downward as if looking for a place to rest in after his learned labors ; and that other Thaddeus,[1] the old man of West Cambridge, who outwatched the rest so long after they had gone to sleep in their own churchyards, that it almost seemed as if he meant to sit up until the morning of the resurrection ; and, bringing up the rear, attenuated but vivacious little Jonathan Homer of Newton, who was, to look upon, a kind of expurgated, reduced, and Americanized copy of Voltaire, but very unlike him in wickedness or wit. The good-humored junior member of our family always loved to make him happy by setting him chirruping about Miles Coverdale's Version, and the Bishop's Bible, and how he wrote to his friend Sir Isaac (Coffin) about something or other, and how Sir Isaac wrote back that he was very much pleased with the contents of his letter, and so on about Sir Isaac, *ad libitum,* — for the admiral was his old friend, and he was proud of him. The kindly little old gentleman was a collector of Bibles, and made himself believe he thought he should publish a learned Commentary some day or other ; but his friends looked for it only in the Greek Calends, — say on the 31st of April, when that should come round, if you would modernize the phrase. I recall also one or two exceptional and infrequent visitors with perfect

[1] Rev. Thaddeus Fiske, who died in 1855 at the age of 93

distinctness: cheerful Elijah Kellogg, a lively missionary from the region of the Quoddy Indians, with much hopeful talk about Sock Bason and his tribe ; also poor old Poor-house-Parson Isaac Smith, his head going like a China mandarin, as he discussed the possibilities of the escape of that distinguished captive whom he spoke of under the name, if I can reproduce phonetically its vibrating nasalities, of " General Mmbongaparty," — a name suggestive to my young imagination of a dangerous, loose-jointed skeleton, threatening us all like the armed figure of Death in my little New England Primer.

I have mentioned only the names of those whose images come up pleasantly before me, and I do not mean to say anything which any descendant might not read smilingly. But there were some of the black-coated gentry whose aspect was not so agreeable to me. It is very curious to me to look back on my early likes and dislikes, and see how as a child I was attracted or repelled by such and such ministers, a good deal, as I found out long afterwards, according to their theological beliefs. On the whole, I think the old-fashioned New England divine softening down into Arminianism was about as agreeable as any of them. And here I may remark, that a mellowing rigorist is always a much pleasanter object to contemplate than a tightening liberal, as a cold day warming up to 32° Fahrenheit is much more agreeable than a warm one chilling down to the same temperature. The least pleasing change is that kind of mental hemiplegia which now and then attacks the rational side of a man at about the same period of life when one side of the body is liable to be palsied, and in fact is, very probably, the same thing as palsy, in another form. The worst of it is that the subjects of it never seem to suspect that they are intellectual invalids, stammerers and cripples at best, but are all the time hitting out at their old friends with the well arm, and calling them hard names out of their twisted mouths.

It was a real delight to have one of those good, hearty, happy, benignant old clergymen pass the Sunday with us, and I can remember some whose advent made the day feel almost like " Thanksgiving." But now and then would come along a clerical visitor with a sad face and a wailing voice, which sounded exactly as if somebody must be lying dead up-stairs, who took no interest in us children, except a painful one, as being in a bad way with our cheery looks, and did more to unchristianize us with his woebegone ways than all his sermons were like to accomplish in the other direction. I remember one in particular, who twitted me so with my blessings as a Christian child, and whined so to me about the naked black children who, like the " Little Vulgar Boy," " had n't got no supper and had n't got no ma," and had n't got no Catechism, (how I wished for the moment I was a little black boy !) that he did more in that one day to make me a heathen than he had ever done in a

month to make a Christain out of an infant Hottentot. What a debt we owe to our friends of the
left centre, the Brooklyn and the Park Street and
the Summer Street ministers; good, wholesome,
sound-bodied, sane-minded, cheerful-spirited men,
who have taken the place of those wailing *poitri-
naires* with the bandanna handkerchiefs round their
meagre throats and a funeral service in their forlorn
physiognomies! I might have been a minister myself, for aught I know, if this clergyman had not
looked and talked so like an undertaker.

All this belongs to one of the side-shows, to
which I promised those who would take tickets to
the main exhibition should have entrance *gratis*. If
I were writing a poem you would expect, as a matter of course, that there would be a digression now
and then.

To come back to the old house and its former
tenant, the Professor of Hebrew and other Oriental
languages. Fifteen years he lived with his family
under its roof. I never found the slightest trace of
him until a few years ago, when I cleaned and
brightened with pious hands the brass lock of " the
study," which had for many years been covered with
a thick coat of paint. On that I found scratched,
as with a nail or fork, the following inscription : —

E PE

Only that and nothing more, but the story told
itself. Master Edward Pearson, then about as high

as the lock, was disposed to immortalize himself in
monumental brass, and had got so far towards it,
when a sudden interruption, probably a smart box
on the ear, cheated him of his fame, except so far
as this poor record may rescue it. Dead long ago.
I remember him well, a grown man, as a visitor at
a later period ; and, for some reason, I recall him
in the attitude of the Colossus of Rhodes, standing
full before a generous wood-fire, not facing it, but
quite the contrary, a perfect picture of the content
afforded by a blazing hearth contemplated from that
point of view, and, as the heat stole through his
person and kindled his emphatic features, seeming
to me a pattern of manly beauty. What a statue
gallery of posturing friends we all have in our
memory ! The old Professor himself sometimes
visited the house after it had changed hands. Of
course, my recollections are not to be wholly trusted,
but I always think I see his likeness in a profile
face to be found among the illustrations of Rees's
Cyclopædia. (See Plates, Vol. IV., Plate 2, Painting, Diversities of the Human Face, Fig. 4.)

And now let us return to our chief picture. In
the days of my earliest remembrance, a row of tall
Lombardy poplars mounted guard on the western
side of the old mansion. Whether, like the cypress,
these trees suggest the idea of the funeral torch or
the monumental spire, whether their tremulous
leaves make us afraid by sympathy with their nerv-
ous thrills, whether the faint balsamic smell of their
leaves and their closely swathed limbs have in them

vague hints of dead Pharaohs stiffened in their cere-
ments, I will not guess; but they always seemed to
me to give an air of sepulchral sadness to the house
before which they stood sentries. Not so with the
row of elms which you may see leading up towards
the western entrance. I think the patriarch of
them all went over in the great gale of 1815; I
know I used to shake the youngest of them with
my hands, stout as it is now, with a trunk that
would defy the bully of Crotona, or the strong man
whose *liaison* with the Lady Delilah proved so disastrous.

The College plain would be nothing without its
elms. As the long hair of a woman is a glory to
her, so are these green tresses that bank themselves against the sky in thick clustered masses, the
ornament and the pride of the classic green. You
know the " Washington elm," or if you do not, you
had better rekindle your patriotism by reading the
inscription, which tells you that under its shadow
the great leader first drew his sword at the head of
an American army. In a line with that you may
see two others: the *coral fan,* as I always called it
from its resemblance in form to that beautiful ma-
rine growth, and a third a little farther along. I
have heard it said that all three were planted at the
same time, and that the difference of their growth
is due to the slope of the ground, — the Washington elm being lower than either of the others.
There is a row of elms just in front of the old
house on the south. When I was a child the one

at the southwest corner was struck by lightning, and one of its limbs and a long ribbon of bark torn away. The tree never fully recovered its symmetry and vigor, and forty years and more afterwards a second thunderbolt crashed upon it and set its heart on fire, like those of the lost souls in the Hall of Eblis. Heaven had twice blasted it, and the axe finished what the lightning had begun.

The soil of the University town is divided into patches of sandy and of clayey ground. The Common and the College green, near which the old house stands, are on one of the sandy patches. Four curses are the local inheritance: droughts, dust, mud, and canker-worms. I cannot but think that all the characters of a region help to modify the children born in it. I am fond of making apologies for human nature, and I think I could find an excuse for myself if I, too, were dry and barren and muddy-witted and " cantankerous," — disposed to get my back up, like those other natives of the soil.

I know this, that the way Mother Earth treats a boy shapes out a kind of natural theology for him. I fell into Manichean ways of thinking from the teaching of my garden experiences. Like other boys in the country, I had my patch of ground, to which, in the spring-time, I intrusted the seeds furnished me, with a confident trust in their resurrection and glorification in the better world of summer. But I soon found that my lines had fallen in a place where a vegetable growth had to run the gauntlet of as many foes and trials as a Christian pilgrim. Flowers would not blow; daffodils perished like criminals in their condemned caps, without their petals ever seeing daylight; roses were disfigured with monstrous protrusions through their very centres, — something that looked like a second bud pushing through the middle of the corolla; lettuces and cabbages would not head; radishes knotted themselves until they looked like centenarians' fingers; and on every stem, on every leaf, and both sides of it, and at the root of everything that grew, was a professional specialist in the shape of grub, caterpillar, aphis, or other expert, whose business it was to devour that particular part, and help murder the whole attempt at vegetation. Such experiences must influence a child born to them. A sandy soil, where nothing flourishes but weeds and evil beasts of small dimensions, must breed different qualities in its human offspring from one of those fat and fertile spots which the wit whom I have once before quoted described so happily [1] that, if I quoted the passage, its brilliancy would spoil one of my pages, as a diamond breastpin sometimes kills the social effect of the wearer, who might have passed for a gentleman without it. Your arid patch of earth should seem to be the natural birthplace of the leaner virtues and the feebler vices, — of temperance and the domestic proprieties on the one hand, with a tendency to light weights in groceries

[1] Possibly in reference to Douglas Jerrold's *mot* of a certain fertile district: " Tickle it with a hoe and it will laugh with a harvest."

and provisions, and to clandestine abstraction from the person on the other, as opposed to the free hospitality, the broadly planned burglaries, and the largely conceived homicides of our rich Western alluvial regions. Yet Nature is never wholly unkind. Economical as she was in my unparadised Eden, hard as it was to make some of my floral houris unveil, still the damask roses sweetened the June breezes, the bladed and plumed flower-de-luces unfolded their close-wrapped cones, and larkspurs and lupins, lady's delights, — plebeian manifestations of the pansy, — self-sowing marigolds, hollyhocks, the forest flowers of two seasons, and the perennial lilacs and syringas, — all whispered to the winds blowing over them that some caressing presence was around me.

Beyond the garden was " the field," a vast domain of four acres or thereabout, by the measurement of after years, bordered to the north by a fathomless chasm, — the ditch the base-ball players of the present era jump over ; on the east by unexplored territory ; on the south by a barren inclosure, where the red sorrel proclaimed liberty and equality under its *drapeau rouge*, and succeeded in establishing a vegetable commune where all were alike, poor, mean, sour, and uninteresting ; and on the west by the Common, not then disgraced by jealous inclosures, which make it look like a cattle-market. Beyond, as I looked round, were the Colleges, the meeting-house, the little square market-house, long vanished ; the burial-ground where

the dead Presidents stretched their weary bones under epitaphs stretched out at as full length as their
subjects ; the pretty church where the gouty tories
used to kneel on their hassocks ; the district school-
house, and hard by it Ma'am Hancock's cottage,
never so called in those days, but rather " ten-
footer ; " then houses scattered near and far, open
spaces, the shadowy elms, round hilltops in the
distance, and over all the great bowl of the sky.
Mind you, this was the WORLD, as I first knew it ;
terra veteribus cognita, as Mr. Arrowsmith would
have called it, if he had mapped the universe of
my infancy.

But I am forgetting the old house again in the
landscape. The worst of a modern stylish mansion
is, that it has no place for ghosts. I watched one
building not long since. It had no proper garret,
to begin with, only a sealed interval between the
roof and attics, where a spirit could not be accom-
modated, unless it were flattened out like Ravel,
Brother, after the mill-stone had fallen on him.
There was not a nook or a corner in the whole
house fit to lodge any respectable ghost, for every
part was as open to observation as a literary man's
character and condition, his figure and estate, his
coat and his countenance, are to his (or her) Bohe-
mian Majesty on a tour of inspection through his
(or her) subjects' keyholes.

Now the old house had wainscots, behind which
the mice were always scampering and squeaking
and rattling down the plaster, and enacting family

scenes and parlor theatricals. It had a cellar where the cold slug clung to the walls, and the misanthropic spider withdrew from the garish day; where the green mould loved to grow, and the long, white potato-shoots went feeling along the floor, if haply they might find the daylight; it had great brick pillars, always in a cold sweat with holding up the burden they had been aching under day and night for a century and more; it had sepulchral arches closed by rough doors that hung on hinges rotten with rust, behind which doors, if there was not a heap of bones connected with a mysterious disappearance of long ago, there well might have been, for it was just the place to look for them. It had a garret, very nearly such a one as it seems to me one of us has described in one of his books; but let us look at this one as I can reproduce it from memory. It has a flooring of laths with ridges of mortar squeezed up between them, which if you tread on you will go to — the Lord have mercy on you! where *will* you go to? — the same being crossed by narrow bridges of boards, on which you may put your feet, but with fear and trembling. Above you and around you are beams and joists, on some of which you may see, when the light is let in, the marks of the conchoidal clippings of the broad-axe, showing the rude way in which the timber was shaped as it came, full of sap, from the neighboring forest. It is a realm of darkness and thick dust, and shroud-like cobwebs and dead things they wrap in their gray folds. For a garret is

like a sea-shore, where wrecks are thrown up and
slowly go to pieces. There is the cradle which the
old man you just remember was rocked in; there
is the ruin of the bedstead he died on; that ugly
slanting contrivance used to be put under his pillow in the days when his breath came hard; there
is his old chair with both arms gone, symbol of the
desolate time when he had nothing earthly left to
lean on; there is the large wooden reel which the
blear-eyed old deacon sent the minister's lady, who
thanked him graciously, and twirled it smilingly,
and in fitting season bowed it out decently to the
limbo of troublesome conveniences. And there
are old leather portmanteaus, like stranded por-
poises, their mouths gaping in gaunt hunger for
the food with which they used to be gorged to
bulging repletion; and old brass andirons, waiting
until time shall revenge them on their paltry sub-
stitutes, and they shall have their own again, and
bring with them the fore-stick and the back-log of
ancient days; and the empty churn, with its idle
dasher, which the Nancys and Phœbes, who have
left their comfortable places to the Bridgets and
Norahs, used to handle to good purpose; and the
brown, shaky old spinning-wheel, which was running, it may be, in the days when they were hanging the Salem witches.

Under the dark and haunted garret were attic
chambers which themselves had histories. On a pane
in the northeastern chamber may be read these
names: " John Tracy," " Robert Roberts," " Thomas

Prince ; " " *Stultus* " another hand had added. When I found these names a few years ago (wrong side up, for the window had been reversed), I looked at once in the Triennial to find them, for the epithet showed that they were probably students. I found them, all under the years 1771 and 1773. Does it please their thin ghosts thus to be dragged to the light of day ? Has " *Stultus* " forgiven the indignity of being thus characterized ?

The southeast chamber was the Library Hospital. Every scholar should have a book infirmary attached to his library. There should find a peaceable refuge the many books, invalids from their birth, which are sent " with the best regards of the Author ; " the respected, but unpresentable cripples which have lost a cover ; the odd volumes of honored sets which go mourning all their days for their lost brother ; the school-books which have been so often the subjects of assault and battery, that they look as if the police court must know them by heart ; these, and still more the pictured story-books, beginning with Mother Goose (which a dear old friend of mine[1] has just been amusing his philosophic leisure with turning most ingeniously and happily into the tongues of Virgil and Homer), will be precious mementos by and by, when children and grandchildren come along. What would I not give for that dear little paper-bound quarto, in large and most legible type,

---

[1] Χηνῳδια [Chenodia], or the Classical Mother Goose. *Argutos inter strepere anser olores.* [By Dr. Jacob Bigelow.] Cambridge: Printed (not Published), University Press, 1871.

on certain pages of which the tender hand that was
the shield of my infancy had crossed out with deep
black marks something awful, probably about BEARS,
such as once tare two-and-forty of us little folks for
making faces, and the very name of which made us
hide our heads under the bed-clothes.

I made strange acquaintances in that book infirmary up in the southeast attic. The "Negro
Plot" at New York helped to implant a feeling in
me which it took Mr. Garrison a good many years
to root out. "Thinks I to Myself," an old novel,
which has been attributed to a famous statesman,[1]
introduced me to a world of fiction which was not
represented on the shelves of the library proper,
unless perhaps by "Cœlebs in Search of a Wife,"
or allegories of the bitter tonic class, as the young
doctor that sits on the other side of the table would
probably call them. I always, from an early age,
had a keen eye for a story with a moral sticking
out of it, and gave it a wide berth, though in my
later years I have myself written a couple of "med-
icated novels," as one of my dearest and pleasantest
old friends wickedly called them, when somebody
asked her if she had read the last of my printed
performances. I forgave the satire for the charming *esprit* of the epithet. Besides the works I have
mentioned, there was an old, old Latin alchemy
book, with the manuscript annotations of some
ancient Rosicrucian, in the pages of which I had a

[1] George Canning. The actual author of the novel was an
English clergyman, Rev. Edward Nares.

17

vague notion that I might find the mighty secret of
the *Lapis Philosophorum*, otherwise called Chaos,
the Dragon, the Green Lion, the *Quinta Essentia*,
the Soap of Sages, the Vinegar of Philosophers,
the Dew of Heavenly Grace, the Egg, the Old Man,
the Sun, the Moon, and by all manner of odd aliases,
as I am assured by the plethoric little book before
me, in parchment covers browned like a meerschaum
with the smoke of furnaces and the thumbing of
dead gold-seekers, and the fingering of bony-handed
book-misers, and the long intervals of dusty slumber on the shelves of the *bouquiniste ;* for next
year it will be three centuries old, and it had already
seen nine generations of men when I caught its eye
(*Alchemiæ Doctrina*) and recognized it at pistol-shot
distance as a prize, among the breviaries and *Heures*
and trumpery volumes of the old open-air dealer
who exposed his treasures under the shadow of St.
Sulpice. I have never lost my taste for alchemy
since I first got hold of the *Palladium Spagyricum*
of Peter John Faber, and sought — in vain, it is
true — through its pages for a clear, intelligible,
and practical statement of how I could turn my
lead sinkers and the weights of the tall kitchen
clock into good yellow gold, specific gravity 19.2,
and exchangeable for whatever I then wanted, and
for many more things than I was then aware of.
One of the greatest pleasures of childhood is found
in the mysteries which it hides from the scepticism
of the elders, and works up into small mythologies
of its own. I have seen all this played over again

in adult life, — the same delightful bewilderment of semi-emotional belief in listening to the gaseous promises of this or that fantastic system, that I found in the pleasing mirages conjured up for me by the ragged old volume I used to pore over in the southeast attic-chamber.

The rooms of the second story, the chambers of birth and death, are sacred to silent memories.

Let us go down to the ground-floor. I should have begun with this, but that the historical reminiscences of the old house have been recently told in a most interesting memoir by a distinguished student of our local history.[1] I retain my doubts about those " dents" on the floor of the right-hand room, " the study " of successive occupants, said to have been made by the butts of the Continental militia's firelocks, but this was the cause the story told me in childhood laid them to. That military consultations were held in that room when the house was General Ward's headquarters, that the Provincial generals and colonels and other men of war there planned the movement which ended in the fortifying of Bunker's Hill, that Warren slept in the house the night before the battle, that President Langdon went forth from the western door and prayed for God's blessing on the men just setting forth on their bloody expedition, — all these things have been told, and perhaps none of them need be doubted.

But now for fifty years and more that room has

[1] See *Old Cambridge and New*, by Thomas C. Amory. Boston, 1871.

been a meeting-ground for the platoons and companies which range themselves at the scholar's word of
command. Pleasant it is to think that the retreating host of books is to give place to a still larger
army of volumes, which have seen service under
the eye of a great commander. For here the noble
collection of him so freshly remembered as our sil-
ver-tongued orator, our erudite scholar, our honored
College President, our accomplished statesman, our
courtly ambassador, are to be reverently gathered
by the heir of his name, himself not unworthy to be
surrounded by that august assembly of the wise of
all ages and of various lands and languages.[1]

Could such a many-chambered edifice have stood
a century and a half and not have had its passages
of romance to bequeath their lingering legends to
the after-time? There are other names on some
of the small window-panes, which must have had
young flesh-and-blood owners, and there is one of
early date which elderly persons have whispered
was borne by a fair woman, whose graces made the
house beautiful in the eyes of the youth of that time.
One especially — you will find the name of Fortes-
cue Vernon, of the class of 1780, in the Triennial
Catalogue — was a favored visitor to the old mansion; but he went over seas, I think they told me,
and died still young, and the name of the maiden
which is scratched on the window-pane was never
changed. I am telling the story honestly, as I re
member it, but I may have colored it unconsciously

---

[1] William Everett, at that time one of the College Faculty.

and the legendary pane may be broken before this for aught I know. At least, I have named no names except the beautiful one of the supposed hero of the romantic story.

It was a great happiness to have been born in an old house haunted by such recollections, with harmless ghosts walking its corridors, with fields of waving grass and trees and singing birds, and that vast territory of four or five acres around it to give a child the sense that he was born to a noble principality. It has been a great pleasure to retain a certain hold upon it for so many years; and since in the natural course of things it must at length pass into other hands, it is a gratification to see the old place making itself tidy for a new tenant, like some venerable dame who is getting ready to entertain a neighbor of condition. Not long since a new cap of shingles adorned this ancient mother among the village — now city — mansions. She has dressed herself in brighter colors than she has hitherto worn, so they tell me, within the last few days. She has modernized her aspects in several ways; she has rubbed bright the glasses through which she looks at the Common and the Colleges; and as the sunsets shine upon her through the flickering leaves or the wiry spray of the elms I remember from my childhood, they will glorify her into the aspect she wore when President Holyoke, father of our long since dead centenarian,[1] looked upon her youthful comeliness.

[1] Dr Edward Augustus Holyoke, who died in 1829, aged 101 years.

The quiet corner formed by this and the neighboring residences has changed less than any place I can remember. Our kindly, polite, shrewd, and humorous old neighbor, who in former days has served the town as constable and auctioneer,[1] and who bids fair to become the oldest inhabitant of the city, was there when I was born, and is living there to-day. By and by the stony foot of the great University will plant itself on this whole territory, and the private recollections which clung so tenaciously and fondly to the place and its habitations will have died with those who cherished them.

Shall they ever live again in the memory of those who loved them here below? What is this life without the poor accidents which made it our own, and by which we identify ourselves? Ah me! I might like to be a winged chorister, but still it seems to me I should hardly be quite happy if I could not recall at will the Old House with the Long Entry, and the White Chamber (where I wrote the first verses[2] that made me known, with a pencil *stans pede in uno*, pretty nearly), and the Little Parlor, and the Study, and the old books in uniforms as varied as those of the Ancient and Honorable Artillery Company used to be, if my memory serves me right, and the front yard with the stars of Bethlehem growing, flowerless, among the grass, and the dear faces to be seen no more there or anywhere on this earthly place of farewells.

---

[1] Royall Morse.

[2] Were not these *Old Ironsides?*

I have told my story. I do not know what special gifts have been granted or denied me; but this I know, that I am like so many others of my fellow-creatures, that when I smile, I feel as if they must; when I cry, I think their eyes fill; and it always seems to me that when I am most truly myself I come nearest to them and am surest of being listened to by the brothers and sisters of the larger family into which I was born so long ago. I have often feared they might be tired of me and what I tell them. But then, perhaps, would come a letter from some quiet body in some out-of-the-way place, which showed me that I had said something which another had often felt but never said, or told the secret of another's heart in unburdening my own. Such evidences that one is in the highway of human experience and feeling lighten the footsteps wonderfully. So it is that one is encouraged to go on writing as long as the world has anything that interests him, for he never knows how many of his fellow-beings he may please or profit, and in how many places his name will be spoken as that of a friend.[1]

[1] A pleasant paper of reminiscences of Cambridge will be found in Lowell's *Fireside Travels*, entitled *Cambridge Thirty Years Ago*. See also Dr. Holmes's *Cinders from the Ashes*, and ᴧ short paper on *The Old Court-House*, by his brother, John Holmes, in *The Cambridge of* 1776; and T. C. Amory's *Old Cambridge and New*, already referred to.

JAMES RUSSELL LOWELL.

INTRODUCTION.

IT has sometimes seemed to the casual observer
that Lowell has had a divided interest in his
literary life, passing from poetry to prose, and back
to poetry, as if he found it difficult to determine
in which direction his power lay. But a closer
student will remark how very large a proportion
of Lowell's prose is the record of his studies in
poetry. His first venture in literature was poetic,
when he published, not long after graduation from
college, the volume of poems, *A Year's Life;* but the
opening words of the dedication of that book hint
at studies which had been begun long before, and
have been carried on with unflagging zeal ever
since. Three years later he published *Conversations on Some of the Old Poets*, a book now out of
print; and any one reading the titles of the papers
which comprise the four volumes of his prose writings will readily see how much literature, and
especially poetic literature, has occupied his attention. Shakspere, Dryden, Lessing, Rousseau,
Dante, Spenser, Wordsworth, Milton, Keats, Car-

lyle, Percival, Thoreau, Swinburne, Chaucer, Emerson, Pope, — these are the principal subjects of his prose, and the range of topics indicates the catholicity of his taste.

It is more correct, therefore, to regard Lowell as primarily a poet, who has published also the results of a scholarship which has busied itself chiefly about poetry. The comments of a poet upon other poets are always of interest, and the first question usually asked of a young poet is : What master has he followed? The answer is generally to be found in the verse itself which betrays the influence of other and older poets. It is not too much to say that while here and there one may trace special influences in Lowell's poetry, — as, for example, of Keats, — the more noticeable influence is in the converging force of the great features of historic poetry, so that there is no echo of any one poet or conscious imitation of a poetic school; but poetry as interpreted by the masters of song, in consenting form and spirit, reappears in his verse.

It must not be inferred from this that the source of Lowell's poetic inspiration is wholly or in great part literary. It is only to say that as a poet he has also been a profound student of poetry ; the great impulses under which poets have been stirred have moved him also. These impulses are nature, humanity, and literature ; we have noticed briefly his studies in literature ; there the immediate result is less distinguishable in his poetry than in his prose, the great bulk of which, as noted, is composed of critical observations on poetry. For his studies in nature we must look most directly to his verse. There will be found the evidence of his keen delight, his quick ear and eye, his fine apprehension; and as poetry offers the most ready outlet for enthusiasm in the phenomena of nature, so Lowell the poet has sung of nature rather than written of her. But one may find a small section of his essays devoted to this field, and the paper which we have taken, *My Garden Acquaintance*, belongs in the group. It is included in his volume, *My Study Windows*, a fanciful title which intimates how divided the poet's attention is between his books and nature; how ready he is to let the fresh air into his library, and how, when observing the world from within the house, he has carried in his mind the thoughts of other lovers of nature. In this group also belongs a part of the contents of *Fireside Travels*.

It was said of the great landscape painter of modern days, by his disciple and interpreter, that in all his pictures he introduced the human figure not for the sake of color, or to hint at proportions, but because to him nature was empty without the thought of humanity. This third great inspiration has been the most prominent in Lowell's poetry, and it has been the cause of an important part of his prose writings. It is not always to be distinguished from the bookish influences which we have noted, for .n studying poetry he has been alive to the personality of the poets; but it finds its strongest expression in a few papers devoted to history and politics, such as his papers on *Witchcraft, New England Two Centuries Ago, A Great Public Character, Abraham Lincoln,* and certain political essays published in magazines, but not collected in his prose works.

Throughout his prose works run the same characteristics to be noted in his poetry; but the form of prose is necessarily more favorable to the exhibition of powers of analysis and of a discursive faculty which leads one to illustrate his subject by frequent reference to matters of history or art. The play upon words also belongs rather to prose than to poetry, and in general we may say that the rambles of a writer are freer and more natural within the unconstrained limits of prose. Thus the associative power of Lowell's mind, that gift which, abundantly fed by reading, enables him to suggest indefinitely new combinations of thought, is most delightfully displayed in his prose. The quickness with which he seizes upon the natural suggestions of his subject and the deftness with which he weaves them into the changing web of his fabric constitute a surprise and delight to the reader, and beneath all the subtlety of thought and richness of fancy there is a substance of common sense and sound judgment which commend themselves to our latest thought upon his work.

My Garden Acquaintance was first published in the *Atlantic Almanac* for 1869.

MY GARDEN ACQUAINTANCE.

ONE of the most delightful books in my father's library was White's Natural History of Selborne. For me it has rather gained in charm with years. I used to read it without knowing the secret of the pleasure I found in it, but as I grow older I begin to detect some of the simple expedients of this natural magic. Open the book where you will, it takes you out of doors. In our broiling July weather one can walk out with this genially garrulous Fellow of Oriel and find refreshment instead of fatigue. You have no trouble in keeping abreast of him as he ambles along on his hobby-horse, now pointing to a pretty view, now stopping to watch the motions of a bird or an insect, or to bag a specimen for the Honorable Daines Barrington or Mr. Pennant. In simplicity of taste and natural refinement he reminds one of Walton; in tenderness toward what he would have called the brute creation, of Cowper. I do not know whether his descriptions of scenery are good or not, but they have made me familiar with his neighborhood. Since I first read him, I have walked over some of his favorite haunts, but I still see them through his eyes rather than by any recollection of actual and personal vision. The book has also the delightfulness of absolute leisure. Mr. White seems never to have had any harder work to do than to study the habits of his feathered fellow-townsfolk, or to watch the ripening of his peaches on the wall. His volumes are the journal of Adam in Paradise,

> " Annihilating all that 's made
> To a green thought in a green shade."

It is positive rest only to look into that garden of his. It is vastly better than to

> " See great Diocletian walk
> In the Salonian garden's noble shade,"

for thither ambassadors intrude to bring with them the noises of Rome, while here the world has no entrance. No rumor of the revolt of the American Colonies seems to have reached him. " The natural term of an hog's life " has more interest for him than that of an empire. Burgoyne may surrender and welcome ; of what consequence is *that* compared with the fact that we can explain the odd tumbling of rooks in the air by their turning over " to scratch themselves with one claw " ? All the couriers in Europe spurring rowel-deep make no stir in Mr. White's little [1] Chartreuse ; but the arrival of the house-martin a day earlier or later than last year is a piece of news worth sending express to all his correspondents.

Another secret charm of this book is its inadvertent humor, so much the more delicious because unsuspected by the author. How pleasant is his

[1] *La Grande Chartreuse* was the original Carthusian monastery in France, where the most austere privacy was maintained.

innocent vanity in adding to the list of the British, and still more of the Selbornian, *fauna !* I believe he would gladly have consented to be eaten by a tiger or a crocodile, if by that means the occasional presence within the parish limits of either of these anthropophagous brutes could have been established. He brags of no fine society, but is plainly a little elated by " having considerable acquaintance with a tame brown owl." Most of us have known our share of owls, but few can boast of intimacy with a feathered one. The great events of Mr. White's life, too, have that disproportionate importance which is always humorous. To think of his hands having actually been thought worthy (as neither Willoughby's nor Ray's were) to hold a stilted plover, the *Charadrius himantopus*, with no back toe, and therefore " liable, in speculation, to perpetual vacillations "! I wonder, by the way, if metaphysicians have no hind toes. In 1770 he makes the acquaintance in Sussex of " an old family tortoise," which had then been domesticated for thirty years. It is clear that he fell in love with it at first sight. We have no means of tracing the growth of his passion ; but in 1780 we find him eloping with its object in a post-chaise. " The rattle and hurry of the journey so perfectly roused it that, when I turned it out in a border, it walked twice down to the bottom of my garden." It reads like a Court Journal : " Yesterday morning H. R. H. the Princess Alice took an airing of half an hour on the terrace of Windsor Castle." This tor·

toise might have been a member of the Royal Society, if he could have condescended to so ignoble
an ambition. It had but just been discovered that
a surface inclined at a certain angle with the plane
of th᠎ horizon took more of the sun's rays. The
tor* ise had always known this (though he unosten-
tatiously made no parade of it), and used accordingly to tilt himself up against the garden-wall in
the autumn. He seems to have been more of a
philosopher than even Mr. White himself, caring
for nothing but to get under a cabbage-leaf when
it rained, or the sun was too hot, and to bury himself alive before frost, — a four-footed Diogenes,
who carried his tub on his back.

There are moods in which this kind of history is
infinitely refreshing. These creatures whom we
affect to look down upon as the drudges of instinct
are members of a commonwealth whose constitution
rests on immovable bases. Never any need of re-
construction there! *They* never dream of settling
it by vote that eight hours are equal to ten, or that
one creature is as clever as another and no more.
They do not use their poor wits in regulating God's
clocks, nor think they cannot go astray so long as
they carry their guide-board about with them, — a
delusion we often practise upon ourselves with our
high and mighty reason, that admirable finger-post
which points every way and always right. It is
good for us now and then to converse with a world
like Mr. White's, where Man is the least important
of animals. But one who, like me, has always lived

in the country and always on the same spot, is
drawn to his book by other occult sympathies. Do
we not share his indignation at that stupid Martin
who had graduated his thermometer no lower than
4° above zero of Fahrenheit, so that in the coldest
weather ever known the mercury basely absconded
into the bulb, and left us to see the victory slip
through our fingers just as they were closing upon
it? No man, I suspect, ever lived long in the
country without being bitten by these meteorologi-
cal ambitions. He likes to be hotter and colder,
to have been more deeply snowed up, to have more
trees and larger blow down than his neighbors.
With us descendants of the Puritans especially,
these weather-competitions supply the abnegated
excitement of the race-course. Men learn to value
thermometers of the true imaginative temperament,
capable of prodigious elations and corresponding
dejections. The other day (5th July) I marked 98°
in the shade, my high water mark, higher by one
degree than I had ever seen it before. I happened
to meet a neighbor ; as we mopped our brows at
each other, he told me that he had just cleared 100°,
and I went home a beaten man. I had not felt the
heat before, save as a beautiful exaggeration of
sunshine ; but now it oppressed me with the prosaic
vulgarity of an oven. What had been poetic intensity became all at once rhetorical hyperbole. I
might suspect his thermometer (as indeed I did,
for we Harvard men are apt to think ill of any
graduation but our own) ; but it was a poor conso-

lation. The fact remained that his herald Mercury, standing a-tiptoe, could look down on mine. I seem to glimpse something of this familiar weakness in Mr. White. He, too, has shared in these mercurial triumphs and defeats. Nor do I doubt that he had a true country-gentleman's interest in the weather-cock ; that his first question on coming down of a morning was, like Barabas's,

" Into what quarter peers my halcyon's bill ? "

It is an innocent and healthful employment of the mind, distracting one from too continual study of himself, and leading him to dwell rather upon the indigestions of the elements than his own. " Did the wind back round, or go about with the sun ? " is a rational question that bears not remotely on the making of hay and the prosperity of crops. I have little doubt that the regulated observation of the vane in many different places, and the interchange of results by telegraph, would put the weather, as it were, in our power, by betraying its ambushes before it is ready to give the assault. At first sight, nothing seems more drolly trivial than the lives of those whose single achievement is to record the wind and the temperature three times a day. Yet such men are doubtless sent into the world for this special end, and perhaps there is no kind of accurate observation, whatever its object, that has not its final use and value for some one or other. It is even to be hoped that the speculations of our newspaper editors and their myriad correspondents upon

18

the signs of the political atmosphere may also fill their appointed place in a well-regulated universe, if it be only that of supplying so many more jack-o'-lanterns to the future historian. Nay, the observations on finance of an M. C. whose sole knowledge of the subject has been derived from a life-long success in getting a living out of the public without paying any equivalent therefor, will perhaps be of interest hereafter to some explorer of our *cloaca maxima*, whenever it is cleansed.

For many years I have been in the habit of noting down some of the leading events of my embowered solitude, such as the coming of certain birds and the like, — a kind of *mémoires pour servir*, after the fashion of White, rather than properly digested natural history. I thought it not impossible that a few simple stories of my winged acquaintances might be found entertaining by persons of kindred taste.

There is a common notion that animals are better meteorologists than men, and I have little doubt that in immediate weather-wisdom they have the advantage of our sophisticated senses (though I suspect a sailor or shepherd would be their match), but I have seen nothing that leads me to believe their minds capable of erecting the horoscope of a whole season, and letting us know beforehand whether the winter will be severe or the summer rainless. I more than suspect that the clerk of the weather himself does not always know very long in advance whether he is to draw an order for hot or cold, dry or moist, and the musquash is scarce likely to be wiser. I have noted but two days' difference in the coming of the song-sparrow between a very early and a very backward spring. This very year I saw the linnets at work thatching, just before a snow-storm which covered the ground several inches deep for a number of days. They struck work and left us for a while, no doubt in search of food. Birds frequently perish from sudden changes in our whimsical spring weather of which they had no foreboding. More than thirty years ago, a cherry-tree, then in full bloom, near my window, was covered with humming-birds benumbed by a fall of mingled rain and snow, which probably killed many of them. It should seem that their coming was dated by the height of the sun, which betrays them into unthrifty matrimony ;

     " So priketh hem Nature in hir corages ; " [1]

but their going is another matter. The chimney-swallows leave us early, for example, apparently so soon as their latest fledglings are firm enough of wing to attempt the long rowing-match that is before them. On the other hand, the wild-geese probably do not leave the North till they are .frozen out, for I have heard their bugles sounding southward so late as the middle of December. What may be called local migrations are doubtless dictated by the chances of food. I have once been visited by large flights of cross-bills ; and whenever the

---

[1] Chaucer's *Canterbury Tales, Prologue,* v. 11.

snow lies long and deep on the ground, a flock of
cedar-birds comes in midwinter to eat the berries
on my hawthorns. I have never been quite able
to fathom the local, or rather geographical partial-
ities of birds. Never before this summer (1870)
have the king-birds, handsomest of flycatchers, built
in my orchard ; though I always know where to
find them within half a mile. The rose-breasted
grosbeak has been a familiar bird in Brookline
(three miles away), yet I never saw one here till
last July, when I found a female busy among my
raspberries and surprisingly bold. I hope she was
prospecting with a view to settlement in our garden.
She seemed, on the whole, to think well of my
fruit, and I would gladly plant another bed if it
would help to win over so delightful a neighbor.

The return of the robin is commonly announced
by the newspapers, like that of eminent or noto-
rious people to a watering-place, as the first au-
thentic notification of spring. And such his appearance in the orchard and garden undoubtedly is.
But, in spite of his name of migratory thrush, he
stays with us all winter, and I have seen him when
the thermometer marked 15 degrees below zero of
Fahrenheit, armed impregnably within,[1] like Emerson's Titmouse, and as cheerful as he. The robin
has a bad reputation among people who do not
value themselves less for being fond of cherries.

---

[1] " For well the soul, if stout within,
    Can arm impregnably the skin."
            The Titmouse, vv. 75, 76.

There is, I admit, a spice of vulgarity in him, and his song is rather of the Bloomfield sort, too largely ballasted with prose. His ethics are of the Poor Richard school, and the main chance which calls forth all his energy is altogether of the belly. He never has those fine intervals of lunacy into which his cousins, the catbird and the mavis, are apt to fall. But for a' that and twice as muckle 's a' that, I would not exchange him for all the cherries that ever came out of Asia Minor. With whatever faults, he has not wholly forfeited that superiority which belongs to the children of nature. He has a finer taste in fruit than could be distilled from many successive committees of the Horticultural Society, and he eats with a relishing gulp not inferior to Dr. Johnson's. He feels and freely exercises his right of eminent domain. His is the earliest mess of green peas ; his all the mulberries I had fancied mine. But if he get also the lion's share of the raspberries, he is a great planter, and sows those wild ones in the woods that solace the pedestrian, and give a momentary calm even to the jaded victims of the White Hills. He keeps a strict eye over one's fruit, and knows to a shade of purple when your grapes have cooked long enough in the sun. During the severe drought a few years ago the robins wholly vanished from my garden. I neither saw nor heard one for three weeks. Meanwhile a small foreign grape-vine, rather shy of bearing, seemed to find the dusty air congenial, and, dreaming perhaps of its sweet Argos across

the sea, decked itself with a score or so of fair
bunches. I watched them from day to day till
they should have secreted sugar enough from the
sunbeams, and at last made up my mind that I
would celebrate my vintage the next morning. But
the robins, too, had somehow kept note of them.
They must have sent out spies, as did the Jews
into the promised land, before I was stirring.
When I went with my basket at least a dozen of
these winged vintagers bustled out from among the
leaves, and alighting on the nearest trees inter-
changed some shrill remarks about me of a de-
rogatory nature. They had fairly sacked the vine.
Not Wellington's veterans made cleaner work of a
Spanish town ; not Federals or Confederates were
ever more impartial in the confiscation of neutral
chickens. I was keeping my grapes a secret to
surprise the fair Fidele with, but the robins made
them a profounder secret to her than I had meant.
The tattered remnant of a single bunch was all my
harvest-home. How paltry it looked at the bottom
of my basket, — as if a humming-bird had laid her
egg in an eagle's nest ! I could not help laughing ;
and the robins seemed to join heartily in the merriment. There was a native grape-vine close by,
blue with its less refined abundance, but my cunning thieves preferred the foreign flavor. Could I
tax them with want of taste ?

The robins are not good solo singers, but their
chorus, as, like primitive fire-worshippers, they hail
the return of light and warmth to the world, is

unrivalled. There are a hundred singing like one. They are noisy enough then, and sing, as poets should, with no afterthought. But when they come after cherries to the tree near my window, they muffle their voices, and their faint *pip, pip, pop !* sounds far away at the bottom of the garden, where they know I shall not suspect them of robbing the great black-walnut of its bitter-rinded store.[1] They are feathered Pecksniffs, to be sure, but then how brightly their breasts, that look rather shabby in the sunlight, shine in a rainy day against the dark green of the fringe-tree ! After they have pinched and shaken all the life of an earthworm, as Italian cooks pound all the spirit out of a steak, and then gulped him, they stand up in honest self-confidence, expand their red waistcoats with the virtuous air of a lobby member, and outface you with an eye that calmly challenges inquiry. " Do *I* look like a bird that knows the flavor of raw vermin ? I throw myself upon a jury of my peers. Ask any robin if he ever ate anything less ascetic than the frugal berry of the juniper, and he will answer that his vow forbids him." Can such an open bosom cover such depravity ? Alas, yes ! I have no doubt his breast was redder at that very moment with the blood of my raspberries. On the whole, he is a doubtful friend in the garden. He makes his dessert of all kinds of berries, and is not averse from early pears.

---

[1] The screech-owl, whose cry, despite his ill name, is one of the sweetest sounds in nature, softens his voice in the same way with the most beguiling mockery of distance. J. R. L.

But when we remember how omnivorous he is, eating his own weight in an incredibly short time, and that Nature seems exhaustless in her invention of new insects hostile to vegetation, perhaps we may reckon that he does more good than harm. For my own part, I would rather have his cheerfulness and kind neighborhood than many berries.

For his cousin, the catbird, I have a still warmer regard. Always a good singer, he sometimes nearly equals the brown thrush, and has the merit of keeping up his music later in the evening than any bird of my familiar acquaintance. Ever since I can remember, a pair of them have built in a gigantic syringa, near our front door, and I have known the male to sing almost uninterruptedly during the evenings of early summer till twilight duskened into dark. They differ greatly in vocal talent, but all have a delightful way of crooning over, and, as it were, rehearsing their song in an undertone, which makes their nearness always unobtrusive. Though there is the most trustworthy witness to the imitative propensity of this bird, I have only once, during an intimacy of more than forty years, heard him indulge it. In that case, the imitation was by no means so close as to deceive, but a free reproduction of the notes of some other birds, especially of the oriole, as a kind of variation in his own song. The catbird is as shy as the robin is vulgarly familiar. Only when his nest or his fledglings are approached does he become noisy and almost aggressive. I have known him to station his young in a thick cornel-bush on the edge of the raspberry-bed, after the fruit began to ripen, and feed them there for a week or more. In such cases he shows none of that conscious guilt which makes the robin contemptible. On the contrary, he will maintain his post in the thicket, and sharply scold the intruder who ventures to steal *his* berries. After all, his claim is only for tithes, while the robin will bag your entire corp if he get a chance.

Dr. Watts's statement that " birds in their little nests agree," like too many others intended to form the infant mind, is very far from being true. On the contrary, the most peaceful relation of the different species to each other is that of armed neutrality. They are very jealous of neighbors. A few years ago I was much interested in the housebuilding of a pair of summer yellow-birds. They had chosen a very pretty site near the top of a tall white lilac, within easy eye-shot of a chamber window. A very pleasant thing it was to see their little home growing with mutual help, to watch their industrious skill interrupted only by little flirts and snatches of endearment, frugally cut short by the common-sense of the tiny housewife. They had brought their work nearly to an end, and had already begun to line it with fern-down, the gathering of which demanded more distant journeys and longer absences. But, alas ! the syringa, immemorial manor of the catbirds, was not more than twenty feet away, and these " giddy neighbors " had, as it appeared, been all along jealously watch-

ful, though silent, witnesses of what they deemed an
intrusion of squatters.   No sooner were the pretty
mates fairly gone for a new load of lining, tnan

> " To their unguarded nest these weasel Scots
>   Came stealing." [1]

Silently they flew back and forth, each gïving a
vengeful dab at the nest in passing.   They did not
fall-to and deliberately destroy it, for they might
have been caught at their mischief.   As it was,
whenever the yellow-birds came back, their enemies were hidden in their own sight-proof bush.
Several times their unconscious victims repaired
damages, but at length, after counsel taken together,
they gave it up.   Perhaps, like other unlettered
folk, they came to the conclusion that the Devil
was in it, and yielded to the invisible persecution
of witchcraft.

The robins, by constant attacks and annoyances,
have succeeded in driving off the blue-jays who used
to build in our pines, their gay colors and quaint,
noisy ways making them welcome and amusing
neighbors.   I once had the chance of doing a kindness to a household of them, which they received
with very friendly condescension.   I had had my
eye for some time upon a nest, and was puzzled by
a constant fluttering of ‘what seemed full-grown
wings in it whenever I drew nigh.   At last I climbed
the tree, in spite of angry protests from the old
birds against my intrusion.   The mystery had a
very simple solution.   In building the nest, a long

[1] Shakspere: *King Henry V.*, act i. scene 2.

piece of packthread had been somewhat loosely woven in. Three of the young had contrived to entangle themselves in it, and had become full-grown without being able to launch themselves upon the air. One was unharmed; another had so tightly twisted the cord about its shank that one foot was curled up and seemed paralyzed; the third, in its struggles to escape, had sawn through the flesh of the thigh and so much harmed itself that I thought it humane to put an end to its misery. When I took out my knife to cut their hempen bonds, the heads of the family seemed to divine my friendly intent. Suddenly ceasing their cries and threats, they perched quietly within reach of my hand, and watched me in my work of manumission. This, owing to the fluttering terror of the prisoners, was an affair of some delicacy; but ere-long I was rewarded by seeing one of them fly away to a neighboring tree, while the cripple, making a parachute of his wings, came lightly to the ground, and hopped off as well as he could with one leg, obsequiously waited on by his elders. A week later I had the satisfaction of meeting him in the pine-walk, in good spirits, and already so far recovered as to be able to balance himself with the .ame foot. I have no doubt that in his old age he accounted for his lameness by some handsome story of a wound received at the famous Battle of the Pines, when our tribe, overcome by numbers, was driven from its ancient camping-ground. Of late years the jays have visited us only at intervals;

and in winter their bright plumage, set off by the snow, and their cheerful cry, are especially welcome. They would have furnished Æsop with a fable, for the feathered crest in which they seem to take so much satisfaction is often their fatal snare. Country boys make a hole with their finger in the snow-crust just lárge enough to admit the jay's head, and, hollowing it out somewhat beneath, bait it with a few kernels of corn. The crest slips easily into the trap, but refuses to be pulled out again, and he who came to feast remains a prey.

Twice have the crow-blackbirds attempted a settlement in my pines, and twice have the robins, who claim a right of preëmption, so successfully played the part of border-ruffians as to drive them away, — to my great regret, for they are the best substitute we have for rooks. At Shady Hill [1] (now, alas! empty of its so long-loved household) they build by hundreds, and nothing can be more cheery than their creaking clatter (like a convention of old-fashioned tavern-signs) as they gather at evening to debate in mass meeting their windy politics, or to gossip at their tent-doors over the events of the day. Their port is grave, and their stalk across the turf as martial as that of a second-rate ghost in Hamlet. They never meddled with my corn, so far as I could discover.

For a few years I had crows, but their nests are an irresistible bait for boys, and their settlement

[1] The home of the Nortons, in Cambridge, who were at the time of this paper in Europe.

was broken up. They grew so wonted as to throw off a great part of their shyness, and to tolerate my near approach. One very hot day I stood for some time within twenty feet of a mother and three children, who sat on an elm bough over my head gasping in the sultry air, and holding their wings half-spread for coolness. All birds during the pairing season become more or less sentimental, and murmur soft nothings in a tone very unlike the grinding-organ repetition and loudness of their habitual song. The crow is very comical as a lover, and to hear him trying to soften his croak to the proper Saint Preux [1] standard, has something the effect of a Mississippi boatman quoting Tennyson. Yet there are few things to my ear more melodious than his caw of a clear winter morning as it drops to you filtered through five hundred fathoms of crisp blue air. The hostility of all smaller birds makes the moral character of the crow, for all his deaconlike demeanor and garb, somewhat questionable. He could never sally forth without insult. The golden robins, especially, would chase him as far as I could follow with my eye, making him duck clumsily to avoid their importunate bills. I do not believe, however, that he robbed any nests hereabouts, for the refuse of the gas-works, which, in our free-and-easy community, is allowed to poison the river, supplied him with dead alewives in abundance. I used to watch him making his periodical visits to the salt-marshes and coming back with a fish in his

[1] See Rousseau's *La Nouvelle Héloise*.

beak to his young savages, who, no doubt, like it in
that condition which makes it savory to the Kana-
kas and other corvine races of men.

Orioles are in great plenty with me. I have seen
seven males flashing about the garden at once. A
merry crew of them swing their hammocks from the
pendulous boughs. During one of these later years,
when the canker-worms stripped our elms as bare as
winter, these birds went to the trouble of rebuilding
their unroofed nests, and chose for the purpose trees
which are safe from those swarming vandals, such as
the ash and the button-wood. One year a pair (disturbed, I suppose, elsewhere) built a second nest in
an elm within a few yards of the house. My friend,
Edward E. Hale, told me once that the oriole rejected from his web all strands of brilliant color,
and I thought it a striking example of that instinct
of concealment noticeable in many birds, though it
should seem in this instance that the nest was amply
protected by its position from all marauders but owls
and squirrels. Last year, however, I had the full-
est proof that Mr. Hale was mistaken. A pair of
orioles built on the lowest trailer of a weeping elm,
which hung within ten feet of our drawing-room
window, and so low that I could reach it from the
ground. The nest was wholly woven and felted
with ravellings of woollen carpet in which scarlet
predominated. Would the same thing have happened in the woods? Or did the nearness of a human dwelling perhaps, give the birds a greater feeling of security? They are very bold, by the way, in

quest of cordage, and I have often watched them stripping the fibrous bark from a honeysuckle growing over the very door. But, indeed, all my birds look upon me as if I were a mere tenant at will, and they were landlords. With shame I confess it, I have been bullied even by a humming-bird. This spring, as I was cleansing a pear-tree of its lichens, one of these little zigzagging blurs came purring toward me, couching his long bill like a lance, his throat sparkling with angry fire, to warn me off from a Missouri-currant whose honey he was sipping. And many a time he has driven me out of a flower-bed. This summer, by the way, a pair. of these winged emeralds fastened their mossy acorn-cup upon a bough of the same elm which the orioles had enlivened the year before. We watched all their proceedings from the window through an opera-glass, and saw their two nestlings grow from black needles with a tuft of down at the lower end, till they whirled away on their first short experimental flights. They became strong of wing in a surprisingly short time, and I never saw them or the male bird after, though the female was regular as usual in her visits to our petunias and verbenas. I do not think it ground enough for a generalization, but in the many times when I watched the old birds feeding their young, the mother always alighted, while the father as uniformly remained upon the wing.

The bobolinks are generally chance visitors, tinkling through the garden in blossoming-time, but this year, owing to the long rains early in the season, their favorite meadows were flooded, and they were driven to the upland. So I had a pair of them domiciled in my grass field. The male used to perch in an apple-tree, then in full bloom, and, while I stood perfectly still close by, he would circle away, quivering round the entire field of five acres, with no break in his song, and settle down again among the blossoms, to be hurried away almost immediately by a new rapture of music. He had the volubility of an Italian charlatan at a fair, and, like him, appeared to be proclaiming the merits of some quack remedy. *Opodeldoc-opodeldoc-try-Doctor-Lincoln's-opodeldoc!* he seemed to repeat over and over again. with a rapidity that would have distanced the deftest-tongued Figaro that ever rattled. I remember Count Gurowski saying once, with that easy superiority of knowledge about this country which is the monopoly of foreigners, that we had no singing-birds! Well, well, Mr. Hepworth Dixon [1] has found the typical America in Oneida and Salt Lake City. Of course, an intelligent European is the best judge of these matters. The truth is there are more singing-birds in Europe because there are fewer forests. These songsters love the neighborhood of man because hawks and owls are rarer, while their own food is more abundant. Most people seem to think, the more trees, the more birds. Even Châteaubriand, who first tried the primitive-forest-cure, and whose description of the wilderness in its imaginative effects is unmatched, fancies the " people of

[1] In his book of travels, *New America.*

the air singing their hymns to him." So far as my own observation goes, the farther one penetrates the sombre solitudes of the woods, the more seldom does he hear the voice of any singing-bird. In spite of Châteaubriand's minuteness of detail, in spite of that marvellous reverberation of the decrepit tree falling of its own weight, which he was the first to notice, I cannot help doubting whether he made his way very deep into the wilderness. At any rate, in a letter to Fontanes, written in 1804, he speaks of *mes chevaux paissant à quelque distance.* To be sure Châteaubriand was apt to mount the high horse, and this may have been but an afterthought of the *grand seigneur*, but certainly one would not make much headway on horseback toward the druid fastnesses of the primæval pine.

The bobolinks build in considerable numbers in a meadow within a quarter of a mile of us. A houseless lane passes through the midst of their camp, and in clear westerly weather, at the right season, one may hear a score of them singing at once. When they are breeding, if I chance to pass, one of the male birds always accompanies me like a constable, flitting from post to post of the railfence, with a short note of reproof continually repeated, till I am fairly out of the neighborhood. Then he will swing away into the air and run down the wind, gurgling music without stint over the unheeding tussocks of meadow-grass and dark clumps of bulrushes that mark his domain.

We have no bird whose song will match the

nightingale's in compass, none whose note is so
rich as that of the European blackbird; but for
mere rapture I have never heard the bobolink's
rival. But his opera-season is a short one. The
ground and tree sparrows are our most constant
performers. It is now late in August, and one of
the latter sings every day and all day long in the
garden. Till within a fortnight, a pair of indigo-
birds would keep up their lively *duo* for an hour
together. While I write, I hear an oriole gay as
in June, and the plaintive *may-be* of the goldfinch
tells me he is stealing my lettuce-seeds. I know
not what the experience of others may have been,
but the only bird I have ever heard sing in the
night has been the chip-bird. I should say he sang
about as often during the darkness as cocks crow.
One can hardly help fancying that he sings in his
dreams.

> " Father of light, what sunnie seed,
> What glance of day hast thou confined
> Into this bird? To all the breed
> This busie ray thou hast assigned;
> Their magnetism works all night,
> And dreams of Paradise and light."

On second thought, I remember to have heard the
cuckoo strike the hours nearly all night with the
regularity of a Swiss clock.

The dead limbs of our elms, which I spare to
that end, bring us the flicker every summer, and
almost daily I hear his wild scream and laugh close
at hand, himself invisible. He is a shy bird, but a
few days ago I had the satisfaction of studying him

through the blinds as he sat on a tree within a few feet of me. Seen so near and at rest, he makes good his claim to the title of pigeon-woodpecker. Lumberers have a notion that he is harmful to timber, digging little holes through the bark to encourage the settlement of insects. The regular rings of such perforations which one may see in almost any apple-orchard seem to give some probability to this theory. Almost every season a solitary quail visits us, and, unseen among the currant-bushes, calls *Bob White, Bob White*, as if he were playing at hide-and-seek with that imaginary being. A rarer visitant is the turtle-dove, whose pleasant coo (something like the muffled crow of a cock from a coop covered with snow) I have sometimes heard, and whom I once had the good luck to see close by me in the mulberry-tree. The wild-pigeon, once numerous, I have not seen for many years.[1] Of savage birds, a hen-hawk now and then quarters himself upon us for a few days, sitting sluggish in a tree after a surfeit of poultry. One of them once offered me a near shot from my study-window one drizzly day for several hours. But it was Sunday, and I gave him the benefit of its gracious truce of God.

Certain birds have disappeared from our neighborhood within my memory. I remember when the whippoorwill could be heard in Sweet Auburn. The night-hawk, once common, is now rare. The brown thrush has moved farther up country. For

[1] They made their appearance again this summer (1870). — J. R. L.

years I have not seen or heard any of the larger
owls, whose hooting was one of my boyish terrors.
The cliff-swallow, strange emigrant, that eastward
takes his way, has come and gone again in my time.
The bank-swallows, wellnigh innumerable during
my boyhood, no longer frequent the crumbly cliff
of the gravel-pit by the river.   The barn-swallows,
which once swarmed in our barn, flashing through
the dusty sun-streaks of the mow, have been gone
these many years.   My father would lead me out
to see them gather on the roof, and take counsel
before their yearly migration, as Mr. White used
to see them at Selborne.   *Eheu fugaces!*   Thank
fortune, the swift still glues his nest, and rolls his
distant thunders night and day in the wide-throated
chimneys, still sprinkles the evening air with his
merry twittering.   The populous heronry in Fresh
Pond meadows has wellnigh broken up, but still a
pair or two haunt the old home, as the gypsies of
Ellangowan their ruined huts, and every evening
fly over us riverwards, clearing their throats with a
hoarse hawk as they go, and, in cloudy weather,
scarce higher than the tops of the chimneys.   Some
times I have known one to alight in one of our
trees, though for what purpose I never could divine.
Kingfishers have sometimes puzzled me in the same
way, perched at high noon in a pine, springing their
watchman's rattle when they flitted away from my
curiosity, and seeming to shove their top-heavy
heads along as a man does a wheelbarrow.

Some birds have left us, I suppose, because the

country is growing less wild. I once found a summer duck's nest within a quarter of a mile of our house, but such a *trouvaille* would be impossible now as Kidd's treasure. And yet the mere taming of the neighborhood does not quite satisfy me as an explanation. Twenty years ago, on my way to bathe in the river, I saw every day a brace of woodcock, on the miry edge of a spring within a few rods of a house, and constantly visited by thirsty cows. There was no growth of any kind to conceal them, and yet these ordinarily shy birds were almost as indifferent to my passing as common poultry would have been. Since bird-nesting has become scientific, and dignified itself as oölogy, that, no doubt, is partly to blame for some of our losses. But some old friends are constant. Wilson's thrush comes every year to remind me of that most poetic of ornithologists. He flits before me through the pine-walk like the very genius of solitude. A pair of pewees have built immemorially on a jutting brick in the arched entrance to the ice-house. Always on the same brick, and never more than a single pair, though two broods of five each are raised there every summer. How do they settle their claim to the homestead? By what right of primogeniture? Once the children of a man employed about the place *oölogized* the nest, and the pewees left us for a year or two. I felt towards those boys as the messmates of the Ancient Mariner did towards him after he had shot the albatross.[1]

[1] In Coleridge's poem of that name.

But the pewees came back at last, and one of them is now on his wonted perch, so near my window that I can hear the click of his bill as he snaps a fly on the wing with the unerring precision a stately Trasteverina shows in the capture of her smaller deer. The pewee is the first bird to pipe up in the morning; and, during the early summer he preludes his matutinal ejaculation of *pewee* with a slender whistle, unheard at any other time. He saddens with the season, and, as summer declines, he changes his note to *eheu, pewee!* as if in lamentation. Had he been an Italian bird, Ovid would have had a plaintive tale to tell about him. He is so familiar as often to pursue a fly through the open window into my library.

There is something inexpressibly dear to me in these old friendships of a lifetime. There is scarce a tree of mine but has had, at some time or other, a happy homestead among its boughs, to which I cannot say,

> "Many light hearts and wings,
> Which now be dead, lodged in thy living bowers."

My walk under the pines would lose half its summer charm were I to miss that shy anchorite, the Wilson's thrush, nor hear in haying-time the metallic ring of his song, that justifies his rustic name of *scythe-whet.* I protect my game as jealously as an English squire. If anybody had oölogized a certain cuckoo's nest I know of (I have a pair in my garden every year), it would have left me a sore place in my mind for weeks. I love to bring these abo·

rigines back to the mansuetude they showed to the early voyagers, and before (forgive the involuntary pun) they had grown accustomed to man and knew his savage ways. And they repay your kindness with a sweet familiarity too delicate ever to breed contempt. I have made a Penn-treaty with them, preferring that to the Puritan way with the natives, which converted them to a little Hebraism and a great deal of Medford rum. If they will not come near enough to me (as most of them will), I bring them close with an opera-glass, — a much better weapon than a gun. I would not, if I could, convert them from their pretty pagan ways. The only one I sometimes have savage doubts about is the red squirrel. I *think* he oölogizes. I *know* he eats cherries (we counted five of them at one time in a single tree, the stones pattering down like the sparse hail that preludes a storm), and that he gnaws off the small end of pears to get at the seeds. He steals the corn from under the noses of my poultry. But what would you have? He will come down upon the limb of the tree I am lying under till he is within a yard of me. He and his mate will scurry up and down the great blackwalnut for my diversion, chattering like monkeys. Can I sign his death-warrant who has tolerated me about his grounds so long? Not I. Let them steal, and welcome. I am sure I should, had I had the same bringing up and the same temptation. As for the birds, I do not believe there is one of them but does more good than harm; and of how many featherless bipeds can this be said?

HENRY DAVID THOREAU.

———◆———

INTRODUCTION.

THERE died at Concord, Massachusetts, in the
year 1862, a man of forty-five who, if one were
to take his word for it, need never have gone out
of the little village of Concord to see all that was
worth seeing in the world. Lowell, in his *My Garden Acquaintance*, reminds the reader of Gilbert
White, who, in his *Natural History of Selborne*, gave
minute details of a lively world found within the
borders of a little English parish. Alphonse Karr,
a French writer, has written a book which contracts
the limit still further in *A Journey round my Garden*, but neither of these writers so completely iso-
lated themselves from the outside world as did
Thoreau, who had a collegiate education at Harvard, made short journeys to Cape Cod, Maine, and
Canada, acted for a little while as tutor in a family
on Staten Island, but spent the best part of his life
as a looker-on in Concord, and during two years of
the time lived a hermit on the shores of Walden
Pond. He made his living, as the phrase goes, by
the occupation of a land surveyor, but he followed

the profession only when it suited his convenience. He did not marry; he never went to church; he never voted; he refused to pay taxes; he sought no society; he declined companions when they were in his way, and when he had anything to say in public, went about from door to door and invited people to come to a hall to hear him deliver his word.

That he had something to say to the world at large is pretty evident from the books which he has left, and it is intimated that the unpublished records of his observation and reflection are more extensive. Thus far his published writings are contained in seven volumes. The first in appearance was *A Week on the Concord and Merrimac Rivers.* It was published in 1849 and built upon the adventures of himself and brother ten years before, when, in a boat of their own construction, they had made their way from Concord down the Concord River to the Merrimac, up that to its source, and back to the starting point. It will readily be seen that such an excursion would not yield a bookful of observation, and though Thoreau notes in it many trivial incidents, a great part of the contents is in the reflections which he makes from day to day. He comes to the little river with its sparse border of population and meagre history, and insists upon measuring antiquity and fame by it. All of his reading he tests by the measure of this stream, and undertakes to show that the terms, big and little, are very much misapplied, and that here on this miniature scale one may read all that is worth knowing in life. His voyage is treated with the gravity which one might use in recording a journey to find the sources of the Nile.

Between the date of the journey and the publication of the book, Thoreau was engaged upon an experiment still more illustrative of his creed of individuality. In 1845 he built a hut in the woods by Walden Pond, and for two years lived a self-contained life there. It was not altogether a lonely life. He was within easy walking distance of Concord village, and the novelty of his housekeeping attracted many visitors, while his friends who valued his conversation sought him out in his hermitage. Besides and beyond this Thoreau had a genius for intercourse with humbler companions. There have been few instances in history of such perfect understanding as existed between him and the lower orders of creation. It has been said of him: " Every fact which occurs in the bed [of the Concord River], on the banks, or in the air over it ; the fishes, and their spawning and nests, their manners, their food ; the shad-flies which fill the air on a certain evening once a year, and which are snapped at by the fishes so ravenously that many of these die of repletion ; the conical heaps of small stones on the river-shallows, one of which heaps will sometime overfill a cart, — these heaps the huge nests of small fishes ; the birds which frequent the stream, heron, duck, sheldrake, loon, osprey ; the snake, muskrat, otter woodchuck, and fox on the banks ; the turtle, frog

hyla, and cricket which made the banks vocal, —
were all known to him, and, as it were, townsmen
and fellow-creatures. . . . . His power of observation seemed to indicate additional senses. He saw
as with a microscope, heard as with ear-trumpet,
and his memory was a photographic register of all
he saw and heard. . . . . His intimacy with animals suggested what Thomas Fuller records of
Butler the apiologist, that ' either he had told the
bees things or the bees had told him ; ' snakes coiled
round his leg ; the fishes swam into his hand, and
he took them out of the water ; he pulled the woodchuck out of its hole by the tail, and took the foxes
under his protection from the hunters." [1]

Walden, published in 1854, is the record of
Thoreau's life in the woods, and inasmuch as that
life was not exhausted in the bare provision against
bodily wants, nor in the observation even of what
lay under the eye and ear, but was busied about
the questions which perplex all who would give an
account of themselves, the record mingles common
fact and personal experience, the world without
and the world within. Thoreau records what he
sees and hears in the woods, but these sights and
sounds are the texts for sermons upon human life.
He undertook to get at the elementary conditions
of living, and to strip himself as far as he could of
all that was unnecessary. In doing this he discovered many curious and ingenious things, and the
unique method which he took was pretty sure to

[1] Emerson's *Biographical Sketch.*

give him glimpses of life not seen by others. But
the method had its disadvantages and chiefly this,
that it was against the common order of things,
and therefore the results reached could not be re-
lied upon as sound and wholesome.

The great value of *Walden*, and indeed of all
Thoreau's books, is not in the philosophy, which is
often shrewd and often strained and arbitrary, but
in the disclosure made of the common facts of the
world about one. He used to say; " I think nothing is to be hoped from you, if this bit of mould
under your feet is not sweeter to you to eat than
any other in this world, or in any world; " and the
whole drift of his writing is toward the develop-
ment of the individual in the place where he happens to be. Thoreau's protesting attitude, and the
stout resistance which he made to all influences
about him except the common ones of nature, betray
themselves in the style of his writing. He has a
way, almost insolent, of throwing out his thoughts,
and growling forth his objections to the conventions
of life, which renders his writing often crabbed and
inartistic. There is a rudeness which seems sometimes affected, and a carelessness which is contemptuous. Yet often his indifference to style is a rugged
insistence on the strongest thought, and in his effort
to express himself unreservedly he reaches a force
and energy which are refreshing.

These two were the only writings of Thoreau
published in his lifetime. He printed contributions
to the magazines from time to time, and out of

these and his manuscripts have been gathered five other volumes, *Excursions in Field and Forest, The Maine Woods, Cape Cod, Letters to Various Persons, A Yankee in Canada.* To *Excursions* was prefixed a biographical sketch by R. W. Emerson, which gives one a very vivid portrait of this unique man. *Cape Cod* is the record of a walk taken the length of the Cape, and that, with *Walden*, are likely to remain as the most finished and agreeable books by the writer. All of his writings, however, will be searched for the evidence which they give of a mind singular for its independence, its resolute confronting of the problems of life, its insight into nature, its isolation, and its waywardness.

The first two papers which follow are from *Walden*, the third from *Cape Cod.*

I.

SOUNDS.

I DID not read books the first summer; I hoed beans. Nay, I often did better than this. There were times when I could not afford to sacrifice the bloom of the present moment to any work, whether of the head or hands. I love a broad margin to my life. Sometimes, in a summer morning, having taken my accustomed bath, I sat in my sunny doorway from sunrise till noon, rapt in a revery, amidst the pines and hickories and sumachs, in undisturbed solitude and stillness, while the birds sang around or flitted noiseless through the house, until by the sun falling in at my west window, or the noise of some traveller's wagon on the distant highway, I was reminded of the lapse of time. I grew in those seasons like corn in the night, and they were far better than any work of the hands would have been. They were not time subtracted from my life, but so much over and above my usual allowance. I realized what the Orientals mean by contemplation and the forsaking of works. For the most part I minded not how the hours went. The day advanced as if to light some work of mine; it was morning, and lo, now it is evening, and nothing memorable is accomplished. Instead of singing like the birds, I silently smiled at my incessant good fortune. As the sparrow had its trill, sitting on the hickory before my door, so had I my chuckle or suppressed warble which he might hear out of my nest. My days were not days of the week, bearing the stamp of any heathen deity, nor were they minced into hours and fretted by the ticking of a clock ; for I lived like the Puri Indians, of whom it is said that " for yesterday, to-day, and to-morrow they have only one word, and they express the variety of meaning by pointing backward for yesterday, forward for to-morrow, and overhead for the passing day." This was sheer idleness to my fellow-townsmen, no doubt ; but if the birds and flowers had tried me by their standard, I should not have been found wanting. A man must find his occasions in himself, it is true. The natural day is very calm, and will hardly reprove his in-dolence.

I had this advantage, at least, in my mode of life over those who were obliged to look abroad for amusement, to society and the theatre; that my life itself was become my amusement and never ceased to be novel. It was a drama of many scenes and without an end. If we were always indeed getting our living, and regulating our lives according to the last and best mode we had learned, we should never be troubled with *ennui*. Follow your genius closely enough, and it will not fail to show you a fresh prospect every hour. Housework was a pleas-aut pastime. When my floor was dirty, I rose early, and, setting all my furniture out of doors on the grass, bed and bedstead making but one budget, dashed water on the floor, and sprinkled white sand from the pond on it, and then with a broom scrubbed it clean and white; and by the time the villagers had broken their fast, the morning sun had dried my house sufficiently to allow me to move in again, and my meditations were almost uninterrupted. It was pleasant to see my whole household effects out on the grass, making a little pile like a gypsy's pack, and my three-legged table, from which I did not remove the books and pen and ink, standing amid the pines and hickories. They seemed glad to get out themselves, and as if unwilling to be brought in. I was sometimes tempted to stretch an awning over them and take my seat there. It was worth the while to see the sun shine on these things, and hear the free wind blow on them; so much more interesting most familiar objects look out of doors than in the house. A bird sits on the next bough, life-everlasting grows under the table, and blackberry vines run round its legs; pine cones, chestnut burs, and strawberry leaves are strewn about. It looked as if this was the way these forms came to be transferred to our furniture, to tables, chairs, and bedsteads, — because they once stood in the midst of them.

My house was on the side of a hill, immediately on the edge of the larger wood, in the midst of a young forest of pitch pines and hickories, and half a

dozen rods from the pond, to which a narrow foot-
path led down the hill. In my front yard grew the
strawberry, blackberry, and life-everlasting, johns-
wort and goldenrod, shrub-oaks and sand-cherry,
blueberry and groundnut. Near the end of May,
the sand-cherry (*cerasus pumila*) adorned the sides
of the path with its delicate flowers arranged in
umbels cylindrically about its short stems, which
last, in the fall, weighed down with good-sized and
handsome cherries, fell over in wreaths like rays
on every side. I tasted them out of compliment
to Nature, though they were scarcely palatable.
The sumach (*rhus glabra*) grew luxuriantly about
the house, pushing up through the embankment
which I had made, and growing five or six feet the
first season. Its broad, pinnate, tropical leaf was
pleasant though strange to look on. The large
buds, suddenly pushing out late in the spring from
dry sticks which had seemed to be dead, developed
themselves as by magic into graceful green and
tender boughs, an inch in diameter ; and sometimes,
as I sat at my window, so heedlessly did they grow
and tax their weak joints, I heard a fresh and
tender bough suddenly fall like a fan to the ground,
when there was not a breath of air stirring, broken
off by its own weight. In August, the large masses
of berries, which, when in flower, had attracted
many wild bees, gradually assumed their bright,
velvety, crimson hue, and by their weight again
bent down and broke the tender limbs.

20

As I sit at my window this summer afternoon, hawks are circling about my clearing; the tantivy of wild pigeons, flying by twos and threes athwart my view, or perching restless on the white-pine boughs behind my house, gives a voice to the air; a fishhawk dimples the glassy surface of the pond and brings up a fish; a mink steals out of the marsh before my door and seizes a frog by the shore; the sedge is bending under the weight of the reedbirds flitting hither and thither; and for the last half hour I have heard the rattle of railroad cars, now dying away and then reviving like the beat of a partridge, conveying travellers from Boston to the country. For I did not live so out of the world as that boy, who, as I hear, was put out to a farmer in the east part of the town, but ere long ran away and came home again, quite down at the heel and homesick. He had never seen such a dull and out-of-the-way place; the folks were all gone off; why, you could n't even hear the whistle! I doubt if there is such a place in Massachusetts now : —

> " In truth, our village has become a butt
> For one of those fleet railroad shafts, and o'er
> Our peaceful plain its soothing sound is — Concord."

The Fitchburg Railroad touches the pond about a hundred rods south of where I dwell. I usually go to the village along its causeway, and am, as it were, related to society by this link. The men on the freight trains, who go over the whole length of the road, bow to me as to an old acquaintance, they pass me so often, and apparently they take me for an employee; and so I am. I too would fain be a track-repairer somewhere in the orbit of the earth.

The whistle of the locomotive penetrates my woods summer and winter, sounding like the scream of a hawk sailing over some farmer's yard, informing me that many restless city merchants are arriving within the circle of the town, or adventurous country traders from the other side. As they come under one horizon, they shout their warning to get off the track to the other, heard sometimes through the circles of two towns. Here come your groceries, country; your rations, countrymen! Nor is there any man so independent on his farm that he can say them nay. And here 's your pay for them! screams the countryman's whistle; timber like long battering rams going twenty miles an hour against the city's walls, and chairs enough to seat all the weary and heavy laden that dwell within them. With such huge and lumbering civility the country hands a chair to the city. All the Indian huckleberry hills are stripped, all the cranberry meadows are raked into the city. Up comes the cotton, down goes the woven cloth; up comes the silk, down goes the woollen; up come the books, but down goes the wit that writes them.

When I meet the engine with its train of cars moving off with planetary motion, — or, rather, ike a comet, for the beholder knows not if with that velocity and with that direction it will ever revisit this system, since its orbit does not look like a returning curve, — with its steam cloud like a banner streaming behind in golden and silver wreaths, like many a downy cloud which I have seen, high in the heavens, unfolding its masses to the light, — as if this travelling demigod, this cloud-compeller, would ere long take the sunset sky for the livery of his train ; when I hear the iron horse make the hills echo with his snort like thunder, shaking the earth with his feet, and breathing fire and smoke from his nostrils (what kind of winged horse or fiery dragon they will put into the new Mythology I don't know), it seems as if the earth had got a race now worthy to inhabit it. If all were as it seems, and men made the elements their servants for noble ends ! If the cloud that hangs over the engine were the perspiration of heroic deeds, or as beneficent as that which floats over the farmer's fields, then the elements and Nature herself would cheerfully accompany men on their errands and be their escort.

I watch the passage of the morning cars with the same feeling that I do the rising of the sun, which is hardly more regular. Their train of clouds stretching far behind and rising higher and higher, going to heaven while the cars are going to Boston, conceals the sun for a minute and casts my distant field into the shade, a celestial train beside which the petty train of cars which hugs the earth is but the barb of the spear. The stabler of the iron horse was up early this winter morning by the light of the stars amid the mountains, to fodder and harness his steed. Fire, too, was awakened thus

early to put the vital heat in him and get him off.
If the enterprise were as innocent as it is early !
If the snow lies deep, they strap on his snow-shoes,
and with the giant plough plough a furrow from
the mountains to the seaboard, in which the cars,
like a following drill-barrow, sprinkle all the restless men and floating merchandise in the country
for seed. All day the fire-steed flies over the country, stopping only that his master may rest, and I
am awakened by his tramp and defiant snort at
midnight, when in some remote glen in the woods
he fronts the elements incased in ice and snow ;
and he will reach his stall only with the morning
star, to start once more on his travels without rest
or slumber. Or perchance, at evening, I hear him
in his stable blowing off the superfluous energy of
the day, that he may calm his nerves and cool his
liver and brain for a few hours of iron slumber.
If the enterprise were as heroic and commanding
as it is protracted and unwearied !

Far through unfrequented woods on the confines
of towns, where once only the hunter penetrated
by day, in the darkest night dart these bright sa-
loons without the knowledge of their inhabitants ;
this moment stopping at some brilliant station-
house in town or city, where a social crowd is gathered, the next in the Dismal Swamp, scaring the
owl and fox. The startings and arrivals of the
cars are now the epochs in the village day. They
go and come with such regularity and precision,
and their whistle can be heard so far, that the farm-

ers set their clocks by them, and thus one well-conducted institution regulates a whole country. Have not men improved somewhat in punctuality since the railroad was invented? Do they not talk and think faster in the depot than they did in the stage-office? There is something electrifying in the atmosphere of the former place. I have been astonished at the miracles it has wrought; that some of my neighbors, who, I should have prophesied, once for all, would never get to Boston by so prompt a conveyance, are on hand when the bell rings. To do things "railroad fashion" is now the by-word; and it is worth the while to be warned so often and so sincerely by any power to get off its track. There is no stopping to read the riot act, no firing over the heads of the mob, in this case. We have constructed a fate, an *Atropos*,[1] that never turns aside. (Let that be the name of your engine.) Men are advertised that at a certain hour and minute these bolts will be shot toward particular points of the compass; yet it interferes with no man's business, and the children go to school on the other track. We live the steadier for it. We are all educated thus to be sons of Tell. The air is full of invisible bolts. Every path but your own is the path of fate. Keep on your own track, then.

---

[1] In the classic mythology there were three Fates who presided over the life and death of mankind: Clotho, that spun the thread of birth, Lachesis, that measured it, and Atropos, the unflexible Fate that cut it off.

What recommends commerce to me is its enterprise and bravery. It does not clasp its hands and pray to Jupiter. I see these men every day go about their business with more or less courage and content, doing more even than they suspect, and perchance better employed than they could have consciously devised. I am less affected by their heroism who stood up for half an hour in the front line at Buena Vista, than by the steady and cheerful valor of the men who inhabit the snow-plough for their winter quarters; who have not merely the three-o'-clock in the morning courage, which Bonaparte thought was the rarest, but whose courage does not go to rest so early, who go to sleep only when the storm sleeps or the sinews of their iron steed are frozen. On this morning of the Great Snow, perchance, which is still raging and chilling men's blood, I hear the muffled tone of their engine bell from out the fog bank of their chilled breath, which announces that the cars *are coming*, without long delay, notwithstanding the veto of a New England northeast snow-storm, and I behold the ploughmen covered with snow and rime, their heads peering above the mould-board which is turning down other than daisies and the nests of field-mice, like bowlders of the Sierra Nevada, that occupy an outside place in the universe.

Commerce is unexpectedly confident and serene, alert, adventurous, and unwearied. It is very natural in its methods withal, far more so than many fantastic enterprises and sentimental experiments, and hence its singular success. I am refreshed and expanded when the freight train rattles past me, and I smell the stores which go dispensing their odors all the way from Long Wharf to Lake Champlain, reminding me of foreign parts, of coral reefs, and Indian oceans, and tropical climes, and the extent of the globe. I feel more like a citizen of the world at the sight of the palm-leaf which will cover so many flaxen New England heads the next summer, the Manilla hemp and cocoa-nut husks, the old junk, gunny bags, scrap iron, and rusty nails. This car-load of torn sails is more legible and interesting now than if they should be wrought into paper and printed books. Who can write so graphically the history of the storms they have weathered as these rents have done ? They are proof-sheets which need no correction. Here goes lumber from the Maine woods, which did not go out to sea in the last freshet, risen four dollars on the thousand because of what did go out or was split up; pine, spruce, cedar, — first, second, third and fourth qualities, so lately all of one quality, to wave over the bear, and moose, and caribou. Next rolls Thomaston lime, a prime lot, which will get far among the hills before it gets slacked. These rags in bales, of all hues and qualities, the lowest condition to which cotton and linen descend, the final result of dress, — of patterns which are now no longer cried up, unless it be in Milwaukee, as those splendid articles, English, French, or American prints, ginghams, muslins, etc., gathered from all quarters both

of fashion and poverty, going to become paper of
one color or a few shades only, on which forsooth
will be written tales of real life, high and low, and
founded on fact! This closed car smells of salt
fish, the strong New England and commercial scent,
reminding me of the Grand Banks and the fisheries.
Who has not seen a salt fish, thoroughly cured for
this world, so that nothing can spoil it, and putting
the perseverance of the saints to the blush? with
which you may sweep or pave the streets, and split
your kindlings, and the teamster shelter himself
and his lading against sun, wind, and rain behind it,
— and the trader, as a Concord trader once did,
hang it up by his door for a sign when he commences business, until at last his oldest customer
cannot tell surely whether it be animal, vegetable,
or mineral, and yet it shall be as pure as a snow-
flake, and if it be put into a pot and boiled, will
come out an excellent dun fish for a Saturday's
dinner. Next Spanish hides, with the tails still
preserving their twist and the angle of elevation
they had when the oxen that wore them were ca-
reering over the pampas of the Spanish main, — a
type of all obstinacy, and evincing how almost hope-
less and incurable are all constitutional vices. I
confess, that practically speaking, when I have
learned a man's real disposition, I have no hopes of
changing it for the better or worse in this state of
existence. As the Orientals say, " A cur's tail may
be warmed, and pressed, and bound round with liga-
tures, and after a twelve years' labor bestowed upon

it, still it will retain its natural form." The only effectual cure for such inveteracies as these tails exhibit is to make glue of them, which I believe is what is usually done with them, and then they will stay put and stick. Here is a hogshead of molasses or of brandy directed to John Smith, Cuttingsville, Vermont, some trader among the Green Mountains, who imports for the farmers near his clearing, and now perchance stands over his bulk-head and thinks of the last arrivals on the coast, how they may affect the price for him, telling his customers this moment, as he has told them twenty times before this morning, that he expects some by the next train of prime quality. It is advertised in the " Cuttingsville Times."

While these things go up other things come down. Warned by the whizzing sound, I look up from my book and see some tall pine, hewn on far northern hills, which has winged its way over the Green Mountains and the Connecticut, shot like an arrow through the township within ten minutes, and scarce another eye beholds it ; going

> " To be the mast
> Of some great ammiral." [1]

And hark ! here comes the cattle train bearing the cattle of a thousand hills, sheepcots, stables, and cow-yards in the air, drovers with their sticks, and shepherd boys in the midst of their flocks, all but the mountain pastures, whirled along like leaves blown from the mountains by the September gales.

[1] Milton: *Paradise Lost*, i. 293, 294.

The air is filled with the bleating of calves and sheep, and the hustling of oxen, as if a pastoral valley were going by. When the old bell-wether at the head rattles his bell, the mountains do indeed skip like rams and the little hills like lambs. A car-load of drovers, too, in the midst, on a level with their droves now, their vocation gone, but still clinging to their useless sticks as their badge of office. But their dogs, where are they? It is a stampede to them; they are quite thrown out; they have lost the scent. Methinks I hear them barking behind the Peterboro' Hills, or panting up the western slope of the Green Mountains. They will not be in at the death. Their vocation, too, is gone. Their fidelity and sagacity are below par now. They will slink back to their kennels in disgrace, or perchance run wild and strike a league with the wolf and the fox. So is your pastoral life whirled past and away. But the bell rings, and I must get off the track and let the cars go by; —

> What's the railroad to me?
> I never go to see
> Where it ends.
> It fills a few hollows,
> And makes banks for the swallows,
> It sets the sand a-blowing,
> And the blackberries a-growing,

but I cross it like a cart-path in the woods. I will not have my eyes put out and my ears spoiled by its smoke and steam and hissing.

Now that the cars are gone by and all the restless world with them, and the fishes in the pond no longer feel their rumbling, I am more alone than ever. For the rest of the long afternoon, perhaps, my meditations are interrupted only by the faint rattle of a carriage or team along the distant highway.

Sometimes, on Sundays, I heard the bells, the Lincoln, Acton, Bedford, or Concord bell, when the wind was favorable, a faint, sweet, and, as it were, natural melody, worth importing into the wilderness. At a sufficient distance over the woods this sound acquires a certain vibratory hum, as if the pine needles in the horizon were the strings of a harp which it swept. All sound heard at the greatest possible distance produces one and the same effect, a vibration of the universal lyre, just as the intervening atmosphere makes a distant ridge of earth interesting to our eyes by the azure tint it imparts to it. There came to me in this case a melody which the air had strained, and which had conversed with every leaf and needle of the wood, that portion of the sound which the elements had taken up and modulated and echoed from vale to vale. The echo is, to some extent, an original sound, and therein is the magic and charm of it. It is not merely a repetition of what was worth repeating in the bell, but partly the voice of the wood; the same trivial words and notes sung by a wood-nymph.

At evening, the distant lowing of some cow in

the horizon beyond the woods sounded sweet and melodious, and at first I would mistake it for the voices of certain minstrels by whom I was sometimes serenaded, who might be straying over hill and dale ; but soon I was not unpleasantly disappointed when it was prolonged into the cheap and natural music of the cow. I do not mean to be satirical, but to express my appreciation of those youths' singing, when I state that I perceived clearly that it was akin to the music of the ccw, and they were at length one articulation of Nature.

Regularly at half-past seven, in one part of the summer, after the evening train had gone by, the whippoorwills chanted their vespers for half an hour, sitting on a stump by my door, or upon the ridge-pole of the house. They would begin to sing almost with as much precision as a clock, within five minutes of a particular time, referred to the setting of the sun, every evening. I had a rare opportunity to become acquainted with their habits. Sometimes I heard four or five at once in different parts of the wood, by accident one a bar behind another, and so near me that I distinguished not only the cluck after each note, but often that singular buzzing sound like a fly in a spider's web, only proportionally louder. Sometimes one would circle round and round me in the woods a few feet distant as if tethered by a string, when probably I was near its eggs. They sang at intervals throughout the night, and were again as musical as ever just before and about dawn.

When other birds are still, the screech owls take up the strain, like mourning women their ancient u-lu-lu.[1] Their dismal scream is truly Ben Jonsonian.[2] Wise midnight hags! It is no honest and blunt tu-whit tu-who of the poets, but, without jesting, a most solemn graveyard ditty, the mutual consolations of suicide lovers remembering the pangs and the delights of supernal love in the infernal groves. Yet I love to hear their wailing, their doleful responses, trilled along the woodside; reminding me sometimes of music and singing-birds; as if it were the dark and tearful side of music, the regrets and sighs that would fain be sung. They are the spirits, the low spirits and melancholy forebodings, of fallen souls that once in human shape night-walked the earth and did the deeds of darkness, now expiating their sins with their wailing hymns or threnodies in the scenery of their transgressions. They give me a new sense of the variety and capacity of that nature which is our common dwelling.   *Oh-o-o-o-o that I never had been bor-r-r-r-n!* sighs one on this side of the pond, and circles with the restlessness of despair to some new perch on the gray oaks.   Then — *that I never had been bor-r-r-r-n!* echoes another on the farther side with tremulous sincerity, and — *bor-r-r-r-n!* comes faintly from far in the Lincoln woods.

[1] The simple form of mourning, an elemental succession of sounds, which both in Greek and Latin gave rise to nouns **and** verbs descriptive of mourning.

[2] As in *The Masque of Queens.*

I was also serenaded by a hooting owl. Near at hand you could fancy it the most melancholy sound in Nature, as if she meant by this to stereotype and make permanent in her choir the dying moans of a human being, — some poor weak relic of mortality who has left hope behind, and howls like an animal, yet with human sobs, on entering the dark valley, made more awful by a certain gurgling melodiousness, — I find myself beginning with the letters gl when I try to imitate it, — expressive of a mind which has reached the gelatinous mildewy stage in the mortification of all healthy and courageous thought. It reminded me of ghouls and idiots and insane howlings. But now one answers from far woods in a strain made really melodious by distance, — *Hoo hoo hoo, hoorer hoo ;* and indeed for the most part it suggested only pleasing associations, whether heard by day or night, summer or winter.

I rejoice that there are owls. Let them do the idiotic and maniacal hooting for men. It is a sound admirably suited to swamps and twilight woods which no day illustrates, suggesting a vast and undeveloped nature which men have not recognized. They represent the stark twilight and unsatisfied thoughts which all have. All day the sun has shone on the surface of some savage swamp, where the single spruce stands hung with usnea lichens, and small hawks circulate above, and the chicadee .isps amid the evergreens, and the partridge and rabbit skulk beneath ; but now a more dismal and fitting day dawns, and a different race of creatures awakes to express the meaning of Nature there.

Late in the evening I heard the distant rumbling of wagons over bridges, — a sound heard farther than almost any other at night, — the baying of dogs, and sometimes again the lowing of some disconsolate cow in a distant barn-yard. In the mean while all the shore rang with the trump of bullfrogs, the sturdy spirits of ancient wine-bibbers and wassailers, still unrepentant, trying to sing a catch in their Stygian lake, — if the Walden nymphs will pardon the comparison, for though there are almost no weeds, there are frogs there, — who would fain keep up the hilarious rules of their old festal tables, though their voices have waxed hoarse and solemnly grave, mocking at mirth, and the wine has lost its flavor, and become only liquor to distend their paunches, and sweet intoxication never comes to drown the memory of the past, but mere saturation and waterloggedness and distention. The most aldermanic, with his chin upon a heart-leaf, which serves for a napkin to his drooling chaps, under this northern shore quaffs a deep draught of the once scorned water, and passes round the cup with the ejaculation *tr-r-r-oonk, tr-r-r-oonk, tr-r-r-oonk!* and straightway comes over the water from some distant cove the same password repeated, where the next in seniority and girth has gulped down to his mark ; and when this observance has made the circuit of the shores, then ejaculates the master of ceremonies, with satisfaction, *tr-r-r-oonk!* and each

in his turn repeats the same down to the least dis-
tended, leakiest, and flabbiest paunched, that there
be no mistake ; and then the bowl goes round again
and again, until the sun disperses the morning mist,
and only the patriarch is not under the pond, but
vainly bellowing *troonk* from time to time, and paus-
ing for a reply.

I am not sure that I ever heard the sound of
cock-crowing from my clearing, and I thought that
it might be worth the while to keep a cockerel for
his music merely, as a singing-bird. The note of
this once wild Indian pheasant is certainly the most
remarkable of any bird's, and if they could be naturalized without being domesticated, it would soon
become the most famous sound in our woods, surpassing the clangor of the goose and the hooting of
the owl ; and then imagine the cackling of the hens
to fill the pauses when their lords' clarions rested !
No wonder that man added this bird to his tame
stock, — to say nothing of the eggs and drumsticks.
To walk in a winter morning in a wood where
these birds abounded, their native woods, and hear
the wild cockerels crow on the trees, clear and shrill
for miles over the resounding earth, drowning the
feeble notes of other birds, — think of it ! It would
put nations on the alert. Who would not be early
to rise, and rise earlier and earlier every successive
day of his life, till he became unspeakably healthy,
wealthy, and wise ? This foreign bird's note is celebrated by the poets of all countries along with the
notes of their native songsters. All climates agree

21

with brave Chanticleer. He is more indigenous even than the natives. His health is ever good, his lungs are sound, his spirits never flag. Even the sailor on the Atlantic and Pacific is awakened by his voice ; but its shrill sound never roused my slumbers. I kept neither dog, cat, cow, pig, nor hens, so that you would have said there was a deficiency of domestic sounds ; neither the churn, nor the spinning wheel, nor even the singing of the kettle, nor the hissing of the urn, nor children crying, to comfort one. An old-fashioned man would have lost his senses or died of *ennui* before this. Not even rats in the wall, for they were starved out, or rather were never baited in, — only squirrels on the roof and under the floor, a whippoorwill on the ridgepole, a blue-jay screaming beneath the window, a hare or woodchuck under the house, a screech-owl or a cat-owl behind it, a flock of wild geese or a laughing loon on the pond, and a fox to bark in the night. Not even a lark or an oriole, those mild plantation birds, ever visited my clearing. No cockerels to crow nor hens to cackle in the yard. No yard ! but unfenced Nature reaching up to your very sills. A young forest growing up under your windows, and wild sumachs and blackberry vines breaking through into your cellar ; sturdy pitchpines rubbing and creaking against the shingles for want of room, their roots reaching quite under the house. Instead of a scuttle or a blind blown off in the gale, — a pine-tree snapped off or torn up by the roots behind your house for fuel. Instead of

no path to the front-yard gate in the Great Snow,
— no gate, — no front yard, — and no path to the
civilized world!

II.

BRUTE NEIGHBORS.

WHY do precisely these objects which we behold
make a world? Why has man just these species
of animals for his neighbors; as if nothing but a
mouse could have filled this crevice? I suspect
that Pilpay & Co.[1] have put animals to their best
use, for they are all beasts of burden, in a sense,
made to carry some portion of our thoughts.

The mice which haunted my house were not the
common ones, which are said to have been introduced into the country, but a wild native kind not
found in the village. I sent one to a distinguished
naturalist, and it interested him much. When I
was building, one of these had its nest underneath
the house, and before I had laid the second floor,
and swept out the shavings, would come out regularly at lunch time and pick up the crumbs at my
feet. It probably had never seen a man before;
and it soon became quite familiar, and would run
over my shoes and up my clothes. It could readily
ascend the sides of the room by short impulses, like

[1] That is, the fable-writers, of whom Pilpay, a Brahmin
enjoys in the East the distinction which has been given to Æsop
in the West.

a squirrel, which it resembled in its motions.   At length, as I leaned with my elbow on the bench one day, it ran up my clothes, and along my sleeve, and round and round the paper which held my dinner, while I kept the latter close, and dodged and played at bo-peep with it ; and when at last I held still a piece of cheese between my thumb and finger, it came and nibbled it, sitting in my hand, and afterward cleaned its face and paws, like a fly, and walked away.

A phœbe soon built in my shed, and a robin for protection in a pine which grew against the house. In June the partridge (*Tetrao umbellus*), which is so shy a bird, led her brood past my windows, from the woods in the rear to the front of my house, clucking and calling to them like a hen, and in all her behavior proving herself the hen of the woods. The young suddenly disperse on your approach, at a signal from the mother, as if a whirlwind had swept them away, and they so exactly resemble the dried leaves and twigs that many a traveller has placed his foot in the midst of a brood, and heard the whir of the old bird as she flew off, and her anxious calls and mewing, or seen her trail her wings to attract his attention, without suspecting their neighborhood.   The parent will sometimes roll and spin round before you in such a dishabille, that you cannot, for a few moments, detect what kind of creature it is.   The young squat still and flat, often running their heads under a leaf, and mind only their mother's directions given from a distance, nor

will your approach make them run again and betray themselves. You may even tread on them, or
have your eyes on them for a minute, without dis-
covering them. I have held them in my open hand
at such a time, and still their only care, obedient to
their mother and their instinct, was to squat there
without fear or trembling. So perfect is this instinct, that once, when I had laid them on the
leaves again, and one accidentally fell on its side, it
was found with the rest in exactly the same position ten minutes afterward. They are not callow
like the young of most birds, but more perfectly
developed and precocious even than chickens. The
remarkably adult yet innocent expression of their
open and serene eyes is very memorable. All intelligence seems reflected in them. They suggest
not merely the purity of infancy, but a wisdom
clarified by experience. Such an eye was not born
when the bird was, but is coeval with the sky it re-
flects. The woods do not yield another such a
gem. The traveller does not often look into such
a limpid well. The ignorant or reckless sportsman
often shoots the parent at such a time, and leaves
these innocents to fall a prey to some prowling
beast or bird, or gradually mingle with the decaying
leaves which they so much resemble. It is said
that when hatched by a hen they will directly disperse on some alarm, and so are lost, for they never
hear the mother's call which gathers them again.
These were my hens and chickens.

It is remarkable how many creatures live wild

and free, though secret, in the woods, and still sus
tain themselves in the neighborhood of towns, suspected by hunters only. How retired the otter
manages to live here! He grows to be four feet
long, as big as a small boy, perhaps without any
human being getting a glimpse of him. I formerly
saw the raccoon in the woods behind where my
house is built, and probably still heard their whin-
nering at night. Commonly I rested an hour or
two in the shade at noon, after planting, and ate
my lunch, and read a little by a spring which was
the source of a swamp and of a brook, oozing from
under Brister's Hill, half a mile from my field.
The approach to this was through a succession of
descending grassy hollows, full of young pitch-
pines, into a larger wood about the swamp. There,
in a very secluded and shaded spot, under a spreading white-pine, there was yet a clean, firm sward to
sit on. I had dug out the spring and made a well
of clear gray water, where I could dip up a pailful
without roiling it, and thither I went for this purpose almost every day in midsummer, when the
pond was warmest. Thither, too, the wood-cock
led her brood, to probe the mud for worms, flying
but a foot above them down the bank, while they
ran in a troop beneath ; but at last, spying me, she
would leave her young and circle round and round
me, nearer and nearer till within four or five feet,
pretending broken wings and legs, to attract my
attention, and get off her young, who would already
have taken up their march, with faint wiry peep,

single file through the swamp, as she directed. Or
I heard the peep of the young when I could not see
the parent bird. There, too, the turtle-doves sat
over the spring, or fluttered from bough to bough
of the soft white-pines over my head; or the red
squirrel, coursing down the nearest bough, was particularly familiar and inquisitive. You only need
sit still long enough in some attractive spot in the
woods that all its inhabitants may exhibit themselves to you by turns.

I was witness to events of a less peaceful character. One day when I went out to my wood-pile,
or rather my pile of stumps, I observed two large
ants, the one red, the other much larger, nearly
half an inch long, and black, fiercely contending
with one another. Having once got hold, they
never let go, but struggled and wrestled and rolled
on the chips incessantly. Looking farther, I was
surprised to find that the chips were covered with
such combatants, that it was not a *duellum*, but a
bellum, a war between two races of ants, the red
always pitted against the black, and frequently
two red ones to one black. The legions of these
Myrmidons covered all the hills and vales in my
wood-yard, and the ground was already strewn with
the dead and dying, both red and black. It was
the only battle which I have ever witnessed, the
only battle-field I ever trod while the battle was
raging; internecine war; the red republicans on
the one hand, and the black imperialists on the
other. On every side they were engaged in deadly

combat, yet without any noise that I could hear, and human soldiers never fought so resolutely. I watched a couple that were fast locked in each other's embraces, in a little sunny valley amid the chips, now at noon-day prepared to fight till the sun went down, or life went out. The smaller red champion had fastened himself like a vise to his adversary's front, and through all the tumblings on that field never for an instant ceased to gnaw at one of his feelers near the root, having already caused the other to go by the board; while the stronger black one dashed him from side to side, and, as I saw on looking nearer, had already divested him of several of his members. They fought with more pertinacity than bull-dogs. Neither manifested the least disposition to retreat. It was evident that their battle-cry was Conquer or die. In the mean while there came along a single red ant on the hillside of this valley, evidently full of excitement, who either had dispatched his foe, or had not yet taken part in the battle; probably the latter, for he had lost none of his limbs; whose mother had charged him to return with his shield or upon it. Or perchance he was some Achilles, who had nourished his wrath apart, and had now come to avenge or rescue his Patroclus.[1] He saw this unequal combat from afar, — for the blacks

[1] In Homer's *Iliad*, Achilles, in a sullen wrath against Agamemnon, remains in his tent and refuses to engage in battle, until Patroclus, his friend whom he armed, has been killed by Hector, when he goes out to avenge the death on the Trojan chief.

were nearly twice the size of the red, — he drew near with rapid pace till he stood on his guard within half an inch of the combatants ; then, watching his opportunity, he sprang upon the black warrior, and commenced his operations near the root of his right fore-leg, leaving the foe to select among his own members ; and so there were three united for life, as if a new kind of attraction had been invented which. put all other locks and cements to shame. I should not have wondered by this time to find that they had their respective musical bands stationed on some eminent chip, and playing their national airs the while, to excite the slow and cheer the dying combatants. I was myself excited somewhat even as if they had been men. The more you think of it, the less the difference. And certainly there is not the fight recorded in Concord history, at least, if in the history of America, that will bear a moment's comparison with this, whether for the numbers engaged in it, or for the patriotism and heroism displayed. For numbers and for carnage it was an Austerlitz or Dresden. Concord Fight ! Two killed on the patriots' side, and Luther Blanchard wounded ! Why here every ant was a Buttrick, — " Fire ! for God's sake fire ! " — and thousands shared the fate of Davis and Hosmer. There was not one hireling there. I have no doubt that it was a principle they fought for, as much as our ancestors, and not to avoid a threepenny tax on their tea ; and the results of this battle will be as important and memorable to those whom it concerns as those of the battle of Bunker Hill, at least.

I took up the chip on which the three I have particularly described were struggling, carried it into my house, and placed it under a tumbler on my window-sill, in order to see the issue. Holding a microscope to the first-mentioned red ant, I saw that, though he was assiduously gnawing at the near fore-leg of his enemy, having severed his remaining feeler, his own breast was all torn away, exposing what vitals he had there to the jaws of the black warrior, whose breast-plate was apparently too thick for him to pierce; and the dark carbuncles of the sufferer's eyes shone with ferocity such as war only could excite. They struggled half an hour longer under the tumbler, and when I looked again the black soldier had severed the heads of his foes from their bodies, and the still living heads were hanging on either side of him like ghastly trophies at his saddle-bow, still apparently as firmly fastened as ever, and he was endeavoring with feeble struggles, being without feelers and with only the remnant of a leg, and I know not how many other wounds, to divest himself of them; which at length, after half an hour more, he accomplished. I raised the glass, and he went off over the window-sill in that crippled state. Whether he finally survived that combat, and spent the remainder of his days in some Hotel des Invalides,[1] I do not know; but I thought that his in-

[1] The Hotel des Invalides in Paris was founded in 1670, by

lustry would not be worth much thereafter. I never learned which party was victorious, nor the cause of the war ; but I felt for the rest of that day as if I had had my feelings excited and harrowed by witnessing the struggle, the ferocity and carnage, of a human battle before my door.

Kirby and Spence [1] tell us that the battles of ants have long been celebrated and the date of them recorded, though they say that Huber is the only modern author who appears to have witnessed them. " Æneas Sylvius," say they, " after giving a very circumstantial account of one contested with great obstinacy by a great and small species on the trunk of a pear-tree," adds that " ' This action was fought in the pontificate of Eugenius the Fourth, in the presence of Nicholas Pistoriensis, an eminent law-yer, who related the whole history of the battle with the greatest fidelity.' A similar engagement between great and small ants is recorded by Olaus Magnus, in which the small ones, being victorious, are said to have buried the bodies of their own sol-diers, but left those of their giant enemies a prey to the birds. This event happened previous to the expulsion of the tyrant Christiern the Second from Sweden." The battle which I witnessed took place in the Presidency of Polk, five years before the passage of Webster's Fugitive-Slave Bill.

Louis XIV., as a home for disabled and infirm soldiers, and in a crypt under the church connected with it is the tomb of Na-poleon.

[1] In their *Introduction to Entomology.*

Many a village Bose, fit only to course a mud-turtle in a victualling cellar, sported his heavy quarters in the woods, without the knowledge of his master, and ineffectually smelled at old fox burrows and woodchucks' holes; led perchance by some slight cur which nimbly threaded the wood, and might still inspire a natural terror in its denizens; — now far behind his guide, barking like a canine bull toward some small squirrel which had treed itself for scrutiny, then, cantering off, bending the bushes with his weight, imagining that he is on the track of some stray member of the jerbilla family. Once I was surprised to see a cat walking along the stony shore of the pond, for they rarely wander so far from home. The surprise was mutual. Nevertheless the most domestic cat, which has lain on a rug all her days, appears quite at home in the woods, and, by her sly and stealthy behavior, proves herself more native there than the regular inhabitants. Once, when berrying, I met with a cat with young kittens in the woods, quite wild, and they all, like their mother, had their backs up and were fiercely spitting at me. A few years before I lived in the woods there was what was called a " winged cat" in one of the farmhouses in Lincoln nearest the pond, Mr. Gillian Baker's. When I called to see her in June, 1842, she was gone a-hunting in the woods, as was her wont (I am not sure whether it was a male or female, and so use the more common pronoun), but her mistress told me that she came into the neigh-

borhood a little more than a year before, in April,
and was finally taken into their house; that she was
of a dark brownish-gray color, with a white spot
on her throat, and white feet, and had a large bushy
tail like a fox; that in the winter the fur grew thick
and flatted out along her sides, forming strips ten
or twelve inches long by two and a half wide, and
under her chin like a muff, the upper side loose, the
under matted like felt, and in the spring these appendages dropped off. They gave me a pair of her
" wings," which I keep still. There is no appearance of a membrane about them. Some thought it
was part flying-squirrel or some other wild animal,
which is not impossible, for, according to natura-
lists, prolific hybrids have been produced by the
union of the marten and domestic cat. This would
have been the right kind of cat for me to keep, if I
had kept any; for why should not a poet's cat be
winged as well as his horse?

In the fall the loon (*Colymbus glacialis*) came, as
usual, to moult and bathe in the pond, making the
woods ring with his wild laughter before I had
risen   At rumor of his arrival all the Mill-dam
sportsmen are on the alert, in gigs and on foot, two
by two and three by three, with patent rifles and
conical balls and spyglasses. They come rustling
through the woods like autumn leaves, at least ten
men to one loon. Some station themselves on this
side of the pond, some on that, for the poor bird
cannot be omnipresent; if he dive here he must
come up there. But now the kind October wind

rises, rustling the leaves and rippling the surface of the water, so that no loon can be heard or seen, though his foes sweep the pond with spy-glasses, and make the woods resound with their discharges. The waves generously rise and dash angrily, taking sides with all waterfowl, and our sportsmen must beat a retreat to town and shop and unfinished jobs. But they were too often successful. When I went to get a pail of water early in the morning I frequently saw this stately bird sailing out of my cove within a few rods. If I endeavored to overtake him in a boat, in order to see how he would manoeuvre, he would dive and be completely lost, so that I did not discover him again, sometimes, till the latter part of the day. But I was more than a match for him on the surface. He commonly went off in a rain.

As I was paddling along the north shore one very calm October afternoon, for such days especially they settle on to the lakes, like the milkweed down, having looked in vain over the pond for a loon, suddenly one, sailing out from the shore toward the middle a few rods in front of me, set up his wild laugh and betrayed himself. I pursued with a paddle and he dived, but when he came up I was nearer than before. He dived again, but I miscalculated the direction he would take, and we were fifty rods apart when he came to the surface this time, for I had helped to widen the interval; and again he laughed long and loud, and with more reason than before. He manoeuvred so cunningly that I could not get within half a dozen rods of him. Each time, when he came to the surface, turning his head this way and that, he coolly surveyed the water and the land, and apparently chose his course so that he might come up where there was the widest expanse of water and at the greatest distance from the boat. It was surprising how quickly he made up his mind and put his resolve into execution. He led me at once to the widest part of the pond, and could not be driven from it. While he was thinking one thing in his brain, I was endeavoring to divine his thought in mine. It was a pretty game, played on the smooth surface of the pond, a man against a loon. Suddenly your adversary's checker disappears beneath the board, and the problem is to place yours nearest to where his will appear again. Sometimes he would come up unexpectedly on the opposite side of me, having apparently passed directly under the boat. So long-winded was he and so unweariable, that when he had swum farthest he would immediately plunge again, nevertheless; and then no wit could divine where in the deep pond, beneath the smooth surface, he might be speeding his way like a fish, for he had time and ability to visit the bottom of the pond in its deepest part. It is said that loons have been caught in the New York lakes eighty feet beneath the surface, with hooks set for trout, — though Walden is deeper than that. How surprised must the fishes be to see this ungainly visitor from another sphere speeding his way amid their schools !

Yet he appeared to know his course as surely under water as on the surface, and swam much faster there. Once or twice I saw a ripple where he approached the surface, just put his head out to reconnoitre, and instantly dived again. I found that it was as well for me to rest on my oars and wait his reappearing as to endeavor to calculate where he would rise; for again and again, when I was straining my eyes over the surface one way, I would suddenly be startled by his unearthly laugh behind me. But why, after displaying so much cunning, did he invariably betray himself the moment he came up by that loud laugh? Did not his white breast enough betray him? He was indeed a silly loon, I thought. I could commonly hear the plash of the water when he came up, and so also detected him. But after an hour he seemed as fresh as ever, dived as willingly and swam yet farther than at first. It was surprising to see how serenely he sailed off with unruffled breast when he came to the surface, doing all the work with his webbed feet beneath. His usual note was this demoniac laughter, yet somewhat like that of a waterfowl; but occasionally, when he had balked me most successfully and come up a long way off, he uttered a long-drawn unearthly howl, probably more like that of a wolf than any bird; as when a beast puts his muzzle to the ground and deliberately howls. This was his looning, — perhaps the wildest sound that is ever heard here, making the woods ring far and wide. I concluded that he laughed in derision of my efforts, confident of his own resources. Though the sky was by this time overcast, the pond was so smooth that I could see where he broke the surface when I did not hear him. His white breast, the stillness of the air, and the smoothness of the water were all against him. At length, having come up fifty rods off, he uttered one of those prolonged howls, as if calling on the god of loons to aid him, and immediately there came a wind from the east and rippled the surface, and filled the whole air with misty rain, and I was impressed as if it were the prayer of the loon answered, and his god was angry with me ; and so I left him disappearing far away on the tumultuous surface.

For hours, in fall days, I watched the ducks cunningly tack and veer and hold the middle of the pond, far from the sportsman ; tricks which they will have less need to practise in Louisiana bayous. When compelled to rise they would sometimes circle round and round and over the pond at a considerable height, from which they could easily see to other ponds and the river, like black motes in the sky ; and, when I thought they had gone off thither long since, they would settle down by a slanting flight of a quarter of a mile on to a distant part which was left free ; but what beside safety they got by sailing in the middle of Walden I do not know, unless they love its water for the same reason that I do.

22

III.

THE HIGHLAND LIGHT.

THIS light-house, known to mariners as the Cape Cod or Highland Light, is one of our " primary sea-coast lights," and is usually the first seen by those approaching the entrance of Massachusetts Bay from Europe. It is forty-three miles from Cape Ann Light, and forty-one from Boston Light. It stands about twenty rods from the edge of the bank, which is here formed of clay. I borrowed the plane and square, level and dividers, of a carpenter who was shingling a barn near by, and using one of those shingles made, of a mast, contrived a rude sort of quadrant, with pins for sights and pivots, and got the angle of elevation of the Bank opposite the light-house, and with a couple of codlines the length of its slope, and so measured its height on the shingle. It rises one hundred and ten feet above its immediate base, or about one hundred and twenty-three feet above mean low water. Graham, who has carefully surveyed the extremity of the Cape, makes it one hundred and thirty feet. The mixed sand and clay lay at an angle of forty degrees with the horizon, where I measured it, but the clay is generally much steeper. No cow nor hen ever gets down it. Half a mile far ther south the bank is fifteen or twenty-five feet higher, and that appeared to be the highest land in

North Truro. Even this vast clay bank is fast wearing away. Small streams of water trickling down it at intervals of two or three rods have left the intermediate clay in the form of steep Gothic roofs fifty feet high or more, the ridges as sharp and rugged-looking as rocks; and in one place the bank is curiously eaten out in the form of a large semicircular crater.

According to the light-house keeper, the Cape is wasting here on both sides, though most on the eastern. In some places it had lost many rods within the last year, and, erelong, the light-house must be moved. We calculated, *from his data,* how soon the Cape would be quite worn away at this point, " for," said he, " I can remember sixty years back." We were even more surprised at this last announcement — that is, at the slow waste of life and energy in our informant, for we had taken him to be not more than forty — than at the rapid wasting of the Cape, and we thought that he stood a fair chance to outlive the former.

Between this October and June of the next year, I found that the bank had lost about forty feet in one place, opposite the light-house, and it was cracked more than forty feet farther from the edge at the last date, the shore being strewn with the recent rubbish. But I judged that generally it was not wearing away here at the rate of more than six feet annually. Any conclusions drawn from the observations of a few years or one generation only are likely to prove false, and the Cape may balk expectation by its durability. In some places even a wrecker's foot-path down the bank lasts several years. One old inhabitant told us that when the light-house was built, in 1798, it was calculated that it would stand forty-five years, allowing the bank to waste one length of fence each year, " but," said he, " there it is " (or rather another near the same site, about twenty rods from the edge of the bank).

The sea is not gaining on the Cape everywhere, for one man told me of a vessel wrecked long ago on the north of Provincetown whose " *bones* " (this was his word) are still visible many rods within the present line of the beach, half buried in sand. Perchance they lie alongside the *timbers* of a whale. The general statement of the inhabitants is, that the Cape is wasting on both sides, but extending itself on particular points on the south and west, as at Chatham and Monomoy Beaches, and at Billingsgate, Long, and Race Points. James Freeman stated in his day that above three miles had been added to Monomoy Beach during the previous fifty years, and it is said to be still extending as fast as ever. A writer in the " Massachusetts Magazine," in the last century, tells us that " when the English first settled upon the Cape, there was an island off Chatham, at three leagues' distance, called Webbs' Island, containing twenty acres, covered with red-cedar or savin. The inhabitants of Nantucket used to carry wood from it ; " but he adds that in his day a large rock alone marked the spot, and the water was six fathoms deep there. The entrance to Nauset Harbor, which was once in Eastham, has now travelled south into Orleans. The islands in Wellfleet Harbor once formed a continuous beach, though now small vessels pass between them. And so of many other parts of this coast.

Perhaps what the Ocean takes from one part of the Cape it gives to another, — robs Peter to pay Paul. On the eastern side the sea appears to be everywhere encroaching on the land. Not only the land is undermined, and its ruins carried off by currents, but the sand is blown from the beach directly up the steep bank where it is one hundred and fifty feet high, and covers the original surface there many feet deep. If you sit on the edge you will have ocular demonstration of this by soon getting your eyes full. Thus the bank preserves its height as fast as it is worn away. This sand is steadily travelling westward at a rapid rate, " more than a hundred yards," says one writer, within the memory of inhabitants now living; so that in some places peat-meadows are buried deep under the sand, and the peat is cut through it; and in one place a large peat-meadow has made its appearance on the shore in the bank covered many feet deep, and peat has been cut there. This accounts for that great pebble of peat which we saw in the surf. The old oysterman had told us that many years ago he lost a " crittur " by her being mired in a swamp near the Atlantic side east of his house, and twenty years ago he lost the swamp itself entirely, but has since seen signs of it appearing on the beach. He also said that he had seen cedar stumps "as big as cart-wheels" (!) on the bottom of the Bay, three miles off Billingsgate Point, when leaning over the side of his boat in pleasant weather, and that that was dry land not long ago. Another told us that a log canoe known to have been buried many years before on the Bay side at East Harbor in Truro, where the Cape is extremely narrow, appeared at length on the Atlantic side, the Cape having rolled over it, and an old woman said, — "Now, you see, it is true what I told you, that the Cape is moving."

The bars along the coast shift with every storm, and in many places there is occasionally none at all. We ourselves observed the effect of a single storm with a high tide in the night, in July, 1855. It moved the sand on the beach opposite the lighthouse to the depth of six feet and three rods in width as far as we could see north and south, and carried it bodily off no one knows exactly where, laying bare in one place a large rock five feet high which was invisible before, and narrowing the beach to that extent. There is usually, as I have said, no bathing on the back side of the Cape, on account of the undertow, but when we were there last, the sea had, three months before, cast up a bar near this light-house, two miles long and ten rods wide, over which the tide did not flow, leaving a narrow cove, then a quarter of a mile long, between it and the shore, which afforded excellent bathing. This cove had from time to time been closed up as the bar travelled northward, in one instance imprisoning four or five hundred whiting and cod, which died there, and the water as often turned fresh and finally gave place to sand. This bar, the inhabitants assured us, might be wholly removed, and the water six feet deep there in two or three days.

The light-house keeper said that when the wind blowed strong on to the shore, the waves ate fast into the bank, but when it blowed off they took no sand away ; for in the former case the wind heaped up the surface of the water next to the beach, and to preserve its equilibrium a strong undertow immediately set back again into the sea which carried with it the sand and whatever else was in the way, and left the beach hard to walk on ; but in the latter case the undertow set on, and carried the sand with it, so that it was particularly difficult for shipwrecked men to get to land when the wind blowed on to the shore, but easier when it blowed off. This undertow, meeting the next surface wave on the bar which itself has made, forms part of the dam over which the latter breaks, as over an upright wall. The sea thus plays with the land, holding a sand-bar in its mouth a while before it swallows it, as a cat plays with a mouse ; but the fatal gripe is sure to come at last. The sea sends its rapacious east wind to rob the land, but before the former has got far with its prey, the land sends its honest west wind to recover some of its own. But, according to Lieutenant Davis, the forms, extent, and distribution of sand-bars and banks are principally determined, not by winds and waves, but by tides.

Our host said that you would be surprised if you were on the beach when the wind blew a hurricane directly on to it, to see that none of the drift-wood came ashore, but all was carried directly northward and parallel with the shore as fast as a man can walk, by the inshore current, which sets strongly in that direction at flood tide. The strongest swimmers also are carried along with it, and never gain an inch toward the beach. Even a large rock has been moved half a mile northward along the beach. He assured us that the sea was never still on the back side of the Cape, but ran commonly as high as your head, so that a great part of the time you could not launch a boat there, and even in the calmest weather the waves run six or eight feet up the beach, though then you could get off on a plank. Champlain and Pourtincourt could not land here in 1606, on account of the swell (*la houlle*), yet the savages came off to them in a canoe. In the Sieur de la Borde's " Relation des Caraibes," my edition of which was published at Amsterdam in 1711, at page 530 he says : —

" Couroumon a Caraibe, also a star [*i. e.* a god], makes the great *lames à la mer*, and overturns canoes. *Lames à la mer* are the long *vagues* which are not broken (*entrecoupees*), and such as one sees come to land all in one piece, from one end of a beach to another, so that, however little wind there may be, a shallop or a canoe could hardly land (*aborder terre*) without turning over, or being filled with water."

But on the Bay side the water even at its edge is often as smooth and still as in a pond. Commonly there are no boats used along this beach. There was a boat belonging to the Highland Light which the next keeper after he had been there a year had not launched, though he said that there was good fishing just off the shore. Generally the Life Boats cannot be used when needed. When the waves run very high it is impossible to get a boat off, however skilfully you steer it, for it will often be completely covered by the curving edge of the approaching breaker as by an arch, and so filled with water, or it will be lifted up by its bows, turned directly over backwards and all the contents spilled out. A spar thirty feet long is served in the same way.

I heard of a party who went off fishing back of Wellfleet some years ago, in two boats, in calm weather, who, when they had laden their boats with fish, and approached the land again, found such a swell breaking on it, though there was no wind, that they were afraid to enter it. At first they thought to pull for Provincetown, but night was coming on, and that was many miles distant. Their case seemed a desperate one. As often as they approached the shore and saw the terrible breakers that intervened, they were deterred. In short, they were thoroughly frightened. Finally, having thrown their fish overboard, those in one boat chose a favorable opportunity, and succeeded, by skill and good luck, in reaching the land, but they were unwilling to take the responsibility of telling the others when to come in, and as the other helmsman was inexperienced, their boat was swamped at once, yet all managed to save themselves.

Much smaller waves soon make a boat "nail-sick," as the phrase is. The keeper said that after a long and strong blow there would be three large waves, each successively larger than the last, and then no large ones for some time, and that, when they wished to land in a boat, they came in on the last and largest wave. Sir Thomas Browne (as quoted in Brand's Popular Antiquities, p. 372), on the subject of the tenth wave being "greater or more dangerous than any other," after quoting Ovid, —

> "Qui venit hic fluctus, fluctus supereminet omnes
> Posterior nono est, undecimo que prior," —

says, "Which, notwithstanding, is evidently false ; nor can it be made out either by observation either upon the shore or the ocean, as we have with diligence explored in both. And surely in vain we expect regularity in the waves of the sea, or in the particular motions thereof, as we may in its general reciprocations, whose causes are constant, and effects therefore correspondent ; whereas its fluctuations are but motions subservient, which winds, storms, shores, shelves, and every interjacency, irregulates."

We read that the Clay Pounds were so called "because vessels have had the misfortune to be pounded against it in gales of wind," which we regard as a doubtful derivation. There are small ponds here, upheld by the clay, which were formerly called the Clay Pits. Perhaps this, or Clay Pounds, is the origin of the name. Water is found in the clay quite near the surface; but we heard of one man who had sunk a well in the sand close by, "till he could see stars at noonday," without finding any. Over this bare Highland the wind has full sweep. Even in July it blows the wings over the heads of the young turkeys, which do not know enough to head against it; and in gales the doors and windows are blown in, and you must hold on to the light-house to prevent being blown into the Atlantic. They who merely keep out on the beach in a storm in the winter are sometimes rewarded by the Humane Society. If you would feel the full force of a tempest, take up your residence on the top of Mount Washington, or at the Highland Light, in Truro.

It was said in 1794 that more vessels were cast away on the east shore of Truro than anywhere in Barnstable County. Notwithstanding that this light-house has since been erected, after almost every storm we read of one or more vessels wrecked here, and sometimes more than a dozen wrecks are visible from this point at one time. The inhabitants hear the crash of vessels going to pieces as they sit round their hearths, and they commonly date from some memorable shipwreck. If the history of this beach could be written from beginning to end, it would be a thrilling page in the history of commerce.

Truro was settled in the year 1700 as *Dangerfield.* This was a very appropriate name, for I afterward read on a monument in the graveyard, near Pamet River, the following inscription : —

Sacred
to the memory of
57 citizens of Truro,
who were lost in seven
vessels, which
foundered at sea in
the memorable gale
of Oct. 3d, 1841.

Their names and ages by families were recorded on different sides of the stone. They are said to have been lost on George's Bank, and I was told that only one vessel drifted ashore on the back side of the Cape, with the boys locked into the cabin and drowned. It is said that the homes of all were " within a circuit of two miles." Twenty-eight inhabitants of Dennis were lost in the same gale ; and I read that " in one day, immediately after this storm, nearly or quite one hundred bodies were taken up and buried on Cape Cod." The Truro Insurance Company failed for want of skippers to take charge of its vessels. But the surviving inhabitants went a fishing again the next year as usual. I found that it would not do to speak of shipwrecks there, for almost every family has lost

some of its members at sea. " Who lives in that
house? " I inquired. " Three widows," was the reply.
The stranger and the inhabitant view the shore with
very different eyes. The former may have come to
see and admire the ocean in a storm ; but the latter looks on it as the scene where his nearest rel-
atives were wrecked. When I remarked to an
old wrecker partially blind, who was sitting on the
edge of the bank smoking a pipe, which he had just
lit with a match of dried beach-grass, that I supposed he liked to hear the sound of the surf, he
answered : " No, I do not like to hear the sound
of the surf." He had lost at least one son in " the
memorable gale," and could tell many a tale of the
shipwrecks which he had witnessed there.

In the year 1717 a noted pirate named Bellamy
was led on to the bar off Wellfleet by the captain
of a *snow* which he had taken, to whom he had offered his vessel again if he would pilot him into
Provincetown Harbor. Tradition says that the latter threw over a burning tar barrel in the night,
which drifted ashore, and the pirates followed it. A
storm coming on, their whole fleet was wrecked,
and more than a hundred dead bodies lay along the
shore. Six who escaped shipwreck were executed.
" At times, to this day " (1793), says the historian
of Wellfleet,[1] " there are King William and Queen
Mary's coppers picked up, and pieces of silver
called cob-money. The violence of the seas moves
the sands on the outer bar, so that at times the iron

[1] Levi Whitman, in *Mass. Hist. Soc. Coll.* 1st series, vol. iii.

caboose of the ship [that is, Bellamy's] at low ebbs
has been seen." Another tells us that, " For many
years after this shipwreck, a man of a very singular
and frightful aspect used every spring and autumn to
be seen travelling on the Cape, who was supposed
to have been one of Bellamy's crew. The pre-
sumption is that he went to some place where
money had been secreted by the pirates, to get such
a supply as his exigencies required. When he died,
many pieces of gold were found in a girdle which
he constantly wore."

As I was walking on the beach here in my last
visit, looking for shells and pebbles, just after that
storm which I have mentioned as moving the sand
to a great depth, not knowing but I might find some
cob-money, I did actually pick up a French crown
piece, worth about a dollar and six cents, near high
water mark, on the still moist sand, just under the
abrupt, caving base of the bank. It was a dark
slate color, and looked like a flat pebble, but still
bore a very distinct and handsome head of Louis
XV., and the usual legend on the reverse, *Sit
Nomen Domini Benedictum* (Blessed be the Name
of the Lord), a pleasing sentiment to read in the
sands of the sea-shore, whatever it might be stamped
on, and I also made out the date, 1741. Of course,
I thought at first that it was that same old button
which I have found so many times, but my knife
soon showed the silver. Afterwards, rambling on
the bars at low tide, I cheated my companion by
holding up round shells (*Scutellæ*) between my

fingers, whereupon he quickly stripped and came off to me.

In the Revolution, a British ship of war called the Somerset was wrecked near the Clay Pounds, and all on board, some hundreds in number, were taken prisoners. My informant said that he had never seen any mention of this in the histories, but that at any rate he knew of a silver watch, which one of those prisoners by accident left there, which was still going to tell the story. But this event is noticed by some writers.

The next summer I saw a sloop from Chatham dragging for anchors and chains just off this shore. She had her boats out at the work while she shuffled about on various tacks, and, when anything was found, drew up to hoist it on board. It is a singular employment, at which men are regularly hired and paid for their industry, to hunt to-day in pleasant weather for anchors which have been lost, — the sunken faith and hope of mariners, to which they trusted in vain ; now, perchance, it is the rusty one of some old pirate's ship or Norman fisherman, whose cable parted here two hundred years ago ; and now the best bower anchor of a Canton or a California ship, which has gone about her business. If the roadsteads of the spiritual ocean could be thus dragged, what rusty flukes of hope deceived and parted chain-cables of faith might again be windlassed aboard ! enough to sink the finder's craft, or stock new navies to the end of time. The bottom of the sea is strewn with anchors, some deeper and some shallower, and alternately covered and uncovered by the sand, perchance with a small length of iron cable still attached, — to which where is the other end? So many unconcluded tales to be continued another time. So, if we had diving-bells adapted to the spiritual deeps, we should see anchors with their cables attached, as thick as eels in vinegar, all wriggling vainly toward their holding-ground. But that is not treasure for us which another man has lost; rather it is for us to seek what no other man has found or can find, — not be Chatham men dragging for anchors.

The annals of this voracious beach! who could write them, unless it were a shipwrecked sailor? How many who have seen it have seen it only in the midst of danger and distress, the last strip of earth which their mortal eyes beheld. Think of the amount of suffering which a single strand has witnessed. The ancients would have represented it as a sea-monster with open jaws, more terrible than Scylla and Charybdis. An inhabitant of Truro told me that about a fortnight after the St. John was wrecked at Cohasset he found two bodies on the shore at the Clay Pounds. They were those of a man, and a corpulent woman. The man had thick boots on, though his head was off, but "it was alongside." It took the finder some weeks to get over the sight. Perhaps they were man and wife, and whom God had joined the ocean currents had not put asunder. Yet by what slight accidents at first may they have been associated in their drifting. Some of the bodies of those passengers were picked up far out at sea, boxed up and sunk ; some brought ashore and buried. There are more consequences to a shipwreck than the underwriters notice. The Gulf Stream may return some to their native shores, or drop them in some out-of-the-way cave of Ocean, where time and the elements will write new riddles with their bones. — But to return to land again.

In this bank, above the clay, I counted in the summer two hundred holes of the bank swallow within a space six rods long, and there were at least one thousand old birds within three times that distance, twittering over the surf. I had never associated them in my thoughts with the beach before. One little boy who had been a-birds-nesting had got eighty swallows' eggs for his share ! Tell it not to the Humane Society. There were many young birds on the clay beneath, which had tumbled out and died. Also there were many crow - blackbirds hopping about in the dry fields, and the upland plover were breeding close by the light-house. The keeper had once cut off one's wing while mowing, as she sat on her eggs there. This is also a favorite resort for gunners in the fall to shoot the golden plover. As around the shores of a pond are seen devil's-needles, butter-flies, etc., so here, to my surprise, I saw at the same season great devil's-needles of a size proportionably larger, or nearly as big as my finger, incessantly coasting up and down the edge of the bank, and butterflies also were hovering over it, and I never saw so many dorr-bugs and beetles of various kinds as strewed the beach. They had apparently flown over the bank in the night, and could not get up again, and some had perhaps fallen into the sea and were washed ashore. They may have been in part attracted by the light-house lamps.

The Clay Pounds are a more fertile tract than usual. We saw some fine patches of roots and corn here. As generally on the Cape, the plants had little stalk or leaf, but ran remarkably to seed. The corn was hardly more than half as high as in the interior, yet the ears were large and full, and one farmer told us that he could raise forty bushels on an acre without manure, and sixty with it. The heads of the rye also were remarkably large. The shadbush (*Amelanchier*), beach plums, and blueberries (*Vaccinium Pennsylvanicum*), like the apple-trees and oaks, were very dwarfish, spreading over the sand, but at the same time very fruitful. The blueberry was but an inch or two high, and its fruit often rested on the ground, so that you did not suspect the presence of the bushes, even on those bare hills, until you were treading on them. I thought that this fertility must be owing mainly to the abundance of moisture in the atmosphere, for I observed that what little grass there was was remarkably laden with dew in the morning, and in summer dense imprisoning fogs frequently last till midday, turning one's beard into a wet napkin about his throat, and the oldest inhabitant may lose his way within a stone's throw of his house or be obliged to follow the beach for a guide. The brick house attached to the light-house was exceedingly damp at that season, and writing-paper lost all its stiffness in it. It was impossible to dry your towel after bathing, or to press flowers without their mildewing. The air was so moist that we rarely wished to drink, though we could at all times taste the salt on our lips. Salt was rarely used at table, and our host told us that his cattle invariably refused it when it was offered them, they got so much ·with their grass and at every breath, but he said that a sick horse or one just from the country would sometimes take a hearty draught of salt water, and seemed to like it and be the better for it.

It was surprising to see how much water was contained in the terminal bud of the sea-side golden rod, standing in the sand early in July, and also how turnips, beets, carrots, etc., flourished even in pure sand. A man travelling by the shore near there not long before us noticed something green growing in the pure sand of the beach, just at high water mark, and on approaching found it to be a bed of beets flourishing vigorously, probably from seed washed out of the Franklin. Also beets and turnips came up in the sea-weed used for manure in many parts of the Cape. This suggests how various plants may have been dispersed over the world to distant islands and continents. Vessels, with seeds in their cargoes, destined for particular ports, where perhaps they were not needed, have been cast away on desolate islands, and though their crews perished, some of their seeds have been preserved. Out of many kinds a few would find a soil and climate adapted to them, — become naturalized and perhaps drive out the native plants at last, and so fit the land for the habitation of man. It is an ill wind that blows nobody any good, and for the time lamentable shipwrecks may thus contribute a new vegetable to a continent's stock, and prove on the whole a lasting blessing to its inhabitants. Or winds and currents might effect the same without the intervention of man. What are the various succulent plants which grow on the beach but such beds of beets and turnips, sprung originally from seeds which perhaps were cast on the waters for this end, though we do not know the Franklin which they came out of? In ancient times some Mr. Bell (?) was sailing this way in his ark with seeds of rocket, saltwort, sandwort, beach-grass, samphire, bayberry, poverty-grass, etc., all nicely labelled with directions, intending to establish a nursery somewhere ; and did not a nursery get established, though he thought that he had failed?

About the light-house I observed in the summer the pretty *Polygala polygama*, spreading ray-wise flat on the ground, white pasture thistles (*Cirsium pumilum*), and amid the shrubbery the *Smilax glauca*, which is commonly said not to grow so far north; near the edge of the banks about half a mile southward, the broom crowberry (*Empetrum Conradii*), for which Plymouth is the only locality in Massachusetts usually named, forms pretty green mounds four or five feet in diameter by one foot high, — soft springy beds for the wayfarer. I saw it afterward in Provincetown, but prettiest of all the scarlet pimpernel, or poor-man's weather-glass (*Anagallis arvensis*), greets you in fair weather on almost every square yard of sand. From Yarmouth, I have received the *Chrysopsis falcata* (golden aster), and *Vaccinium stamineum* (deerberry or squaw huckleberry), with fruit not edible, sometimes as large as a cranberry (Sept. 7).

The Highland Light-house,[1] where we were staying, is a substantial-looking building of brick, painted white, and surmounted by an iron cap. Attached to it is the dwelling of the keeper, one story high, also of brick, and built by government. As we were going to spend the night in a light-house, we wished to make the most of so novel an experience, and therefore told our host that we would like to accompany him when he went to light up. At rather early candle-light he lighted a small Japan lamp, allowing it to smoke rather more than we like on ordinary occasions, and told us to follow him. He led the way first through his bedroom, which was placed nearest to the light-house, and then through a long, narrow, covered passage-way,

[1] The light-house has since been rebuilt, and shows a *Fresnel* light. H. D. T.

between whitewashed walls like a prison entry, into the lower part of the light-house, where many great butts of oil were arranged around; thence we ascended by a winding and open iron stairway, with a steadily increasing scent of oil and lamp-smoke, to a trap-door in an iron floor, and through this into the lantern. It was a neat building, with everything in apple-pie order, and no danger of anything rusting there for want of oil. The light consisted of fifteen argand lamps, placed within smooth concave reflectors twenty-one inches in diameter, and arranged in two horizontal circles one above the other, facing every way excepting directly down the Cape. These were surrounded, at a distance of two or three feet, by large plate-glass windows, which defied the storms, with iron sashes, on which rested the iron cap. All the iron work except the floor was painted white. And thus the light-house was completed. We walked slowly round in that narrow space as the keeper lighted each lamp in succession, conversing with him at the same moment that many a sailor on the deep witnessed the lighting of the Highland Light. His duty was to fill and trim and light his lamps, and keep bright the reflectors. He filled them every morning, and trimmed them commonly once in the course of the night. He complained of the quality of the oil which was furnished. This house consumes about eight hundred gallons in a year, which cost not far from one dollar a gallon; but perhaps a few lives would be saved if better oil were provided. Another light-house keeper said that the same proportion of winter-strained oil was sent to the southermost light-house in the Union as to the most northern. Formerly, when this light-house had windows with small and thin panes, a severe storm would sometimes break the glass, and then they were obliged to put up a wooden shutter in haste to save their lights and reflectors, — and sometimes in tempests, when the mariner stood most in need of their guidance, they had thus nearly converted the light-house into a dark lantern, which emitted only a few feeble rays, and those commonly on the land or lee side. He spoke of the anxiety and sense of responsibility which he felt in cold and stormy nights in the winter ; when he knew that many a poor fellow was depending on him, and his lamps burned dimly, the oil being chilled. Sometimes he was obliged to warm the oil in a kettle in his house at midnight, and fill his lamps over again, — for he could not have a fire in the light-house, it produced such a sweat on the windows. His successor told me that he could not keep too hot a fire in such a case. All this because the oil was poor. A government lighting the mariners on its wintry coast with summer-strained oil, to save expense ! That were surely a summer-strained mercy.

This keeper's successor, who kindly entertained me the next year, stated that one extremely cold night, when this and all the neighboring lights were burning summer oil, but he had been provident enough to reserve a little winter oil against emer-

gencies, he was waked up with anxiety, and found
that his oil was congealed, and his lights almost extinguished; and when, after many hours' exertion,
he had succeeded in replenishing his reservoirs with
winter oil at the wick end, and with difficulty had
made them burn, he looked out and found that the
other lights in the neighborhood, which were usually
visible to him, had gone out, and he heard afterward that the Pamet River and Billingsgate Lights
also had been extinguished.

Our host said that the frost, too, on the windows
caused him much trouble, and in sultry summer
nights the moths covered them and dimmed his
lights ; sometimes even small birds flew against the
thick plate glass, and were found on the ground
beneath in the morning with their necks broken.
In the spring of 1855 he found nineteen small yel-
lowbirds, perhaps goldfinches or myrtle-birds thus
lying dead around the light-house ; and sometimes
in the fall he had seen where a golden plover had
struck the glass in the night, and left the down and
the fatty part of its breast on it.

Thus he struggled, by every method, to keep his
light shining before men. Surely the light-house
keeper has a responsible, if an easy, office. When
his lamp goes out, *he* goes out; or, at most, only
one such accident is pardoned.

I thought it a pity that some poor student did
not live there, to profit by all that light, since he
would not rob the mariner. " Well," he said, " I
do sometimes come up here and read the newspaper

when they are noisy down below." Think of fifteen argand lamps to read the newspaper by!
Government oil! — light, enough, perchance, to
read the Constitution by! I thought that he should
read nothing less than his Bible by that light. I
had a classmate [1] who fitted for college by the lamps
of a light-house, which was more light, we think,
than the University afforded.

When we had come down and walked a dozen
rods from the light-house, we found that we could
not get the full strength of its light on the narrow
strip of land between it and the shore, being too
low for the focus, and we saw only so many feeble
and rayless stars; but at forty rods inland we could
see to read, though we were still indebted to only
one lamp. Each reflector sent forth a separate
"fan" of light, — one shone on the windmill, and
one in the hollow, while the intervening spaces
were in shadow. This light is said to be visible
twenty nautical miles and more, from an observer
fifteen feet about the level of the sea. We could
see the revolving light at Race Point, the end of
the Cape, about nine miles distant, and also the
light on Long Point at the entrance of Provincetown Harbor, and one of the distant Plymouth Harbor Lights, across the Bay, nearly in a range with
the last, like a star in the horizon. The keeper
thought that the other Plymouth Light was concealed by being exactly in a range with the Long

[1] C. G. Thomas, who lately died in Cambridge, where he
was commonly called Light-house Thomas.

Point Light. He told us that the mariner was sometimes led astray by a mackerel fisher's lantern, who was afraid of being run down in the night, or even by a cottager's light, mistaking them for some well-known light on the coast, and, when he discovered his mistake, was wont to curse the prudent fisher or the wakeful cottager without reason.

Though it was once declared that Providence placed this mass of clay here on purpose to erect a light-house on, the keeper said that the light-house should have been erected half a mile farther south, where the coast begins to bend, and where the light could be seen at the same time with the Nauset Lights, and distinguished from them. They now talk of building one there. It happens that the present one is the more useless now, so near the extremity of the Cape, because other light-houses have since been erected there.

Among the many regulations of the Light-house Board, hanging against the wall here, many of them excellent, perhaps, if there were a regiment stationed here to attend to them, there is one requiring the keeper to keep an account of the number of vessels which pass his light during the day. But there are a hundred vessels in sight at once, steering in all directions, many on the very verge of the horizon, and he must have more eyes than Argus, and be a good deal farther-sighted, to tell which are passing his light. It is an employment in some respects best suited to the habits of the gulls which coast up and down here, and circle over the sea.

I was told by the next keeper, that on the 8th of June following, a particularly clear and beautiful morning, he rose about half an hour before sunrise, and having a little time to spare, for his custom was to extinguish his lights at sunrise, walked down toward the shore to see what he might find. When he got to the edge of the bank he looked up, and, to his astonishment, saw the sun rising, and already part way above the horizon. Thinking that his clock was wrong, he made haste back, and though it was still too early by the clock, extinguished his lamps, and when he had got through and come down, he looked out the window, and, to his still greater astonishment, saw the sun just where it was before, two thirds above the horizon. He showed me where its rays fell on the wall across the room. He proceeded to make a fire, and when he had done there was the sun still at the same height. Whereupon, not trusting to his own eyes any longer, he called up his wife to look at it, and she saw it also. There were vessels in sight on the ocean, and their crews, too, he said, must have seen it, for its rays fell on them. It remained at that height for about fifteen minutes by the clock, and then rose as usual and nothing else extraordinary happened during that day. Though accustomed to the coast, he had never witnessed nor heard of such a phenomenon before. I suggested that there might have been a cloud in the horizon invisible to him, which rose with the sun, and his clock was only as accurate as the average; or perhaps, as he denied the possiblity of this, it was such a looming of the sun as is said to occur at Lake Superior and elsewhere. Sir John Franklin, for instance, says in his Narrative, that when he was on the shore of the Polar Sea, the horizontal refraction varied so much one morning that " the upper limb of the sun twice appeared at the horizon before it finally rose."

He certainly must be a sun of Aurora to whom the sun looms, when there are so many millions to whom it *glooms* rather, or who never see it till an hour *after* it has risen. But it behooves us old stagers to keep our lamps trimmed and burning to the last, and not trust to the sun's looming.

This keeper remarked that the centre of the flame should be exactly opposite the centre of the reflectors, and that accordingly, if he was not careful to turn down his wicks in the morning, the sun falling on the reflectors on the south side of the building would set fire to them, like a burning-glass, in the coldest day, and he would look up at noon and see them all lighted! When your lamp is ready to give light, it is readiest to receive it, and the sun will light it. His successor said that he had never known them to blaze in such a case, but merely to smoke.

I saw that this was a place of wonders. In a sea turn or shallow fog while I was there the next summer, it being clear overhead, the edge of the bank twenty rods distant appeared like a mountain pasture in the horizon. I was completely deceived by it, and I could then understand why mariners some-

times ran ashore in such cases, especially in the
night, supposing it to be far away, though they
could see the land. Once since this, being in a
large oyster boat two or three hundred miles from
here, in a dark night, when there was a thin veil of
mist ᴜn land and water, we came so near to running on to the land before our skipper was aware of
it, that the first warning was my hearing the sound
of the surf under my elbow. I could almost have·
jumped ashore, and we were obliged to go about
very suddenly to prevent striking. The distant
light for which we were steering, supposing it a
light-house five or six miles off, came through the
cracks of a fisherman's bunk not more than six rods
distant.

The keeper entertained us handsomely in his solitary little ocean-house. He was a man of singular
patience and intelligence, who, when our queries
struck him, rung as clear as a bell in response.
The light-house lamps a few feet distant shone full
into my chamber, and made it as bright as day,
so I knew exactly how the Highland Light bore all
that night, and I was in no danger of being wrecked.
Unlike the last, this was as still as a summer night.
I thought as I lay there, half awake and half asleep,
looking upward through the window at the lights
above my head, how many sleepless eyes from far
out on the Ocean stream — mariners of all nations
spinning their yarns through the various watches
of the night — were directed toward my couch.

RALPH WALDO EMERSON.

INTRODUCTION.

IN point of quantity Emerson's prose much exceeds his poetry. That has been gathered into two small volumes and further sifted by the author into one; the prose has been more frequently published, and at this date (1880) is comprised in three duodecimo volumes. Its form is either the oration or the essay, with one exception. *English Traits* records the observations of the writer after two journeys to England, and, while it may loosely be classed among essays, has certain distinctive features which separate it from the essays of the same writer; there is in it narrative, reminiscence, and description which make it more properly the note-book of a philosophic traveller.

Under the term oration may be included all those writings of Emerson which were originally delivered as lectures, addresses, orations before literary and learned societies. During much of his literary life he has used the platform as his first and chief mode of communicating what he has had to say, and the speeches there made have frequently afterward been published in book form. It may be said of his essays as well as of his deliberate orations that the writer has never been wholly unmindful of an audience ; he has always been conscious that he was not merely delivering his mind but speaking directly to men. One is aware of a certain pointedness of speech which turns the writer into a speaker and the printed words into a sounding voice. Especially where one has heard Emerson does his impressive manner disclose itself in every sentence that one reads. In the orations, however, this directness of speech is most apparent, and their form is cast for it. The end of the speech is kept more positively before the speaker ; there is also more distinct eloquence, that raising of the voice, by which the volume of an utterance is increased and a note of thought is prolonged. The form of the oration requires, moreover, a somewhat brisker manner and crisper sentences, for the speaker knows that the hearer has no leisure to pursue his way by winding clauses.

Yet the spirit of the essay, the other great division of Emerson's writing, more distinctly enters into the oration. It is true that in whatever he writes Emerson feels his audience, but it is an audience of thinking men, and he is not unwilling to give his best thought and to surrender himself in his work to the leadings of his own thought. Come with me, he seems to say to reader or listener, we will follow courageously in this theme whithersoever Thought leads us ; and thus in essay or oration he seems less desirous of proving a proposition or stating roundly something which he has discovered than of entering upon a subject and letting his mind work freely upon it, gathering suggestions by the way and asking for its association with other subjects. Hence to one unaccustomed to the working of Emerson's mind, a first reading of his writings seems to disclose only a series of lightly connected epigrams or searching questions and answers. The very titles of the essays seem mere suggestions and the end of an essay brings with it no conclusion. In the essay proper he allows himself more freedom than in the oration, and his sentences do not converge so distinctly toward some demonstrable point. The discursive character of his thought is best fitted to the essay form, where it is not necessary to make provision beforehand for every idea which is to be entertained, and where the perfection of form is in the graceful freedom from formalism. The oration may be described as one great sentence; the essay as an unrestricted succession of little sentences.

The single, apparently detached, thoughts impress one with a sense of the author's insight; their very abruptness often lends a positiveness and authority to the statements and convictions, and a ready listener finds himself accepting them almost without consideration, so captivating are they in their brilliant light. Yet something more than a ready listener is needed, if Emerson's writings are to be best used. They call for thought in the reader; they demand that one should stop and ask questions, should translate what one has read into one's own ordinary speech, and inquire again if it is true. They are excellent tonics for the mind, but taken heedlessly they are dangerous. The danger is in the careless use, for carelessness makes half truths of what has been said frankly and fearlessly to the open mind. No one should read Emerson who is not willing to have his own weakness disclosed to him, and who is not prepared also to test what he finds by a standard which is above both writer and reader.

As one reads steadily he is likely to note certain mental characteristics in the writer which mark all his work. One or two of these characteristics have already been mentioned; a more important and pervading one is his loyalty to idealism, and his belief in the power of the soul to work out a noble place for itself. In his oration on *Literary Ethics* he says of the scholar: "He must be a solitary, laborious, modest, and charitable soul. He must embrace solitude as a bride. He must have his glees and his glooms alone. His own estimate must be measure enough, his own praise reward enough for him. And why must the student be solitary and silent? That he may become acquainted with his thoughts. If he pines in a lonely place, hankering for the crowd, for display, he is not in the lonely place; his heart is in the market; he does not see, he does not hear, he does not think. But go cherish your soul; expel companions; set your habits to

24

a life of solitude; then will the faculties rise fair
and full within, like forest trees and field flowers;
you will have results, which, when you meet your
fellow-men, you can communicate, and they will
gladly receive. Do not go into solitude only that
you may presently come into public. Such solitude
denies itself, is public and stale. The public can
get public experience, but they wish the scholar to
replace to them those private, sincere, divine experiences of which they have been defrauded by
dwelling in the street. It is the noble, manlike, just
thought which is the superiority demanded of you,
and not crowds, but solitude, confers this elevation.
Not insulation of place, but independence of spirit
is essential, and it is only as the garden, the cottage,
the forest, and the rock are a sort of mechanical
aids to this that they are of value. Think alone
and all places are friendly and sacred. . . . . Fatal
to the man of letters, fatal to man, is the lust of
display, the seeming that unmakes our being. A
mistake of the main end to which they labor is incident to literary men, who, dealing with the organ
of language, — the subtlest, strongest, and longest-
lived of man's creation, and only fitly used as the
weapon of thought and of justice, — learn to enjoy
the pride of playing with this splendid engine, but
rob it of its almightiness by failing to work with it.
Extricating themselves from the tasks of the world,
the world revenges itself by exposing, at every
turn, the folly of these incomplete, pedantic, useless, ghastly creatures. The scholar will feel that

the richest romance, — the noblest fiction that was ever woven, — the heart and soul of beauty, — lies inclosed in human life. Itself of surpassing value, it is also the richest material for his creations. How shall he know its secrets of tenderness, of terror, of will, and of fate ? How can he catch and keep the strain of upper music that peals from it ? Its laws are concealed under the details of daily action. All action is an experiment upon them. He must bear his share of the common load. He must work with men in houses, and not with their names in books. His needs, appetites, talents, affections, accomplishments are keys that open to him the beautiful museum of human life. Why should he read it as an Arabian tale, and not know in his own beating bosom its sweet and smart? Out of love and hatred ; out of earnings and borrowings, and lendings and losses ; out of sickness and pain ; out of wooing and worshipping ; out of travelling, and voting, and watching, and caring ; out of disgrace and contempt ; comes our tuition in the serene and beautiful laws. Let him not slur his lesson ; let him learn it by heart. Let him endeavor, exactly, bravely, and cheerfully, to solve the problem of that life which is set before *him*. And this, by punctual action, and not by promises or dreams. Believing, as in God, in the presence and favor of the grandest influences, let him deserve that favor, and learn how to receive and use it, by fidelity, also, to the lower observances. . . . . The man of genius should occupy the whole space between God or

pure mind and the multitude of uneducated men.
He must draw from the infinite Reason, on one
side; and he must penetrate into the heart and
sense of the crowd, on the other. From one, he
must draw his strength; to the other he must owe
his aim. The one yokes him to the real, the other
to the apparent. At one pole is Reason, at the
other Common Sense. If he be defective at either
extreme of the scale, his philosophy will seem low
and utilitarian; or it will appear too vague and in-
definite for the uses of life."

In some such terms as these one may define
Emerson's own attitude toward his work. The
openness of his mind to new thought, his loyalty to
high ideals, his eager advocacy of the real, and his
insight into the nature of things have separated him
and made his words often unintelligible, but the se-
renity of his life and the courage of his speech have
endeared him to men, even when they have thought
him fatally oblivious to some aspects of human life.
The essay on *Behavior* is taken from *The Conduct
of Life;* that on *Books* from *Society and Solitude.*

I.

BEHAVIOR.

GRACE, Beauty, and Caprice
Build this golden portal;
Graceful women, chosen men,
Dazzle every mortal:
Their sweet and lofty countenance
His enchanting food;
He need not go to them, their forms
Beset his solitude.
He looketh seldom in their face,
His eyes explore the ground,
The green grass is a looking-glass
Whereon their traits are found.
Little he says to them,
So dances his heart in his breast,
Their tranquil mien bereaveth him
Of wit, of words, of rest.
Too weak to win, too fond to shun
The tyrants of his doom,
The much-deceived Endymion
Slips behind a tomb.

THE soul which animates Nature is not less significantly published in the figure, movement, and gesture of animated bodies, than in its last vehicle of articulate speech. This silent and subtile language is Manners; not *what*, but *how*. Life expresses. A statue has no tongue, and needs none. Good tableaux do not need declamation. Nature tells every secret once. Yes, but in man she tells it all the time, by form, attitude, gesture, mien, face, and parts of the face, and by the whole action of the machine. The visible carriage or action of the individual, as resulting from his organization and his will combined, we call manners. What are they but thought entering the hands and feet, controlling the movements of the body, the speech and behavior ?

There is always a best way of doing everything, if it be to boil an egg. Manners are the happy ways of doing things ; each once a stroke of genius or of love, — now repeated and hardened into usage. They form at last a rich varnish, with which the routine of life is washed, and its details adorned. If they are superficial, so are the dewdrops which give such a depth to the morning meadows. Manners are very communicable ; men catch them from each other. Consuelo, in the romance,[1] boasts of the lessons she had given the nobles in manners, on the stage ; and, in real life, Talma [2] taught Napoleon the arts of behavior. Genius invents fine manners, which the baron and the baroness copy very fast, and, by the advantage of a palace, better the instruction. They stereotype the lesson they have learned into a mode.

The power of manners is incessant, — an element as unconcealable as fire. The nobility cannot in any country be disguised, and no more in a republic or a democracy than in a kingdom. No man

1 Of the same name, by George Sand.
2 A celebrated actor.

can resist their influence. There are certain manners which are learned in good society, of that force, that, if a person have them, he or she must be considered, and is everywhere welcome, though without beauty, or wealth, or genius. Give a boy address and accomplishments, and you give him the mastery of palaces and fortunes where he goes. He has not the trouble of earning or owning them; they solicit him to enter and possess. We send girls of a timid, retreating disposition to the boarding-school, to the riding-school, to the ball-room, or wheresoever they can come into acquaintance and nearness of leading persons of their own sex; where they might learn address, and see it near at hand. The power of a woman of fashion to lead, and also to daunt and repel, derives from their belief that she knows resources and behaviors not known to them; but when these have mastered her secret, they learn to confront her, and recover their self-possession.

Every day bears witness to their gentle rule. People who would obtrude, now do not obtrude. The mediocre circle learns to demand that which belongs to a high state of nature or of culture. Your manners are always under examination, and by committees little suspected, — a police in citizens' clothes, — but are awarding or denying you very high prizes when you least think of it.

We talk much of utilities, but 't is our manners that associate us. In hours of business, we go to him who knows, or has, or does this or that which we want, and we do not let our taste or feeling stand in the way. But this activity over, we return to the indolent state, and wish for those we can be at ease with; those who will go where we go, whose manners do not offend us, whose social tone chimes with ours. When we reflect on their persuasive and cheering force; how they recommend, prepare, and draw people together; how, in all clubs, manners make the members; how manners make the fortune of the ambitious youth; that, for the most part, his manners marry him, and, for the most part, he marries manners; when we think what keys they are, and to what secrets; what high lessons and inspiring tokens of character they convey; and what divination is required in us, for the reading of this fine telegraph, we see what range the subject has, and what relations to convenience, power, and beauty.

Their first service is very low, — when they are the minor morals: but 't is the beginning of civility, — to make us, I mean, endurable to each other. We prize them for their rough-plastic, abstergent force; to get people out of the quadruped state; to get them washed, clothed, and set up on end; to slough their animal husks and habits; compel them to be clean; overawe their spite and meanness, teach them to stifle the base, and choose the generous expression, and make them know how much happier the generous behaviors are.

Bad behavior the laws cannot reach. Society is infested with rude, cynical, restless, and frivolous persons who prey upon the rest, and whom a public opinion concentrated into good manners — forms accepted by the sense of all — can reach : the contradictors and railers at public and private tables, who are like terriers, who conceive it the duty of a dog of honor to growl at any passer-by, and do the honors of the house by barking him out of sight : — I have seen men who neigh like a horse when you contradict them, or say something which they do not understand :— then the overbold, who make their own invitation to your hearth ; the persevering talker, who gives you his society in large, saturating doses ; the pitiers of themselves, — a perilous class ; the frivolous Asmodeus, who relies on you to find him in ropes of sand to twist; the monotones ; in short, every stripe of absurdity ; — these are social inflictions which the magistrate cannot cure or defend you from, and which must be intrusted to the restraining force of custom, and proverbs, and familiar rules of behavior impressed on young people in their school-days.

In the hotels on the banks of the Mississipi, they print, or used to print, among the rules of the house, that "no gentleman can be permitted to come to the public table without his coat"; and in the same country, in the pews of the churches, little placards plead with the worshipper against the fury of expectoration. Charles Dickens self-sacrificingly undertook the reformation of our American manners in unspeakable particulars. I think the lesson was not quite lost ; that it held bad manners up, so that the churls could see the deformity. Unhappily, the book had its own deformities. It ought not to need to print in a reading-room a caution to strangers not to speak loud ; nor to persons who look over fine engravings, that they should be handled like cobwebs and butterflies' wings; nor to persons who look at marble statues, that they shall not smite them with canes. But, even in the perfect civilization of this city, such cautions are not quite needless in the Athenæum and City Library.

Manners are factitious, and grow out of circumstance as well as out of character. If you look at the pictures of patricians and of peasants, of different periods and countries, you will see how well they match the same classes in our towns. The modern aristocrat not only is well drawn in Titian's Venetian doges, and in Roman coins and statues, but also in the pictures which Commodore Perry brought home of dignitaries in Japan. Broad lands and great interests not only arrive to such heads as can manage them, but form manners of power. A keen eye, too, will see nice gradations of rank, or see in the manners the degree of homage the party is wont to receive. A prince who is accustomed every day to be courted and deferred to by the highest grandees, acquires a corresponding expectation, and a becoming mode of receiving and replying to this homage.

There are always exceptional people and modes. English grandees affect to be farmers. Claverhouse is a fop, and, under the finish of dress, and levity of

behavior, hides the terror of his war. But nature
and Destiny are honest, and never fail to leave their
mark, to hang out a sign for each and for every
quality. It is much to conquer one's face, and perhaps the ambitious youth thinks he has got the
whole secret when he has learned that disengaged
manners are commanding. Don't be deceived by a
facile exterior. Tender men sometimes have strong
wills. We had, in Massachusetts, an old statesman,
who had sat all his life in courts and in chairs of
state, without overcoming an extreme irritability
of face, voice, and bearing; when he spoke, his
voice would not serve him; it cracked, it broke, it
wheezed, it piped; little cared he; he knew that
it had got to pipe, or wheeze, or screech his argument and his indignation. When he sat down,
after speaking, he seemed in a sort of fit, and held
on to his chair with both hands; but underneath
all this irritability was a puissant will, firm, and
advancing, and a memory in which lay in order
and method like geologic strata every fact of his
history, and under the control of his will.

Manners are partly factitious, but, mainly, there
must be capacity for culture in the blood. Else all
culture is vain. The obstinate prejudice in favor of
blood, which lies at the base of the feudal and mon-
archical fabrics of the Old World, has some reason
in common experience. Every man — mathema-
tician, artist, soldier, or merchant — looks with confidence for some traits and talents in his own child,
which he would not dare to presume in the child of

a stranger. The Orientalists are very orthodox on this point. "Take a thorn-bush," said the emir Abdel-Kader, "and sprinkle it for a whole year with water; it will yield nothing but thorns. Take a date-tree, leave it without culture, and it will always produce dates. Nobility is the date-tree, and the Arab populace is a bush of thorns."

A main fact in the history of manners is the wonderful expressiveness of the human body. If it were made of glass, or of air, and the thoughts were written on steel tablets within, it could not publish more truly its meaning than now. Wise men read very sharply all your private history in your look and gait and behavior. The whole economy of nature is bent on expression. The tell-tale body is all tongues. Men are like Geneva watches with crystal faces which expose the whole movement. They carry the liquor of life flowing up and down in these beautiful bottles, and announcing to the curious how it is with them. The face and eyes reveal what the spirit is doing, how old it is, what aims it has. The eyes indicate the antiquity of the soul, or, through how many forms it has already ascended. It almost violates the proprieties, if we say above the breath here, what the confessing eyes do not hesitate to utter to every street passenger.

Man cannot fix his eye on the sun, and so far seems imperfect. In Siberia, a late traveller found men who could see the satellites of Jupiter with their unarmed eye. In some respects the animals excel us. The birds have a longer sight, beside the ad vantage by their wings of a higher observatory. A cow can bid her calf, by secret signal, probably of the eye, to run away, or to lie down and hide itself. The jockeys say of certain horses, that " they look over the whole ground." The outdoor life, and hunting, and labor, give equal vigor to the human eye. A farmer looks out at you as strong as the horse ; his eye-beam is like the stroke of a staff. An eye can threaten like a loaded and levelled gun, or can insult like hissing or kicking ; or, in its altered mood, by beams of kindness, it can make the heart dance with joy.

The eye obeys exactly the action of the mind. When a thought strikes us, the eyes fix, and remain gazing at a distance ; in enumerating the names of persons or of countries, as France, Germany, Spain, Turkey, the eyes wink at each new name. There is no nicety of learning sought by the mind which the eyes do not vie in acquiring. " An artist," said Michel Angelo, " must have his measuring tools not in the hand, but in the eye " ; and there is no end to the catalogue of its performances, whether in indolent vision (that of health and beauty), or in strained vision (that of art and labor).

Eyes are bold as lions, — roving, running, leaping, here and there, far and near. They speak all languages. They wait for no introduction ; they are no Englishmen ; ask no leave of age or rank ; they respect neither poverty nor riches, neither learning nor power, nor virtue, nor sex, but intrude, and come again, and go through and through you, in a mo-

ment of time. What inundation of life and thought
is discharged from one soul into another, through
them! The glance is natural magic. The mysterious communication established across a house between two entire strangers, moves all the springs
of wonder. The communication by the glance is
in the greatest part not subject to the control of
the will. It is the bodily symbol of identity of nature. We look into the eyes to know if this other
form is another self, and the eyes will not lie, but
make a faithful confession what inhabitant is there.
The revelations are sometimes terrific. The confession of a low, usurping devil is there made, and
the observer shall seem to feel the stirring of owls,
and bats, and horned hoofs, where he looked for in-
nocence and simplicity. 'T is remarkable, too, that
the spirit that appears at the windows of the house
does at once invest himself in a new form of his
own, to the mind of the beholder.

The eyes of men converse as much as their
tongues, with the advantage, that the ocular dialect
needs no dictionary, but is understood all the world
over. When the eyes say one thing, and the tongue
another, a practised man relies on the language of
the first. If the man is off his centre, the eyes
show it. You can read in the eyes of your companion, whether your argument hits him, though
his tongue will not confess it. There is a look by
which a man shows he is going to say a good thing,
and a look when he has said it. Vain and fogrotten
are all the fine offers and offices of hospitality, if

there is no holiday in the eye. How many furtive inclinations avowed by the eye, though dissembled by the lips! One comes away from a company, in which, it may easily happen, he has said nothing, and no important remark has been addressed to him, and yet, if in sympathy with the society, he shall not have a sense of this fact, such a stream of life has been flowing into him, and out from him, through the eyes. There are eyes, to be sure, that give no more admission into the man than blueberries. Others are liquid and deep, — wells that a man might fall into ; — others are aggressive and devouring, seem to call out the police, take all too much notice, and require crowded Broadways, and the security of millions, to protect individuals against them. The military eye I meet, now darkly sparkling under clerical, now under rustic, brows. 'T is the city of Lacedæmon ; 't is a stack of bayonets. There are asking eyes, asserting eyes, prowling eyes ; and eyes full of fate, — some of good, and some of sinister, omen. The alleged power to charm down insanity, or ferocity in beasts, is a power behind the eye. It must be a victory achieved in the will, before it can be signified in the eye. 'T is very certain that each man carries in his eye the exact indication of his rank in the immense scale of men, and we are always learning to read it. A complete man should need no auxiliaries to his personal presence. Whoever looked on him would consent to his will, being certified that his aims were generous and universal. The reason why

men do not obey us, is because they see the mud at
the bottom of our eye.

If the organ of sight is such a vehicle of power,
the other features have their own. A man finds
room in the few square inches of the face for the
traits of all his ancestors ; for the expression of
all his history, and his wants. The sculptor, and
Winckelmann, and Lavater, will tell you how significant a feature is the nose ; how its form expresses
strength or weakness of will and good or bad temper. The nose of Julius Cæsar, of Dante, and of
Pitt suggest " the terrors of the beak." What refinement, and what limitations, the teeth betray !
" Beware you don't laugh," said the wise mother,
" for then you show all your faults."

Balzac left in manuscript a chapter, which he
called " *Théorie de la démarche*," in which he says :
" The look, the voice, the respiration, and the attitude or walk are identical. But, as it has not
been given to man, the power to stand guard, at
once, over these four different simultaneous expressions of his thought, watch that one which speaks
out the truth, and you will know the whole man."

Palaces interest us mainly in the exhibition of
manners, which in the idle and expensive society
dwelling in them are raised to a high art. The
maxim of courts is that manner is power. A calm
and resolute bearing, a polished speech, and em-
bellishment of trifles, and the art of hiding all uncomfortable feeling, are essential to the courtier ;
and Saint Simon, and Cardinal de Retz, and Roe-

derer, and an encyclopædia of " Mémoires," will instruct you, if you wish, in those potent secrets. Thus, it is a point of pride with kings to remember faces and names. It is reported of one prince, that his head had the air of leaning downwards, in order not to humble the crowd. There are people who come in ever like a child with a piece of good news. It was said of the late Lord Holland, that he always came down to breakfast with the air of a man who had just met with some signal good fortune. In " Notre Dame " the grandee took his place on the dais, with the look of one who is thinking of something else. But we must not peep and eavesdrop at palace-doors.

Fine manners need the support of fine manners in others. A scholar may be a well-bred man, or he may not. The enthusiast is introduced to polished scholars in society, and is chilled and silenced by finding himself not in their element. They all have somewhat which he has not, and, it seems, ought to have. But if he finds the scholar apart from his companions, it is then the enthusiast's turn, and the scholar has no defence, but must deal on his terms. Now they must fight the battle out on their private strength. What is the talent of that character so common, — the successful man of the world, — in all marts, senates, and drawing-rooms ? Manners: manners of power ; sense to see his advantage, and manners up to it. See him approach his man. He knows that troops behave as they are handled at first ; — that is his cheap secret; just what happens to every two persons who meet on any affair, one instantly perceives that he has the key of the situation, that his will comprehends the other's will, as the cat does the mouse; and he has only to use courtesy, and furnish good-natured reasons to his victim to cover up the chain, lest he be shamed into resistance.

The theatre in which this science of manners has a formal importance is not with us a court, but dress-circles, wherein, after the close of the day's business, men and women meet at leisure, for mutual entertainment, in ornamented drawing-rooms. Of course, it has every variety of attraction and merit; but, to earnest persons, to youths or maidens who have great objects at heart, we cannot extol it highly. A well-dressed, talkative company, where each is bent to amuse the other, — yet the high-born Turk who came hither fancied that every woman seemed to be suffering for a chair; that all talkers were brained and exhausted by the de-oxygenated air; it spoiled the best persons: it put all on stilts. Yet here are the secret biographies written and read. The aspect of that man is repulsive; I do not wish to deal with him. The other is irritable, shy, and on his guard. The youth looks humble and manly: I choose him. Look on this woman. There is not beauty, nor brilliant sayings, nor distinguished power to serve you; but all see her gladly; her whole air and impression are healthful. Here come the sentimentalists, and the invalids. Here is Elise, who caught cold in coming into the world, and has always increased it since. Here are creep-mouse manners; and thievish manners. "Look at Northcote," said Fuseli; "he looks like a rat that has seen a cat." In the shallow company, easily excited, easily tired, here is the columnar Bernard: the Alleghanies do not express more repose than his behavior. Here are the sweet, following eyes of Cecile: it seemed always that she demanded the heart. Nothing can be more excellent in kind than the Corinthian grace of Gertrude's manners, and yet Blanche, who has no manners, has better manners than she; for the movements of Blanche are the sallies of a spirit which is sufficient for the moment, and she can afford to express every thought by instant action.

Manners have been somewhat cynically defined to be a contrivance of wise men to keep fools at a distance. Fashion is shrewd to detect those who do not belong to her train, and seldom wastes her attentions. Society is very swift in its instincts, and, if you do not belong to it, resists and sneers at you; or quietly drops you. The first weapon enrages the party attacked; the second is still more effective, but is not to be resisted, as the date of the transaction is not easily found. People grow up and grow old under this infliction, and never suspect the truth, ascribing the solitude which acts on them very injuriously to any cause but the right one.

The basis of good manners is self-reliance. Necessity is the law of all who are not self-possessed. Those who are not self-possessed obtrude and pain us. Some men appear to feel that they belong to a Pariah caste. They fear to offend, they bend and apologize, and walk through life with a timid step.

As we sometimes dream that we are in a well-dressed company without any coat, so Godfrey acts ever as if he suffered from some mortifying circumstance. The hero should find himself at home, wherever he is; should impart comfort by his own security and good-nature to all beholders. The hero is suffered to be himself. A person of strong mind comes to perceive that for him an immunity is secured so long as he renders to society that service which is native and proper to him, — an immunity from all the observances, yea, and duties, which society so tyrannically imposes on the rank and file of its members. " Euripides," says Aspasia, " has not the fine manners of Sophocles: but," she adds, good-humoredly, " the movers and masters of our souls have surely a right to throw out their limbs as carelessly as they please on the world that belongs to them, and before the creatures they have animated." [1]

Manners require time, as nothing is more vulgar than haste. Friendship should be surrounded with ceremonies and respects, and not crushed into corners. Friendship requires more time than poor busy men can usually command. Here comes to me Roland, with a delicacy of sentiment leading and inwrapping him like a divine cloud or holy ghost. 'T is a great destitution to both that this should not

[1] Landor, *Pericles and Aspasia.*

be entertained with large leisures, but contrariwise should be balked by importunate affairs.

But through this lustrous varnish, the reality is ever shining. 'T is hard to keep the *what* from breaking through this pretty painting of the *how*. The core will come to the surface. Strong will and keen perception overpower old manners, and create new ; and the thought of the present moment has a greater value than all the past. In persons of character we do not remark manners, because of their instantaneousness. We are surprised by the thing done, out of all power to watch the way of it. Yet nothing is more charming than to recognize the great style which runs through the action of such. People masquerade before us in their fortunes, titles, offices, and connections, as academic or civil presidents, or senators, or professors, or great lawyers, and impose on the frivolous, and a good deal on each other, by these fames. At least, it is a point of prudent good manners to treat these reputations tenderly, as if they were merited. But the sad realist knows these fellows at a glance, and they know him ; as when in Paris the chief of the police enters a ball-room, so many diamonded pretenders shrink and make themselves as inconspicuous as they can, or give him a supplicating look as they pass. " I had received," said a sibyl, — " I had received at birth the fatal gift of penetration "; and these Cassandras are always born.

Manners impress as they indicate real power. A man who is sure of his point carries a broad and contented expression, which everybody reads. And you cannot rightly train one to an air and manner, except by making him the kind of man of whom that manner is the natural expression. Nature forever puts a premium on reality. What is done for effect is seen to be done for effect; what is done for love is felt to be done for love. A man inspires affection and honor, because he was not lying in wait for these. The things of a man for which we visit him, were done in the dark and the cold. A little integrity is better than any career. So deep are the sources of this surface-action, that even the size of your companion seems to vary with his freedom of thought. Not only is he larger, when at ease, and his thoughts generous, but everything around him becomes variable with expression. No carpenter's rule, no rod and chain, will measure the dimensions of any house or house-lot: go into the house: if the proprietor is constrained and deferring, 't is of no importance how large his house, how beautiful his grounds, — you quickly come to the end of all; but if the man is self-possessed, happy, and at home, his house is deep-founded, indefinitely large and interesting, the roof and dome buoyant as the sky. Under the humblest roof, the commonest person in plain clothes sits there massive, cheerful, yet formidable like the Egyptian colossi.

Neither Aristotle, nor Leibnitz, nor Junius, nor Champollion has set down the grammar-rules of of this dialect, older than Sanscrit; but they who cannot yet read English, can read this. Men take each other's measure, when they meet for the first time, — and every time they meet. How do they get this rapid knowledge, even before they speak, of each other's power and dispositions ? One would say that the persuasion of their speech is not in what they say, — or, that men do not convince by their argument, — but by their personality, by who they are, and what they said and did heretofore. A man already strong is listened to, and everything he says is applauded. Another opposes him with sound argument, but the argument is scouted, until by and by it gets into the mind of some weighty person ; then it begins to tell on the community.

Self-reliance is the basis of behavior, as it is the guaranty that the powers are not squandered in too much demonstration. In this country, where school education is universal, we have a superficial culture, and a profusion of reading and writing and expression. We parade our nobilities in poems and orations, instead of working them up into happiness. There is a whisper out of the ages to him who can understand it, — "Whatever is known to thyself alone has always very great value." There is some reason to believe that, when a man does not write his poetry, it escapes by other vents through him, instead of the one vent of writing; clings to his form and manners, whilst poets have often nothing poetical about them except their verses. Jacobi said, that "when a man has fully expressed his thought, he has somewhat less possession of it."

One would say, the rule is, — What a man is irresistibly urged to say, helps him and us. In explaining his thought to others, he explains it to himself: but when he opens it for show, it corrupts him.

Society is the stage on which manners are shown; novels are their literature. Novels are the journal or record of manners; and the new importance of these books derives from the fact that the novelist begins to penetrate the surface, and treat this part of life more worthily. The novels used to be all alike, and had a quite vulgar tone. The novels used to lead us on to a foolish interest in the fortunes of the boy and girl they described. The boy was to be raised from a humble to a high position. He was in want of a wife and a castle, and the object of the story was to supply him with one or both. We watched sympathetically, step by step, his climbing, until, at last, the point is gained, the wedding-day is fixed, and we follow the gala procession home to the bannered portal, when the doors are slammed in our face, and the poor reader is left outside in the cold, not enriched by so much as an idea, or a virtuous impulse.

But the victories of character are instant, and victories for all. Its greatness enlarges all. We are fortified by every heroic anecdote. The novels are as useful as Bibles, if they teach you the secret, that the best of life is conversation, and the greatest success is confidence, or perfect understanding between sincere people. 'T is a French definition of friendship, *rien que s'entendre*, good understanding. The highest compact we can make with our fellow is,— " Let there be truth between us two for evermore." That is the charm in all good novels, as it is the charm in all good histories, that the heroes mutually understand, from the first, and deal loyally and with a profound trust in each other. It is sublime to feel and say of another, I need never meet, or speak, or write to him: we need not reinforce ourselves, or send tokens of remembrance : I rely on him as on myself : if he did thus, or thus, I know it was right.

In all the superior people I have met, I notice directness, truth spoken more truly, as if everything of obstruction, of malformation, had been trained away. What have they to conceal ? What have they to exhibit ? Between simple and noble persons there is always a quick intelligence : they recognize at sight, and meet on a better ground than the talents and skills they may chance to possess, namely, on sincerity and uprightness. For, it is not what talents or genius a man has, but how he is to his talents, that constitutes friendship and character. The man that stands by himself, the universe stands by him also. It is related of the monk Basle, that, being excommunicated by the Pope, he was, at his death, sent in charge of an angel to find a fit place of suffering in hell ; but, such was the eloquence and good-humor of the monk, that wherever he went he was received gladly, and civ illy treated, even by the most uncivil angels : and, when he came to discourse with them, instead of contradicting or forcing him, they took his part, and adopted his manners : and even good angels came from far, to see him, and take up their abode with him. The angel that was sent to find a place of torment for him attempted to remove him to a worse pit, but with no better success ; for such was the contented spirit of the monk, that he found something to praise in every place and company, though in hell, and made a kind of heaven of it. At last the escorting angel returned with his prisoner to them that sent him, saying that no phlegethon could be found that would burn him ; for that in whatever condition, Basle remained incorrigibly Basle. The legend says, his sentence was remitted, and he was allowed to go into heaven, and was canonized as a saint.

There is a stroke of magnanimity in the correspondence of Bonaparte with his brother Joseph, when the latter was King of Spain, and complained that he missed in Napoleon's letters the affectionate tone which had marked their childish correspondence. "I am sorry," replies Napoleon, "you think you shall find your brother again only in the Elysian Fields. It is natural, that at forty, he should not feel towards you as he did at twelve. But his feelings towards you have greater truth and strength. His friendship has the features of his mind."

How much we forgive in those who yield us the rare spectacle of heroic manners ! We will pardon

them the want of books, of arts, and even of the
gentler virtues. How tenaciously we remember
them! Here is a lesson which I brought along
with me in boyhood from the Latin School, and
which ranks with the best of Roman anecdotes.
Marcus Scaurus was accused by Quintus Varius
Hispanus, that he had excited the allies to take
arms against the Republic. But he, full of firm-
ness and gravity, defended himself in this manner :
"Quintus Varius Hispanus alleges that Marcus
Scaurus, President of the Senate, excited the allies
to arms : Marcus Scaurus, President of the Senate,
denies it. There is no witness. Which do you
believe, Romans ? " " *Utri creditis, Quirites ?* "
When he had said these words, he was absolved by
the assembly of the people.

I have seen manners that make a similar impression with personal beauty; that give the like ex-
hilaration, and refine us like that ; and, in memorable experiences, they are suddenly better than
beauty, and make that superfluous and ugly. But
they must be marked by fine perception, the acquaintance with real beauty. They must always
show self-control : you shall not be facile, apolo-
getic, or leaky, but king over your word ; and every
gesture and action shall indicate power at rest.
Then they must be inspired by the good heart.
There is no beautifier of complexion, or form, or
behavior, like the wish to scatter joy and not pain
around us. 'T is good to give a stranger a meal, or
a night's lodging. 'T is better to be hospitable to

his good meaning and thought, and give courage to a companion. We must be as courteous to a man as we are to a picture, which we are willing to give the advantage of a good light. Special precepts are not to be thought of: the talent of well-doing contains them all. Every hour will show a duty as paramount as that of my whim just now; and yet I will write it, — that there is one topic peremptorily forbidden to all well-bred, to all rational mortals, namely, their distempers. If you have not slept, or if you have slept, or if you have headache, or sciatica, or leprosy, or thunder-stroke, I beseech you, by all angels, to hold your peace, and not pollute the morning, to which all the housemate. bring serene and pleasant thoughts, by corruption and groans. Come out of the azure. Love the day. Do not leave the sky out of your landscape The oldest and the most deserving person should come very modestly into any newly awaked company, respecting the divine communications, out of which all must be presumed to have newly come. An old man, who added an elevating culture to a large experience of life, said to me: " When you come into the room, I think I will study how to make humanity beautiful to you."

As respects the delicate question of culture, I do not think that any other than negative rules can be laid down. For positive rules, for suggestion, Nature alone inspires it. Who dare assume to guide a youth, a maid, to perfect manners? — the golden mean is so delicate, difficult, — say frankly, unattainable. What finest hands would not be clumsy to sketch the genial precepts of the young girl's demeanor? The chances seem infinite against success; and yet success is continually attained. There must not be secondariness, and 't is a thousand to one that her air and manner will at once betray that she is not primary, but that there is some other one or many of her class, to whom she habitually postpones herself. But Nature lifts her easily, and without knowing it, over these impossibilities, and we are continually surprised with graces and felicities not only unteachable, but undescribable.

II.

BOOKS.

It is easy to accuse books, and bad ones are easily found; and the best are but records, and not the things recorded; and certainly there is dilettanteism enough, and books that are merely neutral and do nothing for us. In Plato's " Gorgias," Socrates says: " The shipmaster walks in a modest garb near the sea, after bringing his passengers from Ægina or from Pontus, not thinking he has done anything extraordinary, and certainly knowing that his passengers are the same, and in no respect better than when he took them on board." So it is with books, for the most part; they work no redemption in us. The bookseller might certainly know that his customers are in no respect better for the purchase and consumption of his wares. The volume is dear at a dollar, and; after reading to weariness the lettered backs, we leave the shop with a sigh, and learn, as I did, without surprise, of a surly bank director, that in bank parlors they estimate all stocks of this kind as rubbish.

But it is not less true that there are books which are of that importance in a man's private experience, as to verify for him the fables of Cornelius Agrippa, of Michael Scott, or of the old Orpheus of Thrace, — books which take rank in our life with parents and lovers and passionate experiences, so medicinal, so stringent, so revolutionary, so authoritative, — books which are the work and the proof of faculties so comprehensive, so nearly equal to the world which they paint, that, though one shuts them with meaner ones, he feels his exclusion from them to accuse his way of living.

Consider what you have in the smallest chosen library. A company of the wisest and wittiest men that could be picked out of all countries, in a thousand years, have set in best order the results of their learning and wisdom. The men themselves were hid and inaccessible, solitary, impatient of interruption, fenced by etiquette ; but the thought which they did not uncover to their bosom friend is here written out in transparent words to us, the strangers of another age.

We owe to books those general benefits which come from high intellectual action. Thus, I think, we often owe to them the perception of immortality. They impart sympathetic activity to the moral power. Go with mean people, and you think life is mean. Then read Plutarch, and the world is a proud place, peopled with men of positive quality, with heroes and demigods standing around us, who will not let us sleep. Then, they address the imagination : only poetry inspires poetry. They become the organic culture of the time. College education is the reading of certain books which the common-sense of all scholars agrees will represent the science already accumulated. If you know that, — for instance in geometry, if you have read Euclid and Laplace, — your opinion has some value ; if you do not know these, you are not entitled to give any opinion on the subject. Whenever any sceptic or bigot claims to be heard on the questions of intellect and morals, we ask if he is familiar with the books of Plato, where all his pert objections have once for all been disposed of. If not, he has no right to our time. Let him go and find himself answered there.

Meantime the colleges, whilst they provide us with libraries, furnish no professor of books ; and, I think, no chair is so much wanted. In a library we are surrounded by many hundreds of dear friends, but they are imprisoned by an enchanter in these paper and leathern boxes ; and, though they know us, and have been waiting two, ten, or twenty centuries for us, — some of them, — and are eager to give us a sign, and unbosom themselves, it is the law of their limbo that they must not speak until spoken to; and as the enchanter has dressed them, like battalions of infantry, in coat and jacket of one cut, by the thousand and ten thousand, your chance of hitting on the right one is to be computed by the arithmetical rule of Permutation and Combination, — not a choice out of three caskets, but out of half a million caskets all alike. But it happens in our experience, that in this lottery there are at least fifty or a hundred blanks to a prize. It seems, then, as if some charitable soul, after losing a great deal of time among the false books, and alighting upon a few true ones which made him happy and wise, would do a right act in naming those which have been bridges or ships to carry him safely over dark morasses and barren oceans, into the heart of sacred cities, into palaces and temples. This would be best done by those great masters of books who from time to time appear, — the Fabricii, the Seldens, Magliabecchis, Scaligers, Mirandolas, Bayles, Johnsons, whose eyes sweep the whole horizon of learning. But private readers, reading purely for love of the book, would serve us by leaving each the shortest note of what he found.

There are books; and it is practicable to read them, because they are so few. We look over with a sigh the monumental libraries of Paris, of the Vatican, and the British Museum. In 1858, the number of printed books in the Imperial Library at Paris was estimated at eight hundred thousand volumes; with an annual increase of twelve thousand volumes; so that the number of printed books extant to-day may easily 'exceed a million. It is easy to count the number of pages which a diligent man can read in a day, and the number of years which human life in favorable circumstances allows to reading; and to demonstrate that, though he should read from dawn till dark, for sixty years, he must die in the first alcoves. But nothing can be more deceptive than this arithmetic, where none but a natural method is really pertinent. I visit occasionally the Cambridge Library, and I can seldom go there without renewing the conviction that the best of it all is already within the four walls of my study at home. The inspection of the catalogue brings me continually back to the few standard writers who are on every private shelf; and to these it can afford only the most slight and casual additions. The crowds and centuries of books are only commentary and elucidation, echoes and weakeners of these few great voices of Time.

The best rule of reading will be a method from nature, and not a mechanical one of hours and pages. It holds each student to a pursuit of his native aim, instead of a desultory miscellany. Let him read what is proper to him, and not waste his memory on a crowd of mediocrities. As whole nations have derived their culture from a single book, — as the Bible has been the literature as well as the religion of large portions of Europe, — as

26

Hafiz was the eminent genius of the Persians, Confucius of the Chinese, Cervantes of the Spaniards ; so, perhaps, the human mind would be a gainer, if all the secondary writers were lost, — say, in England, all but Shakspere, Milton and Bacon, — through the profounder study so drawn to those wonderful minds. With this pilot of his own genius, let the student read one, or let him read many, he will read advantageously. Dr. Johnson said : " Whilst you stand deliberating which book your son shall read first, another boy has read both ; read anything five hours a day, and you will soon be learned.''

Nature is much our friend in this matter. Nature is always clarifying her water and her wine. No filtration can be so perfect. She does the same thing by books as by her gases and plants. There is always a selection in writers, and then a selection from the selection. In the first place, all books that get fairly into the vital air of the world were written by the successful class, by the affirming and advancing class, who utter what tens of thousands feel though they cannot say. There has already been a scrutiny and choice for many hundreds of young pens, before the pamphlet or political chapter which you read in a fugitive journal comes to your eye. All these are young adventurers, who produce their performance to the wise ear of Time, who sits and weighs, and, ten years hence, out of a million of pages reprints one. Again it is judged, it is winnowed by all the winds of opinion, and what terrific selection has not passed on it before it can be reprinted after twenty years, — and reprinted after a century ! — it is as if Minos and Rhadamanthus had indorsed the writing. 'T is therefore an economy of time to read old and famed books. Nothing can be preserved which is not good ; and I know beforehand that Pindar, Martial, Terence, Galen, Kepler, Galileo, Bacon, Erasmus, More, will be superior to the average intellect. In contemporaries, it is not so easy to distinguish betwixt notoriety and fame.

Be sure, then, to read no mean books. Shun the spawn of the press or the gossip of the hour. Do not read what you shall learn, without asking, in the street and the train. Dr. Johnson said " he always went into stately shops " ; and good travellers stop at the best hotels ; for, though they cost more, they do not cost much more, and there is the good company and the best information. In like manner, the scholar knows that the famed books contain, first and last, the best thoughts and facts. Now and then, by rarest luck, in some foolish Grub Street is the gem we want. But in the best circles is the best information. If you should transfer the amount of your reading day by day from the newspaper to the standard authors— But who dare speak of such a thing?

The three practical rules, then, which I have to offer, are, — 1. Never read any book that is not a year old. 2. Never read any but famed books. 3. Never read any but what you like ; or, in Shakspere's phrase,

"No profit goes where is no pleasure ta'en :
   In brief, sir, study what you most affect."

Montaigne says, " Books are a languid pleasure " ; but I find certain books vital and spermatic, not leaving the reader what he was : he shuts the book a richer man. I would never willingly read any others than such. And I will venture, at the risk of inditing a list of old primers and grammars, to count the few books which a superficial reader must thankfully use.

Of the old Greek books, I think there are five which we cannot spare : 1. Homer, who, in spite of Pope and all the learned uproar of centuries, has really the true fire, and is good for simple minds, is the true and adequate germ of Greece, and occupies that place as history, which nothing can supply. It holds through all literature, that our best history is still poetry. It is so in Hebrew, in Sanscrit, and in Greek. English history is best known through Shakspere ; how much through Merlin, Robin Hood, and the Scottish ballads ! — the German, through the Nibelungenlied ; — the Spanish, through the Cid. Of Homer, George Chapman's is the heroic translation, though the most literal prose version is the best of all. 2. Herodotus, whose history contains inestimable anecdotes, which brought it with the learned into a sort of disesteem ; but in these days, when it is found that what 's most memorable of history is a few anecdotes, and that we need not be alarmed though we should find it not dull, it is regaining credit. 3. Æschy lus, the grandest of the three tragedians, who has given us under a thin veil the first plantation of Europe. The "Prometheus" is a poem of the like dignity and scope as the Book of Job, or the Norse Edda. 4. Of Plato I hesitate to speak, lest there should be no end. You find in him that which you have already found in Homer, now ripened to thought, — the poet converted to a philosopher, with loftier strains of musical wisdom than Homer reached; as if Homer were the youth, and Plato the finished man; yet with no less security of bold and perfect song, when he cares to use it, and with some harp-strings fetched from a higher heaven. He contains the future, as he came out of the past. In Plato, you explore modern Europe in its causes and seed, — all that in thought, which the history of Europe embodies or has yet to embody. The well-informed man finds himself anticipated. Plato is up with him too. Nothing has escaped him. Every new crop in the fertile harvest of reform, every fresh suggestion of modern humanity, is there. If the student wish to see both sides, and justice done to the man of the world, pitiless exposure of pedants, and the supremacy of truth and the religious sentiment, he shall be contented also. Why should not young men be educated on this book? It would suffice for the tuition of the race, — to test their understanding, and to express their reason. Here is that which is so attractive to all men, — the literature of aristocracy, shall I call it? — the picture of the best persons, sentiments, and manners, by the first master, in the best times, — portraits of Pericles, Alcibiades, Crito, Prodicus, Protagoras, Anaxagoras, and Socrates, with the lovely background of the Athenian and suburban landscape. Or who can overestimate the images with which Plato has enriched the minds of men, and which pass like bullion in the currency of all nations? Read the " Phædo," the " Protagoras," the " Phædrus," the " Timæus," the " Republic," and the " Apology of Socrates." 5. Plutarch cannot be spared from the smallest library; first, because he is so readable, which is much; then, that he is medicinal and invigorating. The lives of Cimon, Lycurgus, Alexander, Demosthenes, Phocion, Marcellus, and the rest, are what history has of best. But this book has taken care of itself, and the opinion of the world is expressed in the innumerable cheap editions, which make it as accessible as a newspaper. But Plutarch's " Morals " is less known, and seldom reprinted.[1] Yet such a reader as I am writing to can as ill spare it as the " Lives." He will read in it the essays " On the Dæmon of Socrates," " On Isis and Osiris," " On Progress in Virtue," " On Garrulity," " On Love," and thank anew the art of printing, and the cheerful domain of ancient thinking. Plutarch charms by the facility of his associations; so that it signifies little where you open his book, you find

---

[1] Since the first publication of this essay the book has been issued under the editorship of Professor Goodwin of Harvard, and with an introduction by Mr. Emerson.

yourself at the Olympian tables. His memory is like the Isthmian Games, where all that was excellent in Greece was assembled, and you are stimulated and recruited by lyric verses, by philosophic sentiments, by the forms and behavior of heroes, by the worship of the gods, and by the passing of fillets, parsley and laurel wreaths, chariots, armor, sacred cups, and utensils of sacrifice. An inestimable trilogy of ancient social pictures are the three " Banquets " respectively of Plato, Xenophon, and Plutarch. Plutarch's has the least approach to historical accuracy ; but the meeting of the Seven Wise Masters is a charming portraiture of ancient manners and discourse, and is as clear as the voice of a fife, and entertaining as a French novel. Xenophon's delineation of Athenian manners is an accessory to Plato, and supplies traits of Socrates ; whilst Plato's has merits of every kind, — being a repertory of the wisdom of the ancients on the subject of love, — a picture of a feast of wits, not less descriptive than Aristophanes, — and, lastly, containing that ironical eulogy of Socrates which is the source from which all the portraits of that philosopher current in Europe have been drawn.

Of course a certain outline should be obtained of Greek history, in which the important moments and persons can be rightly set down ; but the shortest is the best, and if one lacks stomach for Mr. Grote's voluminous annals, the old slight and popular summary of Goldsmith or of Gillies will serve. The valuable part is the age of Pericles and the next generation. And here we must read the "Clouds" of Aristophanes, and what more of that master we gain appetite for, to learn our way in the streets of Athens, and to know the tyranny of Aristophanes, requiring more genius and sometimes not less cruelty than belonged to the official commanders. Aristophanes is now very accessible, with much valuable commentary, through the labors of Mitchell and Cartwright. An excellent popular book is J. A. St. John's "Ancient Greece"; the "Life and Letters" of Niebuhr, even more than his Lectures, furnish leading views; and Winckelmann, a Greek born out of due time, has become essential to an intimate knowledge of the Attic genius. The secret of the recent histories in German and in English is the discovery, owed first to Wolff, and later to Boeckh, that the sincere Greek history of that period must be drawn from Demosthenes, especially from the business orations, and from the comic poets.

If we come down a little by natural steps from the master to the disciples, we have, six or seven centuries later, the Platonists, — who also cannot be skipped, — Plotinus, Porphyry, Proclus, Synesius, Jamblichus. Of Jamblichus the Emperor Julian said, " that he was posterior to Plato in time, not in genius." Of Plotinus, we have eulogies by Porphyry and Longinus, and the favor of the Emperor Gallienus, — indicating the respect he inspired among his contemporaries. If any one who had read with interest the " Isis and Osiris " of Plutarch

should then read a chapter called " Providence," by
Synesius, translated into English by Thomas Tay-
lor, he will find it one of the majestic remains of
literature, and, like one walking in the noblest of
temples, will conceive new gratitude to his fellow-
men, and a new estimate of their nobility. The imaginative scholar will find few stimulants to his brain
like these writers. He has entered the Elysian
Fields ; and the grand and pleasing figures of gods
and demons and demoniacal men, of the " azonic"
and the " aquatic gods," demons with fulgid eyes
and all the rest of the Platonic rhetoric, exalted a
little under the African sun, sail before his eyes.
The acolyte has mounted the tripod over the cave
at Delphi ; his heart dances, his sight is quickened.
These guides speak of the gods with such depth and
with such pictorial details, as if they had been bodily present at the Olympian feasts. The reader of
these books makes new acquaintance with his own
mind ; new regions of thought are opened. Jamblichus's " Life of Pythagoras " works more directly
on the will than others ; since Pythagoras was eminently a practical person, the founder of a school
of ascetics and socialists, a planter of colonies, and
uo wise a man of abstract studies alone.

The respectable and sometimes excellent translations of Bohn's Library have done for literature
what railroads have done for internal intercourse.
I do not hesitate to read all the books I have
named, and all good books, in translations. What
is really best in any book is translatable, -- any

real insight or broad human sentiment. Nay, I observe that, in our Bible, and other books of lofty
moral tone, it seems easy and inevitable to render
the rhythm and music of the original into phrases of
equal melody. The Italians have a fling at trans-
lators, — *i traditori traduttori;* but I thank them.
I rarely read any Latin, Greek, German, Italian,
sometimes not a French book in the original, which
I can procure in a good version. I like to be be-
holden to the great metropolitan English speech,
the sea which receives tributaries from every region
under heaven. I should as soon think of swim-
ming across Charles River when I wish to go to
Boston, as of reading all my books in originals,
when I have them rendered for me in my mother-
tongue.

For history there is great choice of ways to bring
the student through early Rome. If he can read
Livy, he has a good book ; but one of the short
English compends, some Goldsmith or Ferguson,
should be used, that will place in the cycle the
bright stars of Plutarch. The poet Horace is the
eye of the Augustan age; Tacitus, the wisest of
historians; and Martial will give him Roman manners, — and some very bad ones, — in the early
days of the Empire: but Martial must be read, if
read at all, in his own tongue. These will bring
him to Gibbon, who will take him in charge, and
convey him with abundant entertainment down —
with notice of all remarkable objects on the way
— through fourteen hundred years of time. He

cannot spare Gibbon, with his vast reading, — with such wit and continuity of mind, that, though never profound, his book is one of the conveniences of civilization, like the new railroad from ocean to ocean, — and, I think, will be sure to send the reader to his " Memoirs of Himself," and the " Extracts from my Journal," and " Abstracts of my Readings," which will spur the laziest scholar to emulation of his prodigious performance.

Now having our idler safe down as far. as the fall of Constantinople in 1453, he is in very good courses : for here are trusty hands waiting for him. The cardinal facts of European history are soon learned. There is Dante's poem, to open the Italian Republics of the Middle Age ; Dante's " Vita Nuova," to explain Dante and Beatrice ; and Boccaccio's " Life of Dante," — a great man to describe a greater. To help us, perhaps a volume or two of M. Sismondi's " Italian Republics " will be as good as the entire sixteen. When we come to Michel Angelo, his Sonnets and Letters must be read, with his Life by Vasari, or, in our day, by Herman Grimm. For the Church, and the Feudal Institution, Mr. Hallam's " Middle Ages " will furnish, if superficial, yet readable and conceivable outlines.

The " Life of the Emperor Charles V.," by the useful Robertson, is still the key of the following age. Ximenes, Columbus, Loyola, Luther, Erasmus, Melanchthon, Francis I., Henry VIII., Elizabeth, and Henry IV. of France, are his contemporaries. It is a time of seeds and expansions, whereof our recent civilization is the fruit.

If now the relations of England to European affairs bring him to British ground, he is arrived at the very moment when modern history takes new proportions. He can look back for the legends and mythology to the "Younger Edda" and the "Heimskringla" of Snorro Sturleson, to Mallet's "Northern Antiquities," to Ellis's "Metrical Romances," to Asser's "Life of Alfred" and Venerable Bede, and to the researches of Sharon Turner and Palgrave. Hume will serve him for an intelligent guide, and in the Elizabethan era he is at the richest period of the English mind, with the chief men of action and of thought which that nation has produced, and with a pregnant future before him. Here he has Shakspere, Spenser, Sidney, Raleigh, Bacon, Chapman, Jonson, Ford, Beaumont and Fletcher, Herbert, Donne, Herrick; and Milton, Marvell, and Dryden, not long after.

In reading history, he is to prefer the history of individuals. He will not repent the time he gives to Bacon, — not if he read the " Advancement of Learning," the " Essays," the " Novum Organum," the " History of Henry VII.," and then all the " Letters " (especially those to the Earl of Devonshire, explaining the Essex business), and all but his " Apophthegms."

The task is aided by the strong mutual light which these men shed on each other. Thus, the works of Ben Jonson are a sort of hoop to bind all these fine persons together, and to the land to which they belong. He has written verses to or on all his notable contemporaries ; and what with so many occasional poems, and the portrait sketches in his " Discoveries," and the gossiping record of his opinions in his conversations with Drummond of Hawthornden, he has really illustrated the England of his time, if not to the same extent, yet much in the same way, as Walter Scott has celebrated the persons and places of Scotland. Walton, Chapman, Herrick, and Sir Henry Wotton write also to the times.

Among the best books are certain *Autobiographies :* as St. Augustine's Confessions ; Benvenuto Cellini's Life ; Montaigne's Essays ; Lord Herbert of Cherbury's Memoirs ; Memoirs of the Cardinal de Retz ; Rousseau's Confessions ; Linnæus's Diary ; Gibbon's, Hume's, Franklin's, Burns's, Alfieri's, Goethe's, and Haydon's Autobiographies.

Another class of books closely allied to these, and of like interest, are those which may be called *Table-Talks :* of which the best are Saadi's Gulistan ; Luther's Table-Talk ; Aubrey's Lives ; Spence's Anecdotes ; Selden's Table-Talk ; Boswell's Life of Johnson ; Eckermann's Conversations with Goethe ; Coleridge's Table-Talk ; and Hazlitt's Life of Northcote.

There is a class whose value I should designate as *Favorites :* such as Froissart's Chronicles ; Southey's Chronicle of the Cid ; Cervantes ; Sully's Memoirs ; Rabelais ; Montaigne ; Izaak Walton ; Evelyn ; Sir Thomas Browne ; Aubrey ; Sterne ; Horace Walpole : Lord Clarendon ; Doctor Johnson ; Burke, shedding floods of light on his times ; Lamb ; Landor; and De Quincy ; — a list, of course, that may be easily swelled, as dependent on individual caprice. Many men are as tender and irritable as lovers in reference to these predilections. Indeed, a man's library is a sort of harem, and I observe that tender readers have a great pudency in showing their books to a stranger.

The annals of bibliography afford many examples of the delirious extent to which book-fancying can go, when the legitimate delight in a book is transferred to a rare edition or to a manuscript. This mania reached its height about the beginning of the present century. For an autograph of Shakspere one hundred and fifty-five guineas were given. In May, 1812, the library of the Duke of Roxburgh was sold. The sale lasted forty-two days, — we abridge the story from Dibdin, — and among the many curiosities was a copy of Boccaccio published by Valdarfer, at Venice, in 1471 ; the only perfect copy of this edition. Among the distinguished company which attended the sale were the Duke of Devonshire, Earl Spencer, and the Duke of Marlborough, then Marquis of Blanford. The bid stood at five hundred guineas. " A thousand guineas," said Earl Spencer : " And ten," added the Marquis. You might hear a pin drop. All eyes were bent on the bidders. Now they talked apart, now ate a biscuit, now made a bet, but without the least thought of yielding one to the other. But to pass over some details, — the contest proceeded until the Marquis said, "Two thousand pounds." The Earl Spencer bethought him like a prudent general of useless bloodshed and waste of powder, and had paused a quarter of a minute, when Lord Althorp with long steps came to his side, as if to bring his father a fresh lance to renew the fight. Father and son whispered together, and Earl Spencer exclaimed, " Two thousand two hundred and fifty pounds !" An electric shock went through the assembly. " And ten," quietly added the marquis. There ended the strife. Ere Evans let the hammer fall, he paused ; the ivory instrument swept the air : the spectators stood dumb, when the hammer fell. The stroke of its fall sounded on the farthest shores of Italy. The tap of that hammer was heard in the libraries of Rome, Milan, and Venice. Boccaccio stirred in his sleep of five hundred years, and M. Van Praet groped in vain among the royal alcoves in Paris, to detect a copy of the famed Valdarfer Boccaccio.

Another class I distinguish by the term *Vocabularies*. Burton's " Anatomy of Melancholy " is a book of great learning. To read it is like reading in a dictionary. 'T is an inventory to remind us how many classes and species of facts exist, and in observing into what strange and multiplex byways learning has strayed, to infer our opulence. Neither is a dictionary a bad book to read. There is no cant in it, no excess of explanation,· and it is full of suggestion — the raw material of possible poems and histories. Nothing is wanting but a little shuffling, sorting, ligature, and cartilage. Out of a hundred examples, Cornelius Agrippa " On the Vanity of Arts and Sciences " is a specimen of that scribatiousness which grew to be the habit of the gluttonous readers of his time. Like the modern Germans, they read a literature while other mortals read a few books. They read voraciously, and must disburden themselves ; so they take any general topic, as, Melancholy, or Praise of Science, or Praise of Folly, and write and quote without method or end. Now and then out of that affluence of their learning comes a fine sentence from Theophrastus, or Seneca, or Boëthius, but no high method, no inspiring efflux. But one cannot afford to read for a few sentences ; they are good only as strings of suggestive words.

There is another class, more needful to the present age, because the currents of custom run now in another direction, and leave us dry on this side, — I mean the *Imaginative.* A right metaphysics should do justice to the coördinate powers of Imagination, Insight, Understanding, and Will. Poetry, with its aids of Mythology and Romance, must be well allowed for an imaginative creature. Men are ever lapsing into a beggarly habit, wherein everything that is not ciphering, that is, which does not serve the tyrannical animal, is hustled out of sight. Our orators and writers are of the same poverty, and, in this rag-fair, neither the Imagina tion, the great awakening power, nor the Morals, creative of genius and of men, are addressed. But though orator and poet be of this hunger party, the capacities remain. We must have symbols. The child asks you for a story, and is thankful for the poorest. It is not poor to him, but radiant with meaning. The man asks for a novel, — that is, asks leave for a few hours to be a poet, and to paint things as they ought to be. The youth asks for a poem. The very dunces wish to go to the theatre. What private heavens can we not open, by yielding to all the suggestion of rich music! We must have idolatries, mythologies, — some swing and verge for the creative power lying coiled and cramped here, driving ardent natures to insanity and crime if it do not find vent. Without the great arts which speak to the sense of beauty, a man seems to me a poor, naked, shivering creature. These are his becoming draperies, which warm and adorn him. Whilst the prudential and economical tone of society starves the imagination, affronted Nature gets such indemnity as she may. The novel is that allowance and frolic the imagination finds. Everything else pins it down, and men flee for redress to Byron, Scott, Disraeli, Dumas, Sand, Balzac, Dickens, Thackeray, and Reade. Their education is neglected; but the circulating library and the theatre, as well as the trout-fishing, the Notch Mountains, the Adirondack country, the tour to Mont Blanc, to the White Hills, and the Ghauts make such amends as they can.

The imagination infuses a certain volatility and intoxication. It has a flute which sets the atoms of our frame in a dance, like planets; and, once so liberated, the whole man reeling drunk to the music, they never quite subside to their old stony state. But what is the imagination? Only an arm or weapon of the interior energy; only the precursor of the reason. And books that treat the old pedantries of the world, our times, places, professions, customs, opinions, histories, with a certain freedom, and distribute things, not after the usages of America and Europe, but after the laws of right reason, and with as daring a freedom as we use in dreams, put us on our feet again, and enable us to form an original judgment of our duties, and suggest new thoughts for to-morrow.

"Lucrezia Floriani," "Le Péché de M. Antoine," "Jeanne," and "Consuelo," of George Sand, are great steps from the novel of one termination, which we all read twenty years ago. Yet how far off from life and manners and motives the novel still is! Life lies about us dumb; the day, as we know it, has not yet found a tongue. These tories are to the plots of real life what the figures n "La Belle Assemblée," which represent the fashion of the month, are to portraits. But the novel will find the way to our interiors one day, and will not always be the novel of costume merely. I do not think it inoperative now. So much novel-reading cannot leave the young men and maidens untouched; and doubtless it gives some ideal dig-

nity to the day. The young study noble behavior;
and as the player in " Consuelo " insists that he
and his colleagues on the boards have taught
princes the fine etiquette and strokes of grace and
dignity which they practise with so much effect in
their villas and among their dependents, so I often
see traces of the Scotch or the French novel in the
courtesy and brilliancy of young midshipmen, col-
legians, and clerks. Indeed, when one observes
how ill and ugly people make their loves and quar-
rels, 't is pity they should not read novels a little
more, to import the fine generosities, and the clear,
firm conduct, which are as becoming in the unions
and separations which love effects under shingle
roofs as in palaces and among illustrious personages.

In novels the most serious questions are beginning to be discussed. What made the popularity
of " Jane Eyre," but that a central question was
answered in some sort? The question there answered in regard to a vicious marriage will always
be treated according to the habit of the party. A
person of commanding individualism will answer it
as Rochester does, — as Cleopatra, as Milton, as
George Sand do, — magnifying the exception into
a rule, dwarfing the world into an exception. A
person of less courage, that is, of less constitution,
will answer as the heroine does, — giving way to
fate, to conventionalism, to the actual state and do-
ings of men and women.

For the most part, our novel-reading is a passion for results. We admire parks, and high-born beauties, and the homage of drawing-rooms, and parliaments. They make us sceptical, by giving prominence to wealth and social position.

I remember when some peering eyes of boys discovered that the oranges hanging on the boughs of an orange-tree in a gay piazza were tied to the twigs by thread. I fear 't is so with the novelist's prosperities. Nature has a magic by which she fits the man to his fortunes, by making them the fruit of his character. But the novelist plucks this event here, and that fortune there, and ties them rashly to his figures, to tickle the fancy of his readers with a cloying success, or scare them with shocks of tragedy. And so, on the whole, 't is a juggle. We are cheated into laughter or wonder by feats which only oddly combine acts that we do every day. There is no new element, no power, no furtherance. 'T is only confectionery, not the raising of new corn. Great is the poverty of their inventions. *She was beautiful, and he fell in love.* Money, and killing, and the Wandering Jew, and persuading the lover that his mistress is betrothed to another, — these are the mainsprings: new names, but no new qualities in the men and women. Hence the vain endeavor to keep any bit of this fairy gold, which has rolled like a brook through our hands. A thousand thoughts awoke; great rainbows seemed to span the sky, — a morning among the mountains; — but we close the book, and not a ray remains in the memory of evening. But this passion for romance, and this disappointment, show how much we need real elevations and pure poetry : that which shall show us, in morning and night, in stars and mountains, and in all the plight and circumstance of men, the analogons of our own thoughts, and a like impression made by a just book and by the face of Nature.

If our times are sterile in genius, we must cheer us with books of rich and believing men who had atmosphere and amplitude about them.   Every good fable, every mythology, every biography from a religious age, every passage of love, and even philosophy and science, when they proceed from an intellectual integrity, and are not detached and critical, have the imaginative element.   The Greek fables, the Persian history (Firdusi), the " Younger Edda " of the Scandinavians, the " Chronicle of the Cid," the poem of Dante, the Sonnets of Michel Angelo, the English drama of Shakspere, Beaumont and Fletcher, and Ford, and even the prose of Bacon and Milton, — in our time, the Ode of Wordsworth, and the poems and the prose of Goethe, have this enlargement, and inspire hope and generous attempts.

There is no room left, — and yet I might as well not have begun as to leave out a class of books which are the best : I mean the Bibles of the world, or the sacred books of each nation, which express for each the supreme result of their experience. After the Hebrew and Greek Scriptures, which constitute the sacred books of Christendom, these

are the Desatir of the Persians, and the Zoroas-
trian Oracles ; the Vedas and Laws of Menu ;
the Upanishads, the Vishnu Purana, the Bhagvat
Geeta, of the Hindoos ; the books of the Bud-
dhists ; the "Chinese Classic," of four books, containing the wisdom of Confucius and Mencius.
Also such other books as have acquired a semi-ca-
nonical authority in the world, as expressing the
highest sentiment and hope of nations. Such are
the "Hermes Trismegistus," pretending to be
Egyptian remains ; the " Sentences " of Epictetus ;
of Marcus Antoninus ; the " Vishnu Sarma" of the
Hindoos ; the " Gulistan" of Saadi ; the " Imitation of Christ," of Thomas à Kempis ; and the
" Thoughts " of Pascal.

All these books are the majestic expressions of
the universal conscience, and are more to our daily
purpose than this year's almanac or this day's newspaper. But they are for the closet, and to be read
on the bended knee. Their communications are
not to be given or taken with the lips and the end
of the tongue, but out of the glow of the cheek, and
with the throbbing heart. Friendship should give
and take, solitude and time brood and ripen, heroes
absorb and enact them. They are not to be held
by letters printed on a page, but are living characters translatable into every tongue and form of life.
I read them on lichens and bark ; I watch them on
waves on the beach ; they fly in birds, they creep
in worms ; I detect them in laughter and blushes
and eye-sparkles of men and women. These are

Scriptures which the missionary might well carry over prairie, desert, and ocean, to Siberia, Japan, Timbuctoo. Yet he will find that the spirit which is in them journeys faster than he, and greets him on his arrival, — was there already long before him. The missionary must be carried by it, and find it there, or he goes in vain. Is there any geography in these things ? We call them Asiatic, we call them primeval ; but perhaps that is only optical ; for Nature is always equal to herself, and there are as good eyes and ears now in the planet as ever were. Only these ejaculations of the soul are uttered one or a few at a time, at long intervals, and it takes millenniums to make a Bible.

These are a few of the books which the old and the later times have yielded us, which will reward the time spent on them. In comparing the number of good books with the shortness of life, many might well be read by proxy, if we had good proxies ; and it would be well for sincere young men to borrow a hint from the French Institute and the British Association, and, as they divide the whole body into sections, each of which sits upon and reports of certain matters confided to it, so let each scholar associate himself to such persons as he can rely on, in a literary club, in which each shall undertake a single work or series for which he is qualfied. For example, how attractive is the whole literature of the " Roman de la Rose," the " Fabliaux," and the *gaie science* of the French Troubadours ! Yet who in Boston has time for that ?

But one of our company shall undertake it, shall
study and master it, and shall report on it, as under oath ; shall give us the sincere result, as it lies
in his mind, adding nothing, keeping nothing back.
Another member, meantime, shall as honestly
search, sift, and as truly report, on British mythology, the Round Table, the histories of Brut, Merlin, and Welsh poetry ; a third on the Saxon
Chronicles, Robert of Gloucester, and William of
Malmesbury ; a fourth, on Mysteries, Early Drama,
" Gesta Romanorum," Collier, and Dyce, and the
Camden Society.   Each shall give us his grains of
gold, after the washing ; and every other shall then
decide whether this is a book indispensable to him
also.